Women and Political Participation in Northern Ireland

C0-BWX-861

ROBERT LEE MILLER *and* RICK WILFORD
School of Social Sciences
Queen's University
Belfast

FREDA DONOGHUE
National College of Industrial Relations
Dublin

Avebury

Aldershot • Brookfield USA • Hong Kong • Singapore • Sydney

© Robert Lee Miller, Rick Wilford and Freda Donoghue 1996

All rights reserved. No part of this publication may be reproduced, stored in a retrieval system, or transmitted in any form or by any means, electronic, mechanical, photocopying, recording or otherwise without the prior permission of the publisher.

Published by
Avebury
Ashgate Publishing Limited
Gower House
Croft Road
Aldershot
Hants GU11 3HR
England

Ashgate Publishing Company
Old Post Road
Brookfield
Vermont 05036
USA

HQ
1391
.67
M55
1996

British Library Cataloguing in Publication Data

Miller, Robert Lee
    Women and political participation in Northern Ireland
    1. Women in politics – Northern Ireland 2. Political
    participation – Northern Ireland
    I. Title II. Wilford,R.A. (Richard A.) III. Donoghue,
    Freda
    320.9'416'082
ISBN 1 85628 991 5

Printed in Great Britain by
Antony Rowe Ltd, Chippenham, Wiltshire

FLORIDA STATE
UNIVERSITY LIBRARIES

JUN 2 1 2001

TALLAHASSEE, FLORIDA

WOMEN AND POLITICAL PARTICIPATION
IN NORTHERN IRELAND

For the women of Northern Ireland.

Contents

Figures and tables

Acknowledgements

We would first like to thank the members of the ESRC's Research Grants Board and its anonymous referees who expressed their confidence in our research proposal and thereby enabled the study to be undertaken. There were innumerable people we consulted in the formative stages of the research design and whose advice was welcome. These included Elizabeth Meehan, Pippa Norris, John Kremer, Valerie Morgan and Richard Moore. We would also like to thank those people who helped us to sharpen our ideas by participating in the pre-testing phases of the study and Ulster Marketing Surveys whose staff conducted the interviews during the first stage of the study. Most of all we acknowledge the assistance of the respondents, especially those who consented to be reinterviewed. Without their time and cooperation the study could not have been undertaken. Special thanks are due to Eileen Maguire who with insight, experience, efficiency and good humour prepared the manuscript for publication. Finally we would like to thank our families: their patience was sorely tested throughout.

Preface

When next an election comes the seed sown shall be ready to germinate - the seed beneath the snow as Silone calls it, speaking of those seeds of new growths that lie for a while submerged, but living.

Hanna Sheehy-Skeffington, 1943, pp. 143-148

1 Introduction:
The study in context

Introduction

Recent developments in Northern Ireland suggest that the province may be on the verge of an established peace. The Downing Street Declaration of December 1993, the two ceasefires of the late summer and early autumn of 1994 together with the publication by the British and Irish Governments of the framework document in February 1995 have each contributed to a guarded air of optimism. While the process of fashioning a political settlement is still in its troubled infancy, the pace of change has, nevertheless, been impressive and is all the more remarkable in the light of immediately prior events.

August 1994 was a particularly memorable four weeks. On the one hand, the 14th of the month marked the twenty-fifth anniversary of the arrival of the first contingent of British troops to Northern Ireland at the outset of 'the troubles'; on the other, seventeen days later, at midnight on the 31st August, the Provisional IRA (PIRA) announced its 'complete cessation of military activities', encouraging the belief that there may yet be a political resolution to the conflict. However, the month had earlier been disfigured by more ominous signs concerning the province's future. There was, for instance, another round of sectarian murders including that of a pregnant Catholic mother of five children, Kathleen O'Hagan, shot dead in her home by members of a loyalist paramilitary organisation. A few days later another woman, Mairead Farrell, featured in the controversial television documentary, 'Death on the Rock', that was re-broadcast to commemorate the renewal of 'the troubles'. Mairead Farrell was one of three unarmed members of an active service unit of the PIRA shot dead by British special forces in Gibraltar in 1988.

1

Here then are but two of Northern Ireland's many female casualties of political violence, 247 of whom have been killed since 1969 by bombs and bullets (McWilliams, 1995, p. 16). To ask which of them represented the authentic face of womanhood in Northern Ireland would be not only naive but mischievious. Such a question implies that there is a genuinely representative stereotype of womanhood in the province. Yet, despite a rich mythic tradition in Ireland in which women warriors such as Maeve, Skatha, Aoife and Bave feature prominently, the conventional configuration of women's role does not normally encompass their portrayal as active members of a paramilitary organisation. Counterposed against such warlike figures are those of the beautiful and tragic Deirdre; or Cathleen Ni Houlihan, who bequeathed the poetic name for Ireland; and Emer, wife of Cuchulainn, the 'Hound of Ulster'. She was said to possess the six gifts of womanhood: beauty, music, wisdom, sweetness of voice, needlework and chastity (Ellis, 1987; Kavanagh, 1988).

Perhaps the most familiar image is that of 'Mother Ireland', lovingly protective of her land and offspring. Such a potent icon implies that any woman who ventures beyond the hallowed, private terrain of home and family is in some way deviant: either because, guileless, she has been misled by manipulative men; or else suffers from some sort of derangement rendering her mad, bad and dangerous to know. Ireland's mythological landscape is, though, peopled by the two sorts of heroine: Emer's domestic virtues counterbalanced by Skatha's military prowess. Despite the latter's role as Cuchulainn's tutor in the martial arts, such an exemplar is ordinarily perceived to be letting the side of womanhood down: the passive and long-suffering Emer offers a more comfortable role model. But the wilder and more extreme shores of political activity represented by violence and coercion have not been the only territory conventionally regarded as being out of bounds to women. The more settled ground of political participation was also guarded as a male preserve, as the protracted struggle for female suffrage so clearly exemplified.

Sameness and difference

The gendered division of political roles and social spaces has reverberated throughout the history of Western political thought (Coole, 1993) and is rooted in the assertion that women and men are fundamentally different, whether by dint of nature or nurture. The weight of this orthodoxy ascribed to women a concern with family and domestic life, the private world of sentiment, emotion and feeling, and to men the public domain of reason, thought and action. Much of the feminist project has in fact been directed towards the subversion of this duality, undermining the division of the world into female, private spaces and male-monopolised public ones - including the realm of politics.

Equal rights feminists inspired by, among others, Mary Wollstonecraft have sought to eradicate any assertions about essential differences between the sexes, perceiving them to be nothing more than a patriarchal device designed to exclude women from the full exercise of citizen rights. Other feminists, earlier labelled 'welfare' or 'new' feminists have, to the contrary, reiterated and prized female essentialism, a view also shared by certain early socialists (Wilford, 1994). For instance, in 1825 the Irish utopian socialists, William Thompson and Anna Wheeler, portrayed women not merely as equal to men in their claim to civil and political rights, but as morally superior beings whose virtues were integral to the realisation of a communal society (Thompson, 1983).

This debate has not, however, been consigned to history. In the United States, the strategic coalition between equal rights and welfare feminists over women's suffrage was sundered by the protracted and mutable campaign for the Equal Rights Amendment begun in 1923 and which staggered on amidst growing discord until the early 1980s (Berry, 1988). More recently, the appearance of 'maternal revivalism' has offended certain radical feminists who perceive the celebration of motherhood by latter-day family feminists like Germaine Greer and Betty Friedan as tantamount to a surrender to patriarchal values (Stacey, 1986). From yet another perspective, the psychologist Carol Gilligan (1982) contends that women, unlike men, are oriented towards interpersonal relationships and inhabit an ethical universe which emphasises nurture and moral responsibility to others: in short, that women speak in 'a different voice' from that of men.

The debate over sameness and difference has, moreover, been compounded within the contemporary feminist movement by a preoccupation with the politics of identities. Thus, alongside the long-running issue of differences between the sexes, a new discourse has developed that seeks to recognise and authenticate differences among women. In fact, no sooner was the slogan 'sisterhood is global' coined in the early, heady days of second-wave feminism than others began to question its validity (Lovenduski and Randall, 1993). In particular, women drawn from ethnic minorities observed that the assertion of a universal sisterhood, which lumped all women together in a mass of shared interests and values, ignored the lived experiences of women from diverse historic, cultural and material backgrounds. Such critics pointed out that mainstream feminism had defined itself in terms of an agenda that served the interests of white, middle-class, heterosexual women, conveniently and arrogantly ignoring the politics of differences among women occasioned by social class, race, ethnicity and sexuality (Collins, 1990; Hooks, 1981; Lorde, 1984).

In a divided society the assumption of a common identity among women is equally, if not more, hazardous. In Northern Ireland, the mutually reinforcing cleavages of national and religious identity have, for instance, structured attitudes towards feminism and proved to be potent inhibitors upon the emergence of an all-encompassing women's movement. (Evason, 1991; Ward, 1987; McWilliams, 1991 and 1995). This book is not, however, inspired primarily by the desire to understand and explain the character of feminism in Northern Ireland. While it does, we think, have something to contribute to that understanding, its key preoccupation is with the forms and extent of women's political participation within the province. In large measure this study therefore constitutes a topographical exercise, seeking to establish the contours of such participation and thereby to locate women on Northern Ireland's political map.

The rationale in brief

Until comparatively recently the exploration of women's political participation took men's activities in the public realm of politics as the norm: to the extent that they did not measure up to a male-defined model of participation, women were regarded as inadequate political actors - imperfect men, if you will (Lane, 1959; Milbrath, 1968; Blondel, 1970; Milbrath and Goel, 1977; Verba et al, 1980). Much, if not all, of this portrayal turned on the definition of political participation. Male-centred definitions suggested that women were generally less active in the conventionally defined public realm than men, whether as voters, as participants in political institutions or in terms of the frequency with which they discussed and/or expressed an interest in politics. On the strength of a wide range of ostensibly impeccable empirical studies a composite image emerged that portrayed political woman in unflattering terms: she was unknowlegeable, uninterested, largely inactive and, in attitudinal terms, of a conservative and moralising disposition (Randall, 1987.)

In situating women on Northern Ireland's political map the study is in part influenced by the more usual measures of political participation: voting turnout, electoral choice, party membership and involvement in pressure groups and other associational activity. But it is also informed by a keen awareness that the concept of political participation and the very landscape upon which it is surveyed have become contested intellectual terrain (Lovenduski, 1981; Bourque and Grossholtz, 1984; Goot and Reid, 1984). Theoretical critiques marshalled by feminist writers have revised the concept of 'the political' and infused political participation with a much broader meaning than that defined simply by what men do (Siltanen and Stanworth, 1984; Jones, 1988). Persuaded by such critiques, we sought to identify and apply measures of political activity that were sensitive to the criticisms of earlier studies of women's involvements in the public realm. In effect the study attempts to contribute to the redrawing of the map of participation, by extending its boundaries and throwing into relief forms of activity not previously understood to be 'political'.

Chapter Two summarises critiques of traditional studies of political participation and identifies the measures employed to obtain a more accurate portrayal of the activities of both women and men. Thus, while the study is located within the distinctive context of Northern Ireland, we would contend that the indices developed are capable of more general application and can contribute to a more complete account of participation by both women and men.

Chapter Three reports the types, patterns and levels of political activity engaged in by women and men; Chapter Four identifies the characteristics and motives of the most active within the general population; Chapter Five assesses the mutual effects of partners on such activities, and Chapter Six discusses the relationship between women and political parties in Northern Ireland. In Chapter Seven we explore the stereotypes of female and male politicians identified by the general population and relate them to the wider debate concerning sameness and difference: are politicians of each sex perceived to embody distinctive attributes which, *inter alia*, carry different implications for the future of the province? Chapter Eight discusses the understanding and character of feminism(s) identified by the respondents in order, partly, to establish whether a transcendent agenda exists among women in Northern Ireland. Underpinning the study as a whole is the concern to discover the extent of political participation by women and to ascertain whether they participate not less than, but differently from, men (Norris, 1990). The nature and extent of gender gaps within the province and the effects of intervening variables, including religion, upon modes of participation concludes the study.

The two phases of research

In designing the project, we were sensitive to the criticism that in the past the methods used to study political participation have excluded activities theorised to be the common property of women. Both in ignoring the domestic arena and by placing exclusive reliance upon tightly structured questionnaires, orthodox measures of participation have therefore been criticised for performing a disservice to women (Randall, 1991.) In choosing research methods we strove to be free of gender bias by employing initially quantitative techniques and, subsequently, a qualitative approach that created the space for the respondents, both female and male, to speak for themselves. (Full details of the methods employed are provided in the Technical Appendix.)

The first stage of the research involved the application of a carefully piloted and pre-tested questionnaire, employing both closed and open questions, to a probability sample of 1402 women and 384 men. The survey instrument incorporated routine measures of orthodox and less conventional activities but, in addition, was also concerned to identify intra-family modes of political participation. These included control over household finances, the socialisation of children, consumer behaviour, frequency of political discussion and argument within the home and whether political beliefs influence the choice of a partner - perhaps the most intimate of political choices, especially pertinent within the context of Northern Ireland's divided society where inter-marriage between the two religions is still an unusual occurrence.

During this initial stage the mapping of the various modes of participation was supplemented by questions designed to elicit the levels and intensity of participation. In the extra-domestic arena the study sought to establish not only the range and types of organisation(s) - if any - the respondents were involved in but also: the roles they performed within them; the motives for their involvement or non-involvement; whether or not their activities had increased or decreased over time; the reasons for any increase or decrease; and the self-perceived effects of their activities. Within the domestic context the study was concerned to identify the roles performed by parents in relation to childhood socialisation; the mutual effects of partners upon political beliefs and behaviour; and whether partners were supportive or unsupportive of the respondent's participation in the public realm. By adopting such a focus the study was able to identify the interactions between the public and private realms, rather than to treat them in discrete and separate ways.

Besides establishing the background characteristics of the respondents, the questionnaire also included a limited range of attitudinal items. These included attitudes towards political parties, churches, politicians, feminists, the women's movement and support for both legitimate and illegitimate modes of political behaviour. In relation to the latter, we did not seek to establish whether or not the respondents were members of a proscribed organisation(s). However, during the qualitative stage past involvements in such organisations were mentioned voluntarily by a small number of respondents. The remaining areas covered during the initial stage of data-gathering concerned opinions relating to representation by women in the public realm of politics, preferred explanations for their underrepresentation in that realm and perceptions of the extent of discrimination against women in public life.

The analysis of the behavioural data acquired during the first stage of the project generated sub-sets of the original sample, differentiated in terms of their rates and modes of participation. To question these sub-sets a semi-structured technique was adopted, employing a pre-tested and piloted range of open-ended items, to reinterview 59 women and 15 men who, on the study's measures, ranged from the highly participative to the virtually inert. This second phase of the project yielded extensive details of the political 'careers' of the respondents amounting to a series of potted life-histories.

During the qualitative stage we were able to probe the motives for participation or non-participation, to identify whether there were commonalities in terms of the identity of significant others and events among the respondents and also to ascertain the direction of their influence; i.e., whether these events and others had a positive or negative effect upon their orientations towards politics. The re-interviews also provided the opportunity to discuss more sensitive issues with each of the respondents, including their differential experiences of 'the troubles'. Throughout each phase we were concerned to obtain data about the actual forms, level and patterns of participation engaged in by respondents, rather than an apparent willingness to participate.

While we would not claim that the techniques or the measures adopted were fully gender-proofed, we do consider that this triangulated method of data-gathering provides more reliable indicators of political participation than those which focus only upon standard measures of activities within the public realm. Moreover, by acting upon the now venerable premiss that 'the personal is political', the study was able to apply a broader conception of political activity than traditionally has been allowed. There are, however, attendant risks involved in adopting a perspective which understands politics to be a ubiquituous activity. This is not, however, to claim that politics is a limitless form of behaviour: to insist that everything is 'political' would be to deprive the concept of all meaning. Rather, it is to state that politics is a seamless activity enacted in both the public and private realms.

(Dis)Counting women

A generation after the emergence of second-wave feminism this perception of politics seems banal: however, until recently, the parcelling of the world into the public sphere of politics inhabited by men and the private realm of family and domestic life to which women "properly belonged", was commonplace. Such an unreflective division was not merely etched on the popular consciousness but was evident in studies of women and politics. Scholarly accounts of women and political participation tended either to neglect them altogether or to take them for granted: most notoriously on the assumption that deferential wives merely emulated the beliefs and voting behaviour of their husbands and dutiful daughters those of their fathers. Moreover, the absence of women from representative roles in the public sphere tended to be interpreted less as the outcome of discrimination, direct or indirect, by either or both the electorate and party selectorates, but more as proof of their uninterest in political life. These rudiments of 'wisdom' find scant support in the results of this study.

Westminster

Among women, for instance, there are significant levels of support for increases in female representation in both the Parliamentary and local government tiers and for equality at the Cabinet table (See Chapters 6 and 7). This unfulfilled demand among women and, to a lesser extent among men, for increased female representation is set against a bleak historic record within the province. Since its creation under the terms of the Government of Ireland Act of 1920, only three women have served as MPs for Northern Ireland's Westminster constituencies, two during the 1950s and the last in the 1970-February 1974 Parliament[1]. At the seven general elections held during the inter-war period, no women were chosen as prospective parliamentary candidates for the province's 12 seats. In total, 42 women have contested Westminster seats at the 14 general elections held since 1945, one-third of them at the 1992 election[2].

Stormont

Until 1972, when it was summarily prorogued, Northern Ireland also possessed its own Parliament (Stormont), a quasi-federal institution invested with extensive powers. During its existence, there were 12 elections for the 52 seat Parliament, the first two of which, in 1921 and 1925, employed the single transferable vote (STV) method of proportional representation, while the simple majority system was employed from 1929. A total of 1008 candidates sought election to Stormont at the dozen elections, of whom just 37 (four per cent) were women. Including by-elections, over the course of almost fifty years there was a total of 43 female candidacies shared among 20 women, nine of whom were elected. In aggregate, these nine - two-thirds of whom were Ulster Unionists - were returned on 29 occasions, but only one of them, Dehra Parker, achieved ministerial office[3].

Never constituting more than six per cent of candidates, the largest number of women to sit in any one of the 12 Parliaments was four, equivalent to 7.7 per cent of the total membership of the relevant assembly. At the final Stormont election of February 1969, the proportion of women candidates dwindled to two per cent, matching the paltry level achieved at the first held in 1921. In effect, Stormont was a virtual male monopoly, a fact that was all the more apparent when sectarian tension and inter-communal conflict escalated, as was the case at both its birth and eventual demise.

Local government

The one tier of elected office in Northern Ireland that has remained durable, though not intact, is local government. Following the introduction of direct rule in 1972, the widely discredited local government system was subjected to root and branch reform to the point at which it retained only minor and uncontroversial functions. STV elections to the 26 district councils, first contested in May 1973, are held every four years. Since 1977, when reliable candidate data first became available, the proportion of women running for local office has shown a modest upward trend. At the five councils elections held between 1977 and 1993, it rose from 9.5 to 14.1 per cent, while the proportion of successful female candidates increased during the same period from 7.2 to 12 per cent.

The relative success of women in securing election to local councils in Northern Ireland is not untypical. A number of observers have noted that in western Europe and the United States, for instance, women tend to fare better in terms of their representation at sub-national rather than national levels of government. This broad pattern, as Clark (1994, p. 108) suggests, seems to be related to both the prestige of, and the intensity of competition for, the office: 'The more desirable the office and/or the greater the competition for office, the less likely that women will be represented'. This, as she observes, seems confirmed by the fact that in the USA there are more women in state and local elected offices than in national offices.

The moderate increase in the proportion of women councillors in Northern Ireland can be viewed in terms that are consistent with the perceptions of Clark. Local government in the province enjoys low prestige because reform left it with only residual functions, colloquially summed-up as 'bins, bogs and burials'. One consequence of this diminution has been a progressive decline in the total number of candidates - from 1002 in 1977 to 933 in 1993 - even though the number of seats has increased over the same period from 526 to 582. The accompanying increase in both the proportion of women candidates and councillors appears to substantiate Clark's rueful observation. Moreover, the virtual absence of women from the Westminster Parliament and their poor record at Stormont confirm Vallance's (1982) related maxim: 'where power is, women aren't' .

In a study of the region's women councillors undertaken in 1992 (Wilford et al, 1993), it was apparent that the increased proportion of women elected to local councils was perceived by the councillors themselves to be explained in large measure by the reluctance of men to run for office rather than a concerted effort by either women themselves to seek candidacy or of the region's political parties to recruit women as candidates. Women were sought, in some cases as a last resort, in order to complete the electoral slate in the multi-member constituencies. The councillors were also highly critical of their respective parties both in terms of their relative uninterest in 'women's issues' and for their inaction in encouraging women to stand for election: a view also shared by women in the general population (See Chapters 6 and 7).

Regional bodies

The poor record of elected representation by women in the province is compounded by the experience of the three failed regional institutions established by successive British Governments since 1972 (O'Leary et al, 1988). The, as yet, unsuccessful pursuit of a stable, devolved consociation led first to the creation of the 78 seat Northern Ireland Assembly, elected in 1973 by means of STV. The short-lived institution, which was brought to an end in May 1974 by a near insurrection, boasted only four female members, each one of whom was either a pro or anti-power sharing

Unionist. In the following year, STV elections were held for a Constitutional Convention charged to draft an agreed scheme for the government of Northern Ireland, and the same quartet who had been elected to the Assembly were returned. The most recent attempt to create a province-wide institution occurred in 1982 when STV elections were held for a new 78 seat Assembly. The body, which was to limp on until 1986, included only three women (two Unionists and one member of the Social Democratic and Labour Party) who were returned at the 1982 election and a fourth (another Unionist) who was added at a by-election in 1985.

Nominated bodies

Somewhat paradoxically women have, in a representative sense, benefited from the introduction of direct rule, a system of governance widely criticised for establishing the region's democratic deficit. This gain for women is an unintended consequence of creating a host of appointed bodies responsible for administering functions and services that formerly were discharged by local councils. As Darcy et al note (1994), appointment as a method of selection does seem to favour women, partly because it has become increasingly difficult for those dispensing patronage to rationalise the exclusion of women; and partly from the social utility of achieving some semblance of gender balance in their appointments. However, while Darcy and his colleagues suggest that women tend to be better represented in appointed bodies because such positions are 'usually less politically important than elected positions' (1994, p. 157), this general rule applies less well in Northern Ireland.

Expressly intended to be free of sectarian bias and to ensure the efficient administration of public housing, education and the health and personal social services; to oversee the police service; and to monitor the implementation of legislation to combat sex and religious and political discrimination; these appointed agencies were invested with immense symbolic and practical significance. Their membership is determined by the Northern Ireland Office (NIO), whose ministerial teams have used their powers of appointment to the relative advantage of women: in 1991, women constituted 25 per cent of the membership of all nominated bodies in the province. By February 1995 the proportion had increased further: of a total of 2547 positions in 128 bodies, women held 827 appointments, equivalent to 32 per cent of the total (NIO, 1995). Over the last twenty years in Northern Ireland, patronage rather than election has proved a surer route to more equitable representation by women[4].

The context of history and culture

The holding of public office, whether through election or appointment, is only one, rather narrow, measure of political participation which, even in the most propitious of circumstances, is available only to a small proportion of any population. The fact that women have never achieved parity of representation in Northern Ireland may in small measure be explained by the fact that, with very few exceptions, it has been largely bereft of indigenous role models *pour l'encouragement des autres*. It has never had the equivalent of, say, Margaret Thatcher or, more recently, Mary Robinson, whose successful candidacy for the Irish Presidency in 1990 prefaced the election of a record number of women to the Irish Parliament two years later (Galligan, 1993). Of the three women elected to the Westminster Parliament from within Northern Ireland, two - Patricia Ford and Patricia McLoughlin, both Unionists - faded into genteel obscurity while the third, Bernadette McAliskey (nee Devlin), was tainted for the majority of women in the province by her close and continuing association with Irish republicanism.

The mention of republicanism prompts the eruptive issue of Northern Ireland's constitutional status. More precisely for our purposes, it raises the matter of women's role both in the quest for Irish independence and for the retention of the union with Great Britain. The clash of these mutually exclusive goals armed, at the least, with perceived conflicting traditions has yielded little if anything to women.

As an always contested political entity, the province's politics have retained the character of a proxy war. Its conditional place within the UK, coupled with the irredentism of the Republic of Ireland, have infused the terms of political discourse in Northern Ireland with martial values, epitomised on the one side by the 'ballot and the bullet' strategy and on the other by the resolute slogan, 'not an inch: no surrender'. The polity and society of Northern Ireland is, as a consequence, suffused with either/or-isms: a series of dualities that inhibit fine distinctions. The resulting zero-sum nature of its politics - if "we" win, "they" lose - marginalises those concerned with aspects of citizenship, including its gendered character, that are expressed in terms other than those of either 'Irishness' or 'Britishness'.

Unhappy marriages

Despite the apparent promise of the 1916 Proclamation to achieve equal rights and opportunities for all citizens, feminists in the 'Free State' discovered Irish nationalism to be progressively inhospitable to their demands. This culminated in De Valera's 1937 Constitution which extolled the wifely and maternal duties of women; a reactionary prescription that chimed perfectly with contemporary Catholic doctrine, exemplified by the Papal Encyclical of 1930, *Casti Connubi*, that exhorted women to perform their 'natural roles' within hearth and home. The 1937 Constitution revoked Section 3 of the 1922 Treaty Constitution which conferred citizen's rights on all over the age of twenty-one, irrespective of sex, in favour of De Valera's sentimentalised image of a rural, Catholic and resolutely patriarchal Ireland. His vision was of 'a countryside...joyous with the rompings of sturdy children, the contests of athletic youths [and] the laughter of joyous maidens' (Ward, 1983, p. 238).

Women did, of course, perform key roles in the Irish nationalist movement in both the nineteenth and early twentieth-centuries. The Ladies Land League, the Daughters of Erin, (*Inghinidhe na hEireann*), and the Irishwomen's Council (*Cumann na mBan*), all bequeathed a legacy of women's involvement in the struggle for Irish independence. However, the roles performed by these organisations were tolerated only to the extent that they acquiesced in the view that the nationalist cause came first. As Ward (1983, pp. 248-249) observes, the 'rigidly masculine tradition of Irish nationalism' relegated the needs of women to the margins, while feminists were criticised for their 'lack of commitment to the nationalist cause'.

Undaunted by such an unrewarding history, the cause of Irish unification has been actively pursued by women in the republican movement, some of whom have employed violence as a means to that end - and as such they have been singled out as the subjects of either incomprehension or especial condemnation[5]. The decision in the early 1970s by both the Provisional IRA and its political arm, Sinn Fein, to accord women equality within their respective ranks has not, however, resolved the historic tension between feminism and Irish republicanism (see Chapter 6).

Participation by women in the form of the exercise of political violence has been less evident within loyalist than republican paramilitary ranks, which is not to claim that it has not occurred. While there is some anectodal evidence of women's participation in the inner reaches of such organisations and one documented incident (the 'romper room' case of 1974) in which 11 loyalist women were convicted of murdering another woman (Fairweather et al, 1984, p. 283), outward appearances suggest that loyalist coercion is virtually an exclusively male activity.

The subordinate role of women within the unionist/loyalist political tradition has a lengthy ancestry, exemplified during the tumultuous events surrounding the legislative passage of the third Home Rule Bill. In 1912 the

13

Irish Unionists, led by Sir Edward Carson, signified their preparedness to engage in rebellion by organising a military force, the Ulster Volunteers, and by drafting the 'Ulster Covenant', whose signatories dedicated themselves to oppose Home Rule by force. Women were not permitted to sign the Covenant but rather the 'Women's Declaration', itself drafted by two men, James Craig and Thomas Sinclair, which committed them to support the 'uncompromising opposition' of 'the men of Ulster'. (Squires, 1993; Kinghan, 1975.)

This helpmate role was evident in the constitution of the Ulster Women's Unionist Council (UWUC), established in 1911, that defined the Council's main purpose as: 'the maintenance of the Legislative Union between Great Britain and Ireland [to which] all other questions in which individual members may be specially interested shall be subordinated'. The pertinence of the subordination of 'all other questions' is that it embraced the other major Parliamentary issue of the day: female suffrage.

The Home Rule and suffrage issues did, however, become enmeshed in the House of Commons when Philip Snowden, Chairman of the Independent Labour Party, moved an unsuccessful amendment to the Government of Ireland Bill. Snowden, a staunch convert to female suffrage and supporter of Home Rule, sought to link both issues by proposing that the local government, rather than the Parliamentary, register be used for the election of members of the prospective Irish Parliament. Though not immune from gendered assumptions about the sexual division of labour - 'Home Rule is a misnomer so long as those who manage home affairs have no part whatever in Home Rule' (HC Debs, 1912, col 1068) - Snowden's amendment was a clever device. Had it been accepted it would, on his own estimate, have enfranchised approximately 100,000 women in Ireland who were already qualified as municipal voters (HC Debs, 1912, col 1065).

The leader of the Irish Parliamentary Party (IPP), John Redmond, resisted the amendment on the grounds that it would be 'used as a political weapon for the purpose of inflicting injury upon the Home Rule Bill' (HC Debs, 1912, col 1089). He anticipated that it would provide the opportunity to those who were opposed to both Home Rule and female suffrage to unite and jeopardise the passage of the Government of Ireland Bill. Moreover, he did not commit either himself or his party to support votes for women, but rather signalled the intention to allow the IPP a free vote at Westminster on forthcoming Bills designed to enfranchise women. His leading opponent did not even go that far: Carson neither spoke during the debate nor voted on the amendment, which was defeated by 314 votes to 141.

Carson's stance on female suffrage was at best equivocal. As a sign of its intent to oppose Home Rule, the Ulster Unionist Council had drafted articles for a rebel, provisional government to take over the administration of Ulster after the Bill had passed into law. Among those articles was provision for votes for women, the inclusion of which gave a fillip to the suffrage movement throughout Britain, including 'non-militant Suffragists [who] rejoiced with the Women's Social and Political Union, forgetting the scruples they had so often expressed against militancy, in their pride that the rebel Unionist Women of Ulster were to be granted a vote under a Government of Civil War' (Pankhurst, 1977, p. 500). The euphoria was, however, short-lived. Within six months a deputation of suffragists from Ulster travelled to Carson's London home seeking an assurance of the commitment to enfranchise women: it was not forthcoming. According to Sylvia Pankhurst (1977, p. 548), '[H]e plainly stated that as his colleagues were not united on the subject of Votes for Women, he would not raise dissension among them by introducing it. Thus the much applauded promise was withdrawn.'

While women were subsequently fully enfranchised - in the 'Free State' earlier than in Britain and Northern Ireland - one lesson of the suffrage campaign was the subordination of women's political rights to the imperatives of high politics. As the struggle for independence dominated the Irish nationalist movement, so that to maintain the Union eclipsed the question of women's citizenship within Unionism. The lasting primacy of Northern Ireland's constitutional status has tended to reinforce a political division of labour between women and men which, if anything, is even more pronounced within the unionist/loyalist 'family'. The conservatism of its component parties, motivated above all to maintain the constitutional *status quo*, has spilled over into other areas, including the role of women within loyalist paramilitary circles where there appears to be a stark sexual division of labour. Conversely, the formal claim to socialist credentials voiced by contemporary Irish nationalism and republicanism creates the doctrinal space within which demands for gender equality can be articulated with greater ideological force.

Women and movement politics

The historic preparedness of all camps to employ coercion in Northern Ireland has sustained the martial character of its politics, tending to buttress a context within which it has proven difficult for women to enter the formal public realm. However, while largely absent from elected office, women have been to the fore in movement politics throughout the history of the province. In the recent past women were integrally involved in the formation of the Campaign for Social Justice in 1964, the Northern Ireland

15

Civil Rights Association (NICRA) established in 1967 and the radical, student-led group, People's Democracy, formed in 1968. They have also been instrumental in campaigning for the state recognition of integrated education and in a variety of groups opposing the use of violence by paramilitary organisations. Perhaps the most pronounced, if fleeting, impact made by women *en masse* occurred with the formation of the 'Women's Peace Movement' (WPM) - later disengendered and dubbed the 'Peace People' - in August 1976.

Formed in response to the deaths of three children killed by a runaway car whose driver, a gunman, had been shot dead by British troops, the WPM generated an immediate and enormous appeal. One of its founders, Mairead Corrigan, aunt to the dead children, speaking at a huge rally held in Belfast on 21st August 1976 struck the feminised note that was to become its leitmotif: 'I believe it is time for the women to have a go and see what the women, of both sides, working together, can do' (Bew and Gillespie, 1993, p. 113).

The wave of support for the Peace People spread quickly to Britain and beyond, culminating in 1977 with the award of the Nobel Peace Prize to Corrigan and her co-founder, Betty Williams. Here, it seemed, was the effective counterpoint to violence and one which, moreover, prized the essentialist association of women with non-violence. Yet, the movement was swiftly assailed by republicans alienated by its perceived failure to condemn violence perpetrated by the security forces, enabling them to allege that it was effectively pro-British. Within three years the movement was in disarray, driven by internal disputes over policy and the focus of criticism concerning the allocation of the monetary award which accompanied the Nobel Prize (Corrigan, 1991).

In a sense, the unhappy circumstances of its decline are less important than the gendered stereotypes perpetuated by the Peace People. The close identity of women with the movement fed an image of them as peacemakers, or at least peace-seekers, that is much more congenial and unthreatening than the model of the female warrior. Yet, as Rooney and Woods (1992, p. 24) observe 'we should be cautious about placing the burden of peace on women without the power of peacemaking'. While estimable, acting on the basis of mass participation in a peace movement is, in part, an eloquent measure of their exclusion from public office, even though it may be one route to the empowerment of women and the expression of apparent moral strength.

Besides episodic convulsions of mass politics, Northern Ireland is also characterised by an enormous range of local and community-based groups, some of which are dedicated to the promotion of cross-community contact and mutual understanding and respect: themes which are consistent with Anglo-Irish policy following the signing of the Hillsbrough Agreement in November 1985 (Wilford, 1992). In addition, there are a host of organisations concerned to meet the particular needs of women, including refuges for battered women and children, legal advice centres, support groups and self-defined 'mother and toddler' groups (Taillon, 1992a).

The existence of many such organisations which plug the gaps of an inadequate welfare regime, has encouraged the idea that in aggregate they constitute a civic space poised between the more formal realms of political participation and the domestic sphere. In particular, some of those concerned with the study of political participation have argued that this is a characteristically female space which has been virtually ignored in classic studies of political participation (Norris, 1990). This has prompted the speculation that far from being less participative than men, women participate differently: notably in fragmented and informal local or community-based associations. This was one proposition that we were particularly concerned to test and for which was found some supporting evidence. However, some caution has to be exercised in discussing certain of these groups, particularly those concerned with cross-community relations, and also in relation to the assumption that such organisations are typically female.

That there are such groups which have emerged quite unbidden is undoubted. However, the premium placed on such activities by both the British and Irish governments has influenced public policy towards the community and voluntary sectors. The creation of the Central Community Relations Unit within the Northern Ireland Office, the Community Relations Council and the subsequent elevation of community relations as a local authority function in the province, have benefited those groups which have grafted a cross-community perspective onto their remits (Taillon, 1992b). The lure of grant-aid for this purpose is undeniably attractive, but a recent study of women in the rural areas of Northern Ireland suggests that this is an offer many groups can, and do, refuse (Morgan and Fraser, 1994). The picture that emerges from their research is of parallel worlds within which women, Catholic and Protestant, maintain a posture of 'polite avoidance' towards one another.

Sisterhood?

Hope, of course, springs eternal: there is a tenacious belief in the capacity of women to bridge the communal divide and dispense sweet reasonableness. Perhaps the most sanguine expression of this view was articulated by Elizabeth Shannon (1989, p. 249). Addressing herself to feminists, in particular, she did not shirk from drawing an unambiguous distinction between the sexes:

> The ultimate feminist goal in Northern Ireland should be to create unity among the women there and a common voice that refutes terrorism as a way of life. Until that voice is heard, men will recite those ancient wounds with monotonous regularity. Their [men's] history has given them an addiction to revenge as insidious as alcohol or drugs.

This presentation of men as trapped and crazed by history probably does a disservice to many, if not most, of them and at the same time imparts a unity to feminism that has never been constant anywhere, let alone in the context of a divided society. The fact that strategic coalitions of feminists have emerged on single issues (McWilliams, 1995), or that Northern Ireland's female councillors articulate a common agenda of unmet needs (Wilford et al, 1993), is no guarantee of agreement on the rights and wrongs of political violence, not to mention the future of the province's constitutional status.

The susceptibility of feminism to history became glaringly apparent in relation to republican women prisoners in Armagh jail. Their campaign for political status, involving a 'dirty protest' and a hunger-strike, magnified divisions within the women's movement, rupturing any nascent potential for unity (Loughran, 1990.) Some years after the event, a symposium was held in Belfast to reflect on a decade of feminism in the province. The rather gloomy conclusion drawn by its rapporteur was the acknowledgement that feminists had failed 'to talk about our divisions in a manner which makes us face them and not deny them' (Ward, 1987). More recently, a reception held at Belfast's City Hall in 1992 to mark International Women's Week ended in disarray when a number of women staged a protest over the exclusion of women members of Sinn Fein and 'Lesbian Line' from the event.

In Northern Ireland the vaulting ambition connoted by the idea of a universal sisterhood has thus far turned out to be a triumph of hope over experience. Nevertheless, a significant minority of women - and a smaller proportion of men - in the sample embrace the feminist label, although their interpretations of the doctrine did of course vary (See Chapter 8). More to the point, perhaps, we did find that higher proportions of both sexes endorsed an agenda concerned with gender equality and acknowledged the situational inequalities confronting women. Whether or not gender equality is a sufficient platform upon which to overcome those disparities is contested by many feminists: yet, the widespread diffusion of liberal feminist ideas - a belief, for instance, in equal pay, equal rights and equal opportunities - suggests a receptivity to ideas that Northern Ireland's main political parties have as yet only begun to contemplate (See Chapter 6).

Indices of disadvantage

The palpable support for gender equality found alerts us to the, by UK standards, relatively low levels of female participation within the economy and the incidence of occupational segregation. Data from a wide variety of sources has consistently revealed that women in Northern Ireland, especially married women, 'are both less likely to be in employment and to return to work when their children are of school age than are their counterparts in Britain' (Montgomery, 1993, p. 17). While a major recent survey (Kremer and Montgomery, eds., 1993) discloses an increase in the proportion of working mothers, particularly those with pre-school children, the economic activity rate of women as a whole in Northern Ireland is the second-lowest of all the UK regions: the province 'still lags approximately 10 per cent behind the UK as a whole..Projections for the year 2000 indicate that activity rates for women of working age may be 62.1 per cent, while for the UK they may be as high as 73.7 per cent' (Trewsdale and Toman, 1993, p. 89).

If women who are economically active tend to be those who are more likely to be politically active - if only for the reason that employment creates pathways of participation *via* work-related organisations such as trade unions - then these lower rates of employment could be hypothesised to have a detrimental effect upon public political participation. Moreover, as elsewhere in the UK, the growth in the proportion of working women in Northern Ireland has been influenced by changes in the structure of the economy, notably the increase of part-time employment, especially in the service sectors within which women workers are heavily concentrated.

The incidence of part-time employment among women in the province, invariably in low-status, low-paid work, has more than doubled in twenty years: from 19 per cent in 1971 to 39 per cent in 1990. Married women constitute an overwhelming majority (88 per cent) of female part-time employees, while as a whole part-time women workers comprise one-third of all employees in both the clerical and related and the education, health and welfare sectors; just under half (46 per cent) of those in the retail sector; and two-thirds of those employed in catering, cleaning, hairdressing and other personal services (HMSO, 1992). However, the growth in part-time employment has not been paralleled by a decline in trade union membership among women; to the contrary, the proportion of unionised women rose from approximately 25 per cent in the early 1950s, to 44 per cent in 1983 (Evason, 1985; Miller and McDade, 1993).

One factor other than employment status or the availability of a union at the place of work that might be hypothesised to explain a lower incidence of female participation in work-related organisations is an inequitable sexual division of labour in the home. More generally, the presence of pre-school children has been hypothesised to be a situational impediment to women's political participation, which may be all the more marked in Northern Ireland given its unenviable status as the UK region with the lowest level of publicly-funded child-care (EOCNI, 1991). While recent survey evidence confirms such inequity within the domestic realm (Turner, 1993), our findings indicate that motherhood does not necessarily create an insuperable barrier to political participation outside the home, but in some cases can act as a spur to activism (See Chapters 4 and 5).

The dismal record of women's entry into Northern Ireland's elected arenas; their, by UK standards, relatively low level of economic activity; the continuing inability of the feminist movement to overcome historic divisions; the persistence of an unequal sexual division of labour; the paucity of child-care provision, combined with the highest birth-rates in the UK - all can be construed as symptoms of more deeply embedded causes that influence women's political participation. In particular, the crucible within which Northern Ireland's history and cultures interact has produced an amalgam of values that have had an enduring impact upon the political activities of women.

Nationality, religion and participation

A study by Inglehart (1981) was of particular interest to us in this regard. She sought to explain why women throughout Western Europe appeared to be persistently less interested in politics than men. Her analysis of data from eight European countries pointed to the enduring impact of key historic events upon women's interest in politics. In particular, Inglehart hypothesised that the relative politicisation of women reflected the importance of the Reformation: that is whether a nation is shaped primarily by either Protestantism or Catholicism.

Surveying cross-national responses to the question 'When you get together with your friends, would you say you discuss political matters frequently, occasionally or never?', Inglehart noted that while women were 'less politicised' than men in each of the countries surveyed 'the differences were greater *between women of different countries* (her emphasis) than between men and women of the same country' (p. 302). Employing a multiple classification analysis, she concluded that the single most important factor explaining an individual's interest in politics was nationality, followed by level of educational attainment, while sex emerged as of tertiary significance in predicting political interest.

Inglehart was thus encouraged contemplate the historical factors specific to each of the nations which could be considered to have a major bearing on 'political commitment'. One such factor was the date of female enfranchisement: adapting related work by Converse (1969), she hypothesised that the earlier women got the vote, the more 'politicised' they would be. There was partial confirmation of this hypothesis, but also some major exceptions, especially in relation to Germany. Women in Germany were enfranchised during the Weimar Republic but, consistent with Hitler's unreconstructed sexism, they were stripped of political rights during his dictatorship. Those rights were restored after 1945 and during the post-war period women have been reported to have high rates of political interest, although significantly below those of German men.

Thus, despite the discontinuity in their exercise of political rights, a high level of political interest among German women has been sustained, suggesting that the uninterrupted exercise of voting rights is insufficient by itself to explain politicisation. This led Inglehart to focus on the effects of both short term events and long term historical influences upon levels of political interest. In particular, she attributed differences in the political commitment of women to the roles performed both by the Catholic Church and national armies, both of which are 'hierarchical and authoritarian' and 'anti-feminist' (pp. 306-307). It is, she conjectures, the historical influences of these institutions, rather than the date of female enfranchisement itself, which constrains women's interest levels. Of course, as she notes, one of the effects of the values prized by those institutions was the date of female enfranchisement itself: women did secure voting rights earlier in Protestant countries and later in countries where Catholicism and a lengthy tradition of militarism prevailed.

The durability of the authoritarian values and beliefs immanent in both institutions, Inglehart hypothesises, depress women's level of political interest, whereas '[T]hrough its emphasis on literacy and equality, Protestantism provided the intellectual background in general for acceptance of women as equal to men' (p. 315). In the German case, the ostensibly egalitarian effects of Protestantism were mitigated by the impact of Prussian militarism throughout Germany and the presence of a significant proportion of Catholics in the south of the country. But her broad argument is that the differing effects of these religious traditions, combined with a series of short-run crises (in Germany those associated primarily with its then divided territory) interact to either inflate or deflate women's political interest.

With a mixed population, 38.4 per cent of which is Catholic (HMSO, 1992), Northern Ireland offers an interesting test-case of her hypothesis. The historic effects of two religious traditions, one of which preaches the direct equality of all before God, the other celebrating the mediatory role of a male hierarchy, can be hypothesised to have differential effects upon Catholic and Protestant women - and men. Moreover, the chronic sense of crisis occasioned by the constitutional issue, coupled with the pervasiveness of violence, strengthen the utility of the case-study of Inglehart's hypothesis. Thus, among other things we are able to evaluate whether this wider context generates higher levels of political interest and participation among men than women, and whether Catholic women are less interested and participative than Protestant women.

The lower levels of interest in politics among Catholic women does, according to Inglehart, correlate with their later acquisition of voting rights in predominantly Catholic states. In Northern Ireland, Catholics (of both sexes) did not enjoy equal voting rights until 1969 when NICRA's demand for 'one man, one vote' was conceded by the Stormont regime. Such tardiness can be hypothesised as retarding the level of political interest among Catholics of both sexes. Conversely, though, the struggle to achieve such rights, allied to campaigns against other forms of discrimination, whether in relation to employment or the allocation of public housing, could be hypothesised as strengthening rather than weakening political interest.

The mainspring of NICRA was, however, the determination to end religious discrimination: with women prominent in the organisation, there was unintentional irony in the fact that it adopted 'one man, one vote' as its slogan, symbolically marginalising the issue of sex discrimination. As a primarily, though not exclusively, Catholic movement this relegation of sex discrimination by NICRA may be conjectured to have had a differential impact upon Catholic women. Moreover, while the Catholic Church remains resolutely patriarchal in both doctrinal and institutional terms, both the Presbyterian Church and the Church of Ireland ordain women: the latter well in advance of the Church of England. Furthermore, unlike Protestant denominations, the Catholic Church does not sanction the existence of women-only lay organisations: there are no Catholic equivalents of, for instance, the Mother's Union or the Presbyterian Women's Association.

However, a simple dichotomy suggesting that Protestant churches are more receptive to the advancement of women than the Catholic Church does not bear close scrutiny. As Morgan and Fraser (1994, p. 65) observe, while the Presbyterian Church enables women to be trained for the ministry, to be given charge of a congregation or to be elected as elders, many of the rural congregations they studied 'have never had a woman in any of these positions'. They go on to note that both within the Presbyterian Church and the Church of Ireland:

> quite a number of the younger ministers and candidates for ordination …appear to be opposed to women ministers on theological grounds and to support a very traditional model of gender relations in which the role of women is focused exclusively on child rearing and domestic responsibilities.

In other sects, like the Brethren and the Free Presbyterians, patriarchy abounds, with women excluded from their respective ministries. Thus, a simple division between Catholic and non-Catholic needs to be treated with great circumspection, as our analysis will show. Other variables, including age and level of educational achievement (a factor noted by Inglehart to be significant in predicting political interest), intervene to produce a richer and more complicated picture of political participation, in many cases eclipsing the significance of both religion and gender. Moreover, all women in Northern Ireland, irrespective of their religious affiliations, have been subjected to public policies that are emblematic of what McWilliams (1991, p. 96) characterises as the province's 'backyard conservatism' .

In the field of employment, for instance, the marriage-bar in public sector jobs persisted far longer in Northern Ireland than in Britain, thereby excluding women from certain key occupational sectors until the late 1960s. In the realm of reproductive policy, the 1967 Abortion Act, even as amended, still does not extend to the province. Yet, confronted by the historic influences of both Catholicism and Protestant fundamentalism, together with the traditional inclemency of nationalism and unionism to feminism, it is perhaps no surprise to learn that in attitudinal terms women in Northern Ireland are more conservative than women in the more secular climate of Britain on issues such as abortion, divorce, pre and extra-marital sex and pornography (Montgomery and Davies, 1991). In addition, the martial character of its politics and the endemic crises that Northern Ireland has until recently endured, suggest that it is an unpromising context within which women can engage in a wide repertoire of political activities. But, as implied earlier, much turns on the meaning of political participation. As a preface to the presentation of the aggregate results of the survey, we first need to establish the grounds upon which we based our more expansive conception of political participation.

Notes

1. The three women who served as Westminster MPs were: Patricia Ford, Ulster Unionist, Down North, 1953-1955; Patricia McLaughlin, Ulster Unionist, West Belfast, 1955-1959; and Bernadette Devlin, Unity Candidate, Mid-Ulster, 1969-1970 and 1970-February 1974. When first returned Devlin was, and remains, the youngest woman to be elected to Parliament. Devlin was also, in 1979, the first woman in Northern Ireland to run for election to the European Parliament. There were no further female candidates for the European Parliament until 1994, when five women stood for election.
2. From the 1983 General Election Northern Ireland has had 17 Westminster constituencies.
3. Parker was a junior minister in the Ministry of Education between 1937-1944 and attained Cabinet rank in 1949 when she was appointed Minister of Health, a post she held until her resignation in 1957.
4. To compound the irony, despite the increase in the proportion of women serving on nominated bodies only one woman, Baroness Denton, has been appointed to a ministerial post in the Northern Ireland Office. She was appointed in January 1994 as a Parliamentary Under Secretary with responsibility for the economy, agriculture and, somewhat predictably, women's issues.
5. The 'Roll of Honour' published by Sinn Fein's Women's Department lists 16 female republicans killed either by the security forces or loyalist paramilitaries between 1971 and 1992. See *Women In Struggle: 25 Years of Resistance* (1994), Sinn Fein, Dublin, pp. 22-23.

2 The parameters of participation

It's hard to put into words....I have an idea of what political activity should be....It involves working for a party and for the good of the country in every way and every sphere - health and education and so on.

It's people coming together in groups for particular purposes. Politics with a small 'p' embraces everyday life - anything from schooling to church or office - all combine and have an impact on the political situation.

Introduction

Perspectives on participation

The above extracts from interviews with two female respondents conducted during the second phase of the study convey the idea of a spectrum across which political participation is understood to occur. In the first case it is regarded as activity that is confined to the institutional context of a political party, whose *raison d'etre* is properly, if narrowly, perceived as the formulation of public policy; in the second, it is regarded as a more pervasive, even mundane, form of behaviour, equally apparent at school and at work as in the formal realms of politics.

This latter interpretation is consistent with what Norris (1991) identifies as 'the radical theory of political participation'. It understands politics as an expansive activity occurring in a wide range of 'relatively unstructured and fragmented arenas within which women operate'. This perspective developed as a riposte to the 'traditional view' of participation and its articulation of 'standard assumptions about female apathy and passivity' *viz* that women were less involved and less interested in conventional forms of political activity. A third perspective sketched by Norris is 'the revisionist'. While its proponents concede that women may have been less active in the earlier post-war period, they contend first, that the extent of any participation gap in the past was probably overstated; and secondly, that over time the gap has closed as women's life styles and life-chances have improved. On this view, the changes in women's opportunities have provided them with access to the financial, educational and organisational resources that now enable them to participate on the same bases and as frequently as men. Revisionists thus 'emphasise the similarities rather than the differences in the mass political behaviour of women and men' (1994, p. 26).

The tripartite distinction drawn by Norris implies the staged evolution of understanding concerning the relationships between gender and political activity. In Walby's (1988) terms, the first of these can be labelled as the stage of 'ignorance' or of 'exclusion', wherein women's political activities were asserted either to be of minor importance or were taken for granted and simply discounted. This 'time of legends' inspired the twin myths of the politically inert and conservative woman (see Goot and Reid, 1975, for the definitive critique of this phase), a period broadly consistent with the traditional perspective identified by Norris. A second stage, one of emerging feminist critiques, challenged the myths that had become part of conventional wisdom, and sought to redress the balance by insisting upon the inclusion of women in empirical studies and more generally by importing gender awareness into scholarly research. Exponents of the critiques contested the ostensibly firm empirical findings which asserted the innate inactivity of women, either by observing that this portrayal was based upon the exaggerated reporting of a limited number of studies (Bourque and Grossholtz, 1984), or by challenging the proposition that women are inherently conservative (Goot and Reid, 1984).

As early as the 1970s some authors observed that the apparent finding that women are less active may be flawed by the adoption of male-defined criteria of political activity (e.g., Freeman, 1976; Randall, 1982; Lovenduski, 1986). Though it is true that women are conspicuous by their absence from political party hierarchies and/or from both the pursuit and holding of public office, this could plausibly indicate exclusion from such forms of participation rather than a lack of either interest or commitment (Lovenduski and Norris, 1993). Considerations of other forms of political activity, such as 'grassroots' work for political parties and involvement in locally-based political issues outside formal political structures, may well result in a different picture of the relative level of activity of the two sexes (Coote and Pattullo, 1990).

Such criticisms fanned a new wave of research, compatible with the revisionist perspective, that has been characterised by the presentation of data on the political activities of women and/or the analysis of existing indices of participation by gender. Moreover, the emphasis upon the obstacles impeding women's political activity, notably those created by an inequitable division of domestic labour, and the challenge posed to the orthodox equation that correlates the 'political' with the public world, are further examples of a more gender conscious approach to the study of politics. This stage can perhaps be styled as one of 'incorporation' whereby women, previously neglected, became included in existing streams of research.

While in no way wishing to discount the importance or timely nature of the inclusion paradigm, labelling it 'the' feminist stage is something of a misnomer. Besides doing an injustice to the sheer energy and diversity of feminist discourse epitomised, for instance, by the current preoccupation with the politics of identity, the measures of political activity upon which this phase is based have their origins in studies of male-centred political activity. Pointing out that women are more constrained in the public realm by domestic demands can be (and has been) misinterpreted as an alibi for rationalising the current under-representation of women in formal political processes (Leijenaar and Niemoller, 1991). The advocacy of means of equalising the burdens of family and home may take priority over the drive for a more equal inclusion of women into these processes; e.g., calling for an equitable division of labour in the home and better childcare facilities rather than advocating that political parties advance women through their ranks and put more of them forward as candidates.

It is essential that women should be included in studies of political activity on an equal basis with men. This does not mean, however, simply extending the sample or other data collection instrument to the female half of the population and/or breaking down all tables and figures by the variable of sex. In the light of feminist critiques of social science research procedure, the basic design of a research project, the methods of research employed and the rationale underlying them, the determination of the information to be collected and the relationship between the information and the conceptual background to the research, all need to be reconsidered. Routinely comparing and contrasting research results for women and men can lead one to miss more significant differences - or similarities - within both the female and the male groups that eclipse differences between the sexes.

A fourth stage of research that is more solidly rooted in the radical perspective of participation is now emergent and, though it risks the charge of hubris, we would contend that the research project reported here falls within the ambit of this embryonic fourth stage. The range of the data collected, its inclusion of the private as well as the public realm, together with the use of a triangulated research design, we hope point to the direction of future large-scale research concerning gender and politics.

Below, the aggregate findings from the quantitative stage of the study are presented and constitute a first step toward answering the questions prompted by Norris's outline of the three perspectives concerning gender and political participation. This stage included conventional measures of political activities common to standard studies of participation and which, by themselves, disclose some support for the traditional perspective; i.e., that women are less participative than men. However, as with a major British study (Parry et al, 1992), we also found, *inter alia*, that on these measures the extent of any participation gap between women and men is narrow and that most people, for most of the time, are inactive. In that respect, there is also some negative support for the revisionist perspective. Such findings are reminiscent of Milbrath's (1965) original tripartite categorisation of Americans into the 'apathetic', 'spectators'' and 'gladiators'. As in the United States, relatively small proportions of the population in Northern Ireland, whether women or men, emerge in gladiatorial terms: that is, perform a wide array of conventional political actions. To that extent Northern Ireland may be unexceptional: the overwhelming majority of both sexes are either inert or content to watch from the sidelines, akin to spectators at a sporting event or viewers slumped in an armchair in front of the television.

However, as Parry and his colleagues observe, this three-fold classification suggests a uni-dimensional pattern of participation, with a few highly active individuals standing at the apex of a pyramid, below which is a largely passive mass (1992, p. 17). As a corrective to Milbrath, the studies by Verba and his co-researchers (1972; 1978) indicated that political participation is a multi-dimensional phenomena: that different individuals tend to concentrate their energies and interests on particular types of activities. Participation is not, from this view, monopolised by a relatively small group of combatants, rather different individuals tend to specialise in specific modes of activity. Some might be active as campaigners, others merely as voters, the least exacting form of participation. Some may emerge as local or communal activists while yet others engage in particularised contacting, approaching public representatives about issues of direct concern to themselves and their families.

This multi-faceted approach has informed this study. Furthermore, it is not wholly inconsistent with the radical perspective on political participation whose exponents encourage the inclusion of types of activity commonly ignored by traditional studies. Thus, the study tested both the proposition that politics is a multi-dimensional activity and that it occurs in multiple arenas, not only those that both popular and social scientific orthodoxy define as its proper forms and realms.

Boundary problems

There are, however, risks associated with such an arena-based approach since it raises the question of boundary definition in a challenging way: where does political participation begin and end? The familiar means of ring-fencing this dilemma is to propose that political participation by citizens is directed towards influencing the policies and decisions of those in positions of authority, whether elected representatives or officials. This is a defensible and necessary element of, and motive for, participation and one that we, like Parry and his colleagues, include - although it does make the risky assumption that all citizens possess the same basic resources, opportunities, knowledge and skills that can be marshalled in order to exert such influence. Moreover, from the radical perspective, it appears unacceptably limiting. Individuals may, for instance, engage in certain activities because they believe they are, *faute de mieux*, filling a gap left by the inaction of government. Alternatively, the creation of and involvement in a mother and toddler group or a local amenity association, for example, may be undertaken for reasons of sociability, creating a network of friendships that otherwise would not exist. Such motives, while not overtly instrumental may yet be interpreted as embodying an indirectly political dimension.

In a divided society, certain forms of participation have a decidedly anti-state motive. While the exercise of coercion is an uncivil act, it nevertheless clearly is intended to influence policy. But, because of its disregard of the law, can such behaviour be deprived of 'political' content? In re-interviewing the activists within our sample, among the frequently encountered phrases were: 'there is no politics in Northern Ireland'; or 'politics, it's all about religion'; or 'it's the provos and the UVF, that's politics'. The equation, 'politics = sectarianism' conveys an explicit understanding among the relevant respondents that political attempts to achieve conflict resolution have had, until recently, to yield to paramilitarism. Not to include such behaviour within the remit of the study would have been to invite ridicule. However, to attempt to obtain an understanding of the extent of such activities *via* a large-scale quantitative study of the general population would, to say the least, have been ingenuous. Certain cues[1] were, however, built into the questionnaire, enabling the matter of political violence to be raised at the qualitative stage. Yet, it has to be acknowledged that this provides only the briefest glimpse into the bleaker reaches of political participation.

Other forms of behaviour including, for instance, the political socialisation of children, can also be construed as a form of political activity even though it has no direct or immediate effects upon decision makers. The promotion of civic (or uncivic) virtues by parents may, however, have long-run implications, not the least of which is to encourage or discourage their children from joining the ranks of activists, whether in conventional or unconventional ways.

The domestic arena, normally excluded from studies of participation, may also be the only context within which people engage in political discussion or argument. This may be particularly significant in Northern Ireland where there is an unspoken and common assumption that neither politics nor religion are discussed at large and in public (See Chapters 4 and 5). In a divided society the home may be the only 'safe' venue for the ventilation of political beliefs and ideas. While this is not participation in the sense of seeking to influence those in authority, it may have an indirect effect upon, for instance, voting behaviour - a proposition that was tested during the first phase of the research. Furthermore, exploring the incidence of political discussions within the domestic realm provides a measure of political interest and enables one to gauge the reciprocal effects between partners upon their political beliefs. More importantly, the extent to which husbands and/or wives support the more tangible and public forms of participation each may engage in is an important resource that can either facilitate or impede a more overtly participative role (See Chapter 5).

A more basic approach to the boundary issue is to ask people whether they consider that the activities in which they are engaged and the organisations to which they belong 'have something to do with politics'. This was asked of those within the wider sample who were active in at least one organisation and probed in more detail during the qualitative phase of the study. While this approach runs the risk of methodological individualism, it does at least enable us to assess the extent to which respondents adopt a broad or narrow understanding of political activity: in a perhaps prosaic sense, it allows one to explore whether the personal is perceived as political, and by whom.

Towards defining political participation

As indicated above, our working definition of participation is that activity which is undertaken in order to influence policy and decision makers. However, this still implies a direct and conscious link in the mind(s) of the individual or group between action and the intended target. But need there be such a consciously understood linkage? Verba and his colleagues raised this issue by adopting the following definition of political activity: 'those legal acts by private citizens that are *more or less directly* aimed at influencing the selection of governmental personnel and/or the actions that they take' (Verba and Nie, 1972, p2; Verba, Nie and Kim, 1978, p. 1) [our emphasis]. At first sight the vagueness of the phrase 'more or less directly' seems a sufficiently broad-brush approach and yet the definition confines itself to legitimate behaviour concerned either with voting, campaign activity, 'communal activity' (a combination of contacting government officials on 'some general social issue' and group activities directed toward the same end), and 'particularised contacts' (the citizen contacting officials about a 'particularised problem' - that is, 'one limited to himself (*sic*) or his (*sic*) family' (Verba, Nie and Kim, 1978, pp. 53-4). While a step in a more generous direction, the particular stress on legality immediately excludes a whole range of activities from consideration - and not just in the context of Northern Ireland where the prevailing legal norms are themselves at issue.

Barnes and Kaase et al (1979, p. 42) moved a step further towards a more extensive understanding by defining political participation as 'all voluntary activities by individual citizens intended to influence *either directly or indirectly* political choices at various levels of the political system' [our emphasis]. Moreover, they incorporate both conventional and unconventional forms of activity, the latter including involvement in protest politics. Similarly, Goel and Smith (1980, p. 76) embrace both 'traditional behaviours' such as voting and joining a political party and 'non-traditional behaviours', including social protest and social activism: 'We find', they state, 'a conceptual communality among all these behaviours'. Christy (1987, pp. 21-22) also drew a distinction between conventional and unconventional activities. Among the former she included voting, campaign activities, communications activities (following politics in the media or discussing politics), communal activity (participation in local affairs) and contacting public officials. The unconventional activities encompassed petitioning, boycotts, legal demonstrations 'as well as more aggressive types of behaviour such as illegal strikes or violent confrontations'.

Christy's broader approach, though, is not emulated by Parry (1992, p. 16). Theirs is a rather more restrictive definition limited to 'taking part in the formulation, passage and implementation of public policies'. Moreover it reasserts the directness of activities; i.e., 'action by citizens which is aimed at influencing decisions...taken by public representatives and officials'. Though Parry et al are sensitive to forms of behaviour that some would regard as political participation they discount, for instance, workplace activities or the incidence of political discussion in the home. More generally, the exclusion of the domestic arena from their remit ignores the more ubiquitous understanding of politics common among feminists and also tends to obliterate the more indirect linkages between the private and public spheres. Parry, Moyser and Day thereby arrive at a rather narrower five-fold operationalisation of political activity: voting; party campaigning; group activity; contacting; and protesting.

This study's approach is a hybrid one, incorporating many elements common to these earlier studies. Besides the more routine measures of voting, party membership, pressure group activity, campaigning and contact behaviour, it also includes membership in work-related organisations, voluntary bodies, church bodies and the range of unconventional activities identified by Christy (1987). Moreover, we are more disposed to allow of indirectness between individuals and policy makers. In that respect the approach is nearer to Barnes and Kaase and their colleagues than Parry et al. In particular, the study incorporates a range of domestic activities within its ambit as well as encompassing illegal activities.

The inclusion of the domestic arena as a site of political activity creates the opportunity to explore interactions between the public and private realms; in particular, to ascertain the extent to which the home supplies both opportunities and constraints for involvement in a variety of forms of public participation. This was a central concern of the study by Ballhausen et al (1986), whose research was a valuable source of inspiration. Based initially on questionnaire interviews with 533 women in Hanover active in political parties, trade unions, welfare organisations, church bodies, women's groups and other voluntary agencies, Ballhausen and her colleagues complemented the structured phase of their research with follow-up in-depth interviews. This enabled the research team to question the respondents about the levels and extent of their activities, the history of their involvement and the obstacles to their participation and how these were negotiated. This two-pronged approach seemed a most valuable method. Nevertheless, while an extremely valuable source, the study was somewhat limited for our purposes by being confined to women who were already active - moreover, the study equated political activity with formal organisational involvement. A main concern of our project was to undertake a study of the types and level of activity within the general population as a whole rather than among women pre-selected on the basis of known and possibly unrepresentative activities.

While any single definition of political participation is contestable, the inclusion of social, domestic and indirect activities seems to us to be merited. If nothing else it offers the opportunity to test the radical assertion that women engage in different types of activity from men. Such activities are invariably understood to be informal, unconventional, local, voluntary, communal, oriented towards self-help or self-improvement and, in organisational terms, are considered to be essentially improvised in character. From this perspective, necessity among women may appear as the mother of political invention.

Underlying the radical perspective on participation is the metaphor of the iceberg. That below the 'waterline' of observable modes of activity there lie realms of behaviour, the dimensions and forms of which are less easily fathomed. So portrayed, the task is to plumb these depths in order to obtain an inclusive picture of political activity, not only that which bobs conveniently on the surface. The wide-trawl approach that we adopt does provide the opportunity to discover whether there are such submerged modes of participation and whether they are gendered. The three perspectives neatly delineated by Norris provide us with a framework within which to organise our data. Are women in Northern Ireland more or less participative than men? Moreover is it the case, as the advocates of the radical theory claim, that women do not participate less than, but differently from, men? Do they inhabit 'unstructured and transitory groups' which, while overlooked in traditional studies, 'can be seen as political since...they address policy issues of public concern' (Norris, 1991), even in an indirect way?

Motives for participation

Adopting a definition of participation that restricts it to direct attempts to influence those in authority imparts a wholly instrumental motive to the politically active. Yet instrumentality is not the only motive for political participation. Some people become active in certain organisations for expressive reasons that do not serve their tangible interests. As Parry et al state: '[they] act in order to express their feelings or display their stance about a matter' (1992, p. 15). Attachments to particular causes, for instance environmentalism, are often cited as examples of such activities, and certainly seem detached from the pursuit of material gain. While not doubting the validity of the distinction, differentiating between instrumental and expressive motives is not always easy.

For example, in Northern Ireland flying the Union flag or the Irish Tricolour from one's home is not merely an act of symbolic expression but an overt and mutually exclusive statement of national and political identity: among other things, it signals where its occupants believe their material interests are better served - as either an integral part of the United Kingdom or, alternatively, of a united Ireland. Instrumental and expressive motives do not, moreover, exhaust the possible causes of political activism. Parry and his colleagues cite two other possible reasons: the communitarian and the educative. The former stresses concern for the community of which the individual is a part, whereby a shared interest in the immediate environment acts as a spur to participation. The latter emphasises the desire to develop civic virtues and skills as the mainspring of activism, although as they acknowledge the felt need for self development may be better understood as an effect of, rather than a reason for, participation (1992, p. 14).

Disentangling such motives is a tricky affair, but it was attempted during both phases of the research. Among other things this enables us to test whether there are gender differences in the motivations among the politically active. The quantitative phase of the study does provide data enabling comparisons of motives to be made between the sexes while, in turn, the qualitative phase offered the opportunity to probe more deeply about the reasons for participation. Relatedly, the in-depth interviews also enabled the exploration of whether or not women and men articulate different orientations towards politics - a view favoured by, among others, the proponents of a 'women's culture'.

The hypothesised existence and character of a women's culture is, as Randall notes (1991, p. 528), characteristic of 'standpoint' feminism. Its exponents contend that the distinctive experiences of women create the possibility for not just a different but a superior way of seeing, understanding and changing the world. It is an experiential approach that portrays women as an oppressed group or class. Yet, according to standpoint theorists, this marginalised vantage point offers a clearer, unimpeded view of existing power relations and of the need for change. Women, as it were, are said to have a wider angle of vision than men who, advantaged by patriarchy, only perceive the world through lenses distorted by the motive of retaining their dominance. Thus, while men are asserted to be motivated by the need to maintain the prevailing sexual *status quo*, standpoint feminism portrays women as potential subversives, seeing, thinking and acting differently from men.

There is nothing inherently essentialist about this view of women in the sense that they are presented as being 'naturally' different from men: such hypothesised differences may result from either ascribed traits or acquired responsibilities; from distinctive socialisation processes; differing processes of personality formation; or to their generalised experience of oppression. But, whatever the apparent cause or causes, this perspective asserts that women's oppressed status encourages them to behave differently, including in the public realm of politics; that the values they bring to politics, their orientations to the political agenda, their preferred styles of political discourse and of decision making are different from those of men.

Buoyed by an explicit claim to superiority, standpoint theory essays a vaulting aspiration for women. According to its adherents, success in achieving significant levels of representation supplies women with the opportunity and the confidence to express their different voice and hence a distinctive agenda, rather than to slavishly emulate men. In practical terms, the realisation of this different and superior capacity to effect change in the public realm of politics is dependent upon women achieving a critical mass in representative institutions - an, as yet, unrealised goal in Northern Ireland.

Despite its view of women as an oppressed class, for some feminists the attraction of the concept of women's culture is that it does not portray them solely as the enduring and permanent victims of male patriarchy. Hedlund (1988), for instance, depicts the concept of women's culture in dualistic terms. While she recognises that it has a negative dimension that embraces elements such as passivity, a lack of self-confidence and dependence on men, Hedlund also identifies the positive aspects of this culture: an emphasis on connectedness, on care for others, a concern to represent women's interests and a behavioural style that is cooperative and unaggressive.

The study (Wilford et al, 1993) of women councillors in Northern Ireland is reminiscent of Hedlund's in the sense that it too identified the lineaments of a women's culture, and in startlingly similar dualistic terms. The crucial difference between the councillors in Northern Ireland and those studied by Hedlund in Sweden, however, is that in the former case women are marginalised in numerical terms and subscribe to an agenda that is submerged beneath the perceived preoccupation among men with security and constitutional issues. In Hedlund's terms, women's culture among female councillors in Northern Ireland can be described as 'an invisible sphere suppressed in the world of men' (p. 101) but which 'carries a potential for change and liberation that affects the entire society' (p. 82).

Both phases of the study reported here enable us to ascertain whether the dual elements of women's culture can be identified among women within the general population. The implications of the existence of a women's culture that is independent of the male world and which may transcend the cleavages of national and religious identity are quite profound: not least within the context of a society that is inching its way towards a political settlement which, if realised, will create the space and the opportunity for a more normal political agenda to develop.

This discussion is taken up later. First we report the findings of the quantitative phase of the study.

Measures of participation

The core of the interview schedule administered during the first stage of the research comprised a wide range of items designed to provide information about a broad array of political activities consistent with the radical theory of participation. Throughout, respondents were asked to report their actual behaviour, not their aspirations or apparent willingness to participate. The various items are summarised below by means of seven types of political activity.

Types of activity

Party activity In relation to electoral turnout and partisanship the respondents, besides being invited to state their party affiliation, were asked: if they had voted at the previous local, General and European elections; whether they belonged to a political party; if they had held office within a political party; and whether they had sought or held public office.

Grassroots activity Respondents were asked a battery of questions in relation to work on behalf of a political party. These included campaigning, canvassing, fund-raising, assisting in a variety of clerical roles, distributing party literature and the donation of money to a party.

Informal political activity A range of contacting activity among the respondents was explored: whether for instance they had written to public representatives and officials about specific matters, and the frequency of such activity. Similarly, we also enquired whether and how often they write letters to the press about political issues. A number of communal activities are also incorporated in this category. These included attendance at local council meetings and neighbourhood meetings concerning local issues; working with others to tackle local problems; circulating petitions; attendance at lawful marches, demonstrations and rallies; the withholding of rents, rates or taxes as a means of political protest; and occupying a building or blocking traffic as a means of protest.

Group activity and organisational involvement Besides membership of political parties, the study also sought to identify the involvement of respondents in a wide range of other organisations. The groups explicitly mentioned were trade unions, staff or professional associations, employers associations, charitable bodies, voluntary groups, church-based organisations, welfare groups, women's groups, school-based groups and environmental groups. In addition, respondents were invited to identify any other organisations in which they were active. They were also asked to specify the extent of their participation within the organisation(s) to which they belonged in order to discover whether they were active participants or passive members. For example, in the case of trade unions, respondents were asked if they had ever been on strike or on a picket line; their frequency of attendance at branch meetings; their participation in voting at union meetings; and whether they had ever tabled a proposal or motion for decision. In relation to charitable bodies, respondents were asked whether they donate significant amounts of money, or whether they engage in voluntary work on behalf of such an organisation.

Consumer activity In addition, the study sought to establish whether the respondents actively expressed their political beliefs in the guise of a consumer. For instance, whether they chose to purchase 'green' products and on what basis (i.e., cost or environmental consciousness); whether they engaged in environmentally friendly behaviour by, for example, recycling materials, choosing to purchase a vehicle that used lead-free fuel or refusing to use products such as pesticides that are harmful to the environment. Respondents were also asked whether they avoided purchasing certain products on political grounds, for instance goods originating in countries whose regimes they disapproved of.

Socialising activity Within the context of the family parents were asked a number of questions relating to the socialisation of children. More precisely, the extent to which they tried to persuade their children to share their own religious beliefs, political opinions and views about both sexual behaviour and sexual equality. Relatedly, parents were asked whether they censored their children's access to the visual media. In particular, whether and at what ages they controlled exposure to news programmes, programmes that the respondents perceived to be politically biased and television films and/or videos with either or both an explicitly sexual or violent content.

The parents among our respondents were also asked whether they encouraged their children to join particular organisations, including the youth wings of political parties; whether they ensured that their children attended church on a regular basis and whether they accompanied them to religious services. Initiation into a religious identity is, in Northern Ireland, reinforced by the educational system which at both primary and secondary level is still largely segregated on religious grounds. In addition single-sex schools are the norm. Against that background, respondents were asked to rank, from a given list, the two most important characteristics of a school they would choose for their children, both girls and boys. Among other things, this item affords an insight into whether they subject their children to differential gender role socialisation.

Discussive activities Consistent with the study's concern to include more indirect means of political participation, a number of questions was also posed that were designed to elicit the extent of political interest among the respondents. These ranged from their readiness to discuss political issues with family, friends or workmates; the frequency of political discussions; whether they initiate conversations about politics; and whether or not they are prepared to argue about politics with family members and others. Other within-family items did have a more direct relationship to political activity. For instance, respondents were asked whether the voting intentions of their partners would influence their own choice of electoral candidate.

The choice of these items was preceded by an intensive pre-testing phase during which a variety of strategies for collecting the data were tried and often discarded. Among the other items that were retained were questions directed to those respondents who were active in at least one organisation and which concerned the effects of their involvement, including the extent to which they perceived themselves to have become more or less politically efficacious as a consequence of their activities. The questionnaire also explored whether there were domestic constraints and/or opportunities upon their activities, including the extent to which their spouse/partner supported their participative behaviour in the wider public realm. Respondents were, in addition, asked whether there had been any significant others or events that had influenced their activities and the nature of that perceived influence; i.e., whether positive or negative.

Many of these items, particularly the latter, provided signposts for the second qualitative phase during which they could be explored in much greater depth. This latter stage also enabled us to investigate other areas in more detail, including the motives for activity, changes in the modes and extent of political participation in the respondents' life course and the effects of 'the troubles' upon their involvements. Other items in the questionnaire, including those of an essentially attitudinal nature, are discussed elsewhere in the text.

Results

The first section of the results present an ordering of the activities into a coherent pattern of types of participation. The data-reduction procedure employed to realise this task is a factor analysis, applied first to the whole sample and then separately to the female and male respondents. The distributions for the female and male samples across the factors representing different types of pubic participation will be presented followed by presentations of the intensity of participation, both in terms of the extent of involvement in organisations and the distribution of unusually high and unusually low levels of participation by sex. Then the amount of correlation between different types of participation will be assessed. Finally, distributions by sex across the individual components constitutes the factors of participation are presented.

Table 2.1 displays the results of factor analyses carried out on the female and male respondents combined and weighted into a single dataset. Coherent, and interpretable, factors of behaviour result.[2]

Table 2.1
Political participation factors: both sexes

	Polit activ- ism	Charit- able activity	Voting/ Sociali sation	Asser- tive	Envir- onmen- talist	Religi- ous activist	Wom. Move- ment
Letter writing	0.754	0.155	0.074	0.245	0.150	0.136	0.023
Unconventional activities	**0.801**	0.261	0.133	**0.384**	0.047	0.260	-0.031
Political party activities	**0.629**	0.108	0.205	0.180	-0.157	0.346	0.009
Running for office	**0.480**	0.231	0.129	0.162	0.094	**0.720**	0.023
Pressure group membership	**0.567**	0.222	-0.073	-0.039	0.009	-0.174	0.081
Charitable group membership	0.178	**0.867**	0.080	0.112	0.049	0.160	0.047
Charitable activities index	0.232	**0.844**	0.171	0.209	0.136	0.180	0.093
Voting activity	0.134	0.027	**0.762**	0.091	-0.121	0.086	0.083
Socialisation index	-0.013	0.184	**0.738**	-0.016	0.197	0.087	0.014
Discusses politics	0.284	0.254	-0.060	**0.722**	0.061	0.074	0.014
Wins political arguments	0.056	0.024	0.081	**0.770**	0.095	0.098	0.025
Trade union activism index	0.287	0.200	0.196	**0.444**	-0.379	0.072	-0.181
'Green' index	0.110	0.315	0.012	**0.409**	**0.458**	-0.021	**0.442**
Environmental group member	0.297	0.381	-0.087	0.197	**0.575**	-0.075	0.230
School activity group member	0.053	0.026	0.216	0.129	**0.672**	0.282	-0.214
Church group membership	0.028	0.236	0.082	0.108	0.120	**0.800**	0.135
'Women's' grp membership	0.046	0.034	0.124	-0.009	-0.048	0.142	**0.858**
Eigenvalue	3.489	1.491	1.322	1.138	1.090	1.001	1.012
% variance	20.5	8.8	7.8	6.7	6.4	5.9	6.0

Kaiser-Meyer-Olkin measure of sampling adequacy is 0.765

The first, 'Political activism', comprises a combination of each of the overtly political activities covered in the interview schedule with the exception of voting. Thus, this factor consists of: first, an index of 'unconventional' political activities ranging from circulating petitions to protest activities; second, an index based upon letter writing to public officials and the media; third, an index of grassroots activities on behalf of a political party; fourth, membership in pressure groups; and, fifth, whether the respondent has contested or held an office in the public realm. Rather than appearing as distinct types of behaviour, overtly political activities fall into a single pattern. Involvement in charitable organisations constitutes a second factor, 'Charitable activity', and consists of two components: membership of charitable organisations; and an index of charitable activities. The third factor is a combination of an index of voting at local, national and European levels and an index of whether the respondent, if they have children, has attempted to induct them into shared values concerning partisanship, sexual politics and morality.[3] The fourth factor can be understood as an indicator of personal or individual assertiveness. It includes an index based primarily upon the respondents' scores on those questions relating to the discussion of politics with friends and family members and, if these discussions develop into argument, whether respondents expect their own views to prevail. Participation in 'ecological consumerism' and product boycotts are further features of this factor as is 'trade union activism'. The 'green index' of ecological consumerism, membership in environmental organisations and membership in groups associated with the schools attended by one's children make up a fifth, 'Environmentalist', factor. The index of ecological consumerism also supplies a minority component of the sixth factor, 'Women's movement', which is predominantly made up of membership in women's groups. Finally, the seventh factor, 'Religious activist', consists of components derived from membership in church groups together with the index of office seeking or office holding.

Tables 2.2a and 2.2b provide the results of factor analyses carried out to develop estimates of the parameters of public participation for women and men separately. One will note that, both in terms of the variables that make up the factors and their coefficients, the results for the female and male samples are remarkably congruent. In both instances, six factors resulted, four of which are virtually identical across gender: political activism; charitable activity; voting/socialisation; and assertiveness. The main divergences between the female and male samples occur only for the remaining two factors, environmentalist and women's movement, where a major reason underlying the difference between the sexes must be that men, by definition, cannot normally appear in one of the avenues for women's participation, i.e. membership in women's groups.

Table 2.2a
Political participation factors: women

	Political activism	Charit- able activity	Voting/ Sociali sation	Asser- tiveness	Religious woman	Militant
Letter writing	**0.715**	0.274	0.003	0.252	0.097	0.143
Unconventional activities	**0.751**	0.189	0.027	0.302	0.109	0.255
Political party activities	**0.595**	-0.049	0.168	0.112	0.215	0.115
Running for office	**0.432**	**0.391**	0.006	0.054	**0.478**	**0.406**
Pressure group membership	**0.562**	0.262	-0.043	-0.019	-0.071	-0.166
Charitable group membership	0.117	**0.833**	0.051	0.128	0.115	0.154
Charitable activities index	0.211	**0.792**	0.186	0.321	0.166	0.136
Voting activity	0.136	-0.028	**0.758**	0.025	0.113	0.146
Socialisation index	-0.003	0.154	**0.751**	0.039	0.089	0.038
Discusses politics	**0.368**	0.238	-0.002	**0.647**	-0.061	0.129
Wins political arguments	0.095	0.039	0.076	**0.727**	0.023	0.192
Trade union activism index	0.227	0.016	0.114	0.125	-0.084	**0.620**
'Green' index	0.101	0.295	-0.043	**0.712**	0.189	0.041
Environmental group member	0.299	**0.466**	-0.210	0.288	0.069	-0.085
School activity group member	0.013	0.150	0.079	0.181	0.169	**0.661**
Church group membership	0.087	0.293	0.056	0.003	**0.669**	0.339
'Women's' grp membership	0.099	-0.051	0.163	0.124	**0.742**	-0.213
Eigenvalue	3.401	1.308	1.413	1.178	1.024	1.007
% variance	20.0	7.7	8.3	6.9	6.0	5.9

Kaiser-Meyer-Olkin measure of sampling adequacy is 0.767

Table 2.2b
Political participation factors: men

	Political activism	Charit-able activity	Voting/ Sociali sation	Asser-tive	Religious activist	Envir-onmen-talist
Letter writing	**0.773**	0.063	0.105	0.177	0.216	0.197
Unconventional activities	**0.819**	0.357	0.179	0.350	0.347	0.124
Political party activities	**0.624**	0.248	0.243	0.127	**0.422**	-0.065
Running for office	**0.438**	0.177	0.187	0.132	**0.810**	0.137
Pressure group membership	**0.589**	0.182	-0.040	0.074	-0.152	-0.024
Charitable group membership	0.201	**0.866**	0.122	0.143	0.155	0.088
Charitable activities index	0.231	**0.808**	0.156	0.118	0.240	0.209
Voting activity	0.164	0.025	**0.774**	0.130	0.086	-0.130
Socialisation index	-0.032	0.207	**0.741**	-0.048	0.094	0.266
Discusses politics	0.209	0.261	-0.074	**0.746**	0.171	0.132
Wins political arguments	0.073	-0.063	0.127	**0.776**	0.096	0.151
Trade union activism index	0.328	0.372	0.170	**0.451**	-0.027	-0.276
'Green' index	0.067	0.272	0.042	0.274	0.086	**0.523**
Environmental group member	0.187	0.318	0.006	0.245	0.047	**0.679**
School activity group member	0.066	-0.076	0.118	-0.033	0.193	**0.683**
Church group membership	0.003	0.220	0.055	0.175	**0.853**	0.140
Eigenvalue	3.665	1.229	1.114	1.308	1.096	1.456
% variance	22.9	7.7	7.0	8.2	6.8	9.1

Kaiser-Meyer-Olkin measure of sampling adequacy is 0.736

Membership in the latter is one of the two main components in a factor unique to the female sample, *viz.* 'religious woman', which incorporates membership in church or church-based groups. This juxtaposition, while it may appear eccentric, does make sense in a Northern Irish context. Analysis of the in-depth interviews discloses that many women's groups, particularly in rural areas, are associated with church activities (Also, see Morgan and Fraser, 1994). The male-only factor, 'religious activist', made up primarily of church group membership and running for office, resembles the 'religious woman' factor, with women's group membership excluded. The sixth factors for each sex are quite different. For women, the factor has been labelled 'activist'; it represents a combination of the trade union activities index, school activity group membership and office seeking. For men, the factor does appear to have a clear 'environmentalist' component; it is made up of membership in environmental groups, the 'green activities' index and membership in school activity groups.

Given this broad symmetry between the types of activity engaged in by women and men, what about levels of activity? One of the features of the criticism of the supposed 'finding' that women are less active than men has been that this may merely be an artefact of male-defined conceptions of what constitutes 'genuine' political activity (Goot and Reid, 1975; Bourque and Grossholz, 1984; Norris, 1991). An implication of this critique is that if broader, less male-defined or male-identified conceptions of political activity are used, women may well prove to be at least as, if not more, active than men. Table 2.3 provides information that allows one to assess this possibility. The individual scorings of each respondent on each factor was computed by multiplying the coefficients for the variables making up the factor by the respondent's coding on each variable. The higher the score on a given factor, the more active an individual is on the types of activities represented by that factor.

Table 2.3 shows that women display a statistically significant higher level of activity on two of the six factors where a meaningful comparison between the sexes is possible: charitable activity and voting/socialisation. Women are also significantly higher on the women's movement factor (a predictable result given that a major component of this factor is membership in women's groups). Furthermore, the mean scores for women on two other factors, environmentalist and religious activist, are higher than those for men, though these differences are not statistically significant.

Table 2.3
Distribution of political participation factors: both sexes

	Political active[a]	Charit-able activ.[a]	Voting/ Sociali-sation[b]	Asser-tive[a]	Environ-mental-ist	Women Move-ment[a]	Religi-ous activist
Minimum							
Women	-48.2	-71.2	-233.2	-79.6	-62.9	-55.1	-32.1
Men	-48.2	-71.2	-233.2	-77.5	-62.9	-55.1	-32.1
1st quartile							
Women	-48.2	-71.2	-58.2	-73.5	-62.9	-55.1	-32.1
Men	-48.2	-71.2	-87.6	-71.9	-62.9	-55.1	-32.1
Median							
Women	-48.2	-10.2	17.0	-69.8	-21.9	-10.5	-32.1
Men	-27.0	-10.2	-1.2	12.7	-35.5	-25.4	-32.1
Mean							
Women	-11.1	9.0	7.8	-15.5	3.4	9.1	3.4
Men	11.1	-9.0	-8.2	15.4	-3.4	-9.1	-3.4
3rd quartile							
Women	-8.5	50.9	73.9	18.6	5.5	19.2	-32.1
Men	15.3	-10.2	69.3	101.6	-8.2	4.3	-32.1
90th percentile							
Women	61.4	37.6	108.0	107.9	60.1	49.0	75.6
Men	114.4	-10.2	105.6	196.7	46.4	34.1	-32.1
95th percentile							
Women	117.3	198.7	143.2	194.2	242.5	78.7	175.4
Men	223.0	198.7	142.1	200.1	218.0	63.8	175.4
Maximum							
Women	612.0	702.9	233.1	380.1	711.3	796.2	1022.1
Men	846.5	407.5	233.1	559.3	760.4	781.3	1138.2

[a] Means for women and men are significantly different at 0.001 level.
[b] Means for women and men are significantly different at 0.01 level. [ANOVA]

There does, then, appear to be support for a gender-based division of participation with women more involved in realms which are associated with assumed female essentialism (a nurturing disposition leading to 'caring' activities); while men are more involved in formally 'public'

45

activities and also emerge (on their own assessments) as more assertive in the realm of personal relationships. Men as a group score higher on political activism, the factor that, voting apart, encompasses all overtly political activities of both a conventional and unconventional sort. Men also are significantly higher on the 'assertive' factor; that is, the measure of willingness to discuss and argue about politics in their personal relationships. These higher scores for men on overtly political indicators of activity are broadly congruent with international results (Christy, 1987, p. 147).

Surveying the distribution of extremely high or extremely low activity across the factors of types of activity, the distributions of all seven of the factors display extreme upward skews; compared to the highest levels of activity for each factor, the average/modal amount of activity is very low. Only a small minority of people of either sex are, on the measures, highly active. Hence, a contrast between inactive/private women and active/public men is misleading: low levels of activity are the norm for both sexes.

Table 2.4
Extent of involvement in an organisation by sex*

	F	M
No involvement in any organisation/group	9.7	6.3
General agreement with goals of organisation but plays no active role	73.8	79.2
Sometimes contributes time or money	4.8	4.9
Active, regularly contributes time or money	8.1	5.5
'Grassroots' level, helps direct others but does not make major decisions	1.6	0.8
'Middle' level	1.2	1.6
At or close to top; plays a part in policy-making	0.8	1.8
Total	100.0	100.0
(N)	(1301)	(384)

* Difference between sexes significant at 0.05 level. [X^2]

Not too much should be made of the differences between the sexes, however, even when these differences are statistically significant. For instance, looking at the extent involvement in any organisation (Table 2.4), while fewer men show no involvement in any organisation or group, and more women report themselves to be active in at least one organisation, the overwhelming majority of both men and women, place themselves in the same category: a largely inactive role in an organisation whose goals they generally agree with. Commonly, both men and women are passive members of such bodies.

This is confirmed by Table 2.5, which is based upon a count of the number of factors for which each respondent had extremely low or high scores. Extremely low scores are defined as values equal to or less than the fifth percentile; extremely high scores are upper outliers, equal to or greater than the ninety-fifth percentile.[4]

Table 2.5
Distribution of number of levels of extremely high and extremely low activity by sex*

| | High | | Low | |
	F	M	F	M
None	68.4	73.4	7.8	7.0
One	21.6	16.1	20.5	22.9
Two	6.6	7.3	27.1	22.9
Three	2.1	2.1	20.5	19.0
Four	1.1	0.5	10.5	12.2
Five	0.2	0.3	10.2	14.3
Six	0.1	0.3	3.2	1.3
Seven	0.0	0.0	0.2	0.3
Total	100.0	100.0	100.0	100.0
(N)	(1301)	(384)	(1301)	(384)
Mean number of activities	0.5	0.4	2.5	2.6

* The differences between women and men for both the distributions $[X^2]$ and the mean numbers of high and low activities [ANOVA] are not statistically significant.

Little or no high activity is typical for both sexes: for example, only 1.4 per cent of women and only 1.1 per cent of men are 'high actives' on four or more factors. Over two-thirds of both the female and male respondents, 68 per cent and 73 per cent respectively, are not 'high actives' on any factor. Due partly to the highly skewed distributions of the activity factors, low activity - or even apathy - is a more common phenomenon. Only 7.8 per cent of women and 7.0 per cent percent of men do not score as a 'low active' on at least one factor. Furthermore, 24.1 per cent of the women and 28.1 per cent of the men can be typed as 'low actives' on four or more factors. That is, multiple low activity is a comparatively common feature of both the female and male samples, with approximately a quarter of each showing low levels of activity on a majority of the composite measures. Moreover, the differences between the sexes for both high and low activity in terms of both distribution and level are not statistically significant.

The above results in Table 2.3 to 2.5 imply that individuals show patterns of low, moderate or high activity across all of the factors. This is confirmed by Table 2.6, a correlation matrix of the scores of respondents on the seven types of activity. All of the activity factors are positively associated at a moderate level, with the majority of the associations being highly significant. The only partial exception is 'assertiveness' in personal relationships, which is not significantly associated with activity in the women's movement[5] and associates positively but at less than the 0.001 level with the 'environmentalist' and 'charitable activity' factors.

Table 2.6
Pearson correlations between the participation factors

	Political activity	Charitable activity	Voting/ Socialisation	Assertive	Environmentalist	Women Movement	Religious activist
Political activity	—	.146[a]	.300[a]	.272[a]	.254[a]	.123[a]	.481[a]
Charitable activity		—	.165[a]	.090[b]	.110[a]	.119[a]	.159[a]
Voting/ Socialisaton			—	.147[a]	.287[a]	.162[a]	.300[a]
Assertiveness				—	.055[c]	.033	.102[a]
Environmentalist					—	.324[a]	.232[a]
Women's movement						—	.161[a]
Religious activist							—

[a] Significant at 0.001 level.
[b] Significant at 0.01 level.
[c] Significant at 0.05 level.

48

The individual items that make up the components of each of the activity factors are now considered. Turning first to the 'political activity' factor in Table 2.7, which demonstrates a higher level of activity for men, we see that there is a higher level of contacting, significant at the 0.01 level, and that this is due first to more men writing 'several times (or more)' to public officials, 'such as a local councillor or someone in the Civil Service'; and secondly to more men having 'written a letter to a newspaper about a political issue'. One should note, however, that for all three types of contacting the vast majority, a minimum of 85 per cent, said they had 'never' written letters on political matters.

Table 2.7
Components of the 'political activity' factor by sex (%)

| | (a) *Contacting*[b] | | |
	Never	Once	Several times
Letter to MP			
Women	88.3	10.3	1.4
Men	86.5	10.7	2.9
Letter to public official[b]			
Women	89.3	8.7	2.1
Men	85.4	9.6	4.9
Letter to newspaper[a]			
Women	98.0	1.4	0.6
Men	95.3	3.4	1.3

| | (b) *Unconventional activities (%)* | | |
	Never	Once	Several times
Attended local council meeting[a]			
Women	94.2	4.1	1.7
Men	90.6	6.2	3.1
Attended other public meetings			
Women	82.9	10.9	6.2
Men	82.0	11.5	6.5

Table 2.7 cont...

	Never	Once	Several times
Work with others on local problems			
Women	92.9	4.1	3.0
Men	89.6	6.2	4.2
Circulated petition			
Women	92.6	6.0	1.4
Men	91.1	6.8	2.1
Attended lawful demonstration[c]			
Women	90.2	7.2	2.6
Men	75.7	13.3	11.0
Withheld rates, rents, taxes as polit. protest			
Women	98.4	1.3	0.1
Men	97.7	1.8	0.5
Other unconventional activities[b]			
Women	97.7	1.8	0.5
Men	94.2	4.2	1.6

(c) *Involved in a political party[a] (%)*		
	Women	Men
Contributed money to a party or campaign[c]	3.7	9.4
Helped out in an election (e.g., canvassed, sent out literature, took voters to polls, monitored, postered etc)[b]	4.7	8.7
Helped with fundraising[c]	2.8	6.8
Helped with paperwork (e.g., typing, kept minutes, accounts, other 'clerical' work)[a]	2.2	4.5
Member of a political party	1.6	2.1

Table 2.7 cont...

(d) *Pressure groups*

	Women	Men
Mean number of memberships in pressure groups	0.009	0.008
Standard deviation	0.092	0.088

[a] Difference between sexes significant at 0.05 level.
[b] Difference between sexes significant at 0.01 level.
[c] Difference between sexes significant at 0.001 level.

The second component of the political activity factor includes activities that the literature (e.g., Barnes and Kaase et al, 1979; Goel and Smith, 1980; Christy, 1987; Parry, Moyser and Day, 1992) has come to term 'unconventional'. Reflecting Northern Ireland's history over the last quarter century, the significant difference (X^2, $p < 0.001$) in favour of a higher level of activity for men appears most strongly in the proportions who have 'ever attended a lawful political demonstration or rally': almost a quarter of men, compared to less than ten per cent of women, have done so at least once. Men have also participated more in each of the other items that comprise this component, particularly those 'other unconventional activities' engaged in as a form of political protest such as occupying a building, blocking traffic or participating in an unofficial strike (5.8 per cent of men reporting at least once compared to 2.3 per cent of women, X^2, $p < 0.01$). The modal level of participation in all categories for both women and men, however, is 'never'.

The third component of the political activity factor concerns involvement with political parties. The overall level of involvement favours men (ANOVA, $p < 0.001$). They are, for instance, three times more likely than women to have 'contributed money to a political party or to a candidate's election campaign for office' (X^2, $p < 0.001$) and to have 'helped with fund-raising'. The hypothesis that women are more involved in grassroots party political activity is not supported. Significantly higher (X^2, $p < 0.01$) proportions of men, rather than women, claimed to have helped out during an election (e.g., sent out campaign literature, canvassed for a candidate, taken voters to the polls, monitored a polling station, put up posters, distributed leaflets, etc) and to have 'helped with paperwork' (e.g., kept minutes of meetings, typing, accounts and clerical-type office work) (X^2, $p < 0.05$). The only category of political party involvement for which men do not display a higher level of involvement is that of party membership: only small proportions of either sex are party members.[6] The most noteworthy feature of these findings is that the level of involvement in political parties by both women and men is negligible. This is also true of pressure groups: only miniscule proportions of each sex belong to such organisations.

The higher level of 'charitable activity' (Table 2.8) shown by women is explained by the significantly (ANOVA, $p < 0.001$) larger number of memberships of charitable groups. Women are more likely (33.3 per cent compared to 26 per cent of men, X^2, $p < 0.01$) to have been involved at some time 'in an unpaid, voluntary capacity in supporting or helping a charity' and are currently twice as likely to perform unpaid charitable work (X^2, $p < 0.001$). Men's relationship with charitable organisations takes a different form: they are more likely to donate money rather than to invest time and effort in voluntary charitable activities.

Table 2.8
Components of the 'charitable activity' factor by sex

(a) *Number of charity groups*[c]		
	F	M
Mean number of memberships in charitable groups	0.151	0.076
Standard deviation	0.459	0.293

(b) *Involved in charitable activities*[a] *(%)*		
Donation of significant amounts to charity	50.1	51.3
Ever performed unpaid voluntary work or help for a charity[b]	33.3	26.0
Currently an unpaid charity worker[c]	12.0	6.8

[a] Difference between sexes significant at 0.05 level.
[b] Difference between sexes significant at 0.01 level.
[c] Difference between sexes significant at 0.001 level.

Women also demonstrate a higher level of activity on the 'voting/socialisation' factor. (See Table 2.9)

Table 2.9
Voting components of the 'voting/socialisation' factor by sex[a]

	% voting in three elections	
	F	M
Previous General Election	77.1	73.0
Previous District Council election[b]	71.7	66.8
Previous European Parliament election	65.4	62.0

[a] The variables making up the 'socialisation' index appear in Tables 5.8a and 5.8b.
[b] Difference between sexes significant at 0.05 level.

Women display a greater propensity to vote in elections at all levels, but these differences are only significant for the previous local government election. On the socialisation index, women display more effort overall, which is largely explained by the larger proportions of women who have attempted to persuade their children to adopt their views on religion, sexual behaviour and sex equality. Notably, the only category where men show a higher (though not significantly higher) level of effort is in attempting to persuade their children to share their 'own political point of view'. (See Chapter 5 for a more extensive discussion of socialisation.)

Turning to employment related activities (Table 2.10), of those in paid work, men are more likely than women to belong, or have belonged, to a trade union or staff association in their present/last job. Of those currently in unions, a greater proportion of men 'always' attend union meetings. Of those who have ever been in unions, men are more likely (X^2, $p < 0.01$) to have voted or to have at some time put forward a proposal or motion at a union or staff association meeting. Among those who are or have ever been in paid employment, men are also more likely (X^2, $p < 0.001$) to have been on strike and to have picketed their place of work.

Table 2.10
Trade union components of the 'assertive' factor by sex[a]

| | In last fulltime job, member of:[b] | | |
	Union	Staff association	Neither
Women	39.4	3.7	56.9
Men	47.6	2.5	49.9

| | Frequency of attendance at union meetings | | | |
	Always	Often	Seldom	Never
Women	5.4	6.6	25.7	62.2
Men	15.4	3.8	26.9	53.8

	Women	Men
Ever gone on strike[c]	17.7	29.9
Ever stood in a picket line[c]	8.0	16.6
Ever voted in a union or staff association meeting[b]	39.7	72.0
Ever put forward a proposal or motion[b]	13.8	40.0

[a] The variables relating to the political discussion and efficacy appear in Tables 5.1, 5.3 and 5.4.
[b] Difference between sexes significant at 0.01 level.
[c] Difference between sexes significant at 0.001 level. $[X^2]$

The overall scores for women on the 'environmentalist' factor, though higher were not significantly different from those of men. This is demonstrated by disaggregating the factor into its component items. (Table 2.11)

Men show a slightly higher, though non-significant, average membership in environmental groups. Women display higher scores on average on a 'green index' due to their more 'activist' responses on two individual items; *viz.,* buying unleaded petrol and avoiding the use of pesticides. In each instance, a significantly higher (X^2, $p < 0.01$) percentage of women claim to do so 'to help the environment'.

Table 2.11
Components of the 'environmentalist' factor by sex

(a) *Environmental groups*	F	M
Mean number of memberships in environmental groups	0.049	0.055
Standard deviation	0.236	0.239

(b) *'Green' index** Buying 'ecological' products (%)	Always buy 'green'	Prefer 'green'	Buy on cost & quality only
Organic produce			
Women	6.4	32.4	61.2
Men	5.3	34.3	60.4
'Environmentally friendly' products			
Women	20.2	35.2	44.6
Men	20.7	36.0	43.2
Recycled products			
Women	12.7	36.6	50.7
Men	15.2	37.1	47.8

(c) *'Ecological' activities (%)*	To help environ.	Health reasons or to save money	Does not do
Return material for recycling			
Women	40.6	3.9	55.5
Men	37.8	2.9	59.8
Buying unleaded petrol*			
Women	40.8	7.2	52.0
Men	36.5	8.4	54.9
Avoid pesticide use*			
Women	39.1	14.5	45.7
Men	34.6	13.0	52.4

Table 2.11 cont...

(d) Avoids purchasing certain nation's goods as a form of protest (%)

	Yes	Yes, but depends on cost & quality	No
Women	12.5	3.8	83.7
Men	11.8	5.0	83.2

* Difference between sexes significant at 0.01 level. [X^2]

Items that may be considered indicators of 'consumer activism' do not display differences between the sexes. As far as purchasing 'environmentally friendly' products is concerned, the modal response of both sexes is to prefer to 'buy on grounds of cost and quality only'. Similarly, over 80 per cent of men and women do not participate in consumer boycotts of any country's goods as a form of protest.

The lack of a significant difference between the sexes on the 'religious activist' factor (Table 2.12) can be explained by the countervailing results for its two components.

Table 2.12
Components of the 'religious activist' factor

(a) 'Running for office' index

	Women	Men
Mean number of public offices nominated for, ran for or held (including offices within a political party)	0.104	0.156
Standard deviation	0.429	0.601

(b) Memberships in church groups

	Women	Men
Mean number of memberships in church groups*	0.117	0.057
Standard deviation	0.349	0.244

* Difference between sexes significant at 0.001 level. [ANOVA]

While women show a higher average membership in church groups ($p < 0.001$), men display a higher, though statistically non-significant, score on the 'office-seeking' index. As expected, women show a significantly higher membership in 'women's groups' although the overall level of participation is low, as indicated by the low average number of memberships across the whole of the female sample.[7]

Table 2.13
Component of the 'women's movements' factor

	Women	Men
Mean number of memberships in 'women's' groups*	0.025	0.008
Standard deviation	0.155	0.088

* Difference between sexes significant at 0.01 level. [ANOVA]

Conclusions

In some respects the above results can be said to be modest since they do not challenge in a fundamental way the findings of other studies of gender and political participation. In general, taking into consideration a wide range of conventional and unconventional activities, together with the assertion of political viewpoints in personal relationships, the level of women's activity emerges as somewhat below that of men. This result holds despite the inclusion of a wider range of such activities than those normally embraced by studies of political participation. However, when the net of participation is cast wider, women are found to be more active on some indices: charitable activities; voting; socialisation; and, predictably, participation in the women's movement itself. Surprisingly, in the area of consumer-related and environmental activities, neither women nor men are found to predominate.

These findings must be tempered, however, with the realisation that the main sources of the differences between men and women reside in the multiple activities of a small minority. The modal behaviour for both sexes on virtually all indices is a very moderate involvement that approaches apathy. The extended view of political activity employed by this study does, however, challenge the general view in the literature that the politically active are made up of a minority of only five to ten per cent of the population. While the norm for the samples is moderate activity, more than one in four do rate as highly active on at least one of the seven types of activity.

The next task is to ascertain the causes and correlations of the types of political activity (and inactivity) and the formative events and experiences that lead respondents to a level of participation beyond the norm.

Notes

1. Among the cues included in the survey instrument were the following: **In general, would you say that individuals should obey the law without exception, or are there circumstances where people could follow their consciences even if it means breaking the law?; [Are you] worried about the personal danger to yourself or your family of being involved in political activities in Northern Ireland?; Can you identify any individuals, experiences, events or groups that have had an important influence on your political opinions?**. While such indicators may seem rather obtuse, during the pre-testing and piloting phases of the questionnaire design they proved to be the most proficient means of probing this delicate area of potential activity.

2. Using OBLIM rotation on SPSS - a VARIMAX rotation produced the same substantive results. In order to avoid artefactual effects, the codings of the individual variables comprising the factors were standardised to a mean of zero and a standard deviation of one. Otherwise, the component variables that have a wide range would have had a disproportionate effect on the individual factor 'scores'. The clearest example of this would be the 'Voting/Socialisation' factor, where the 'voting index' ranges from 0 to 3 with a small standard deviation, while the 'socialisation index' ranges from 0 to 16 with a large standard deviation and a pronounced upward skew. When the standardised figures were compared with the equivalent 'unstandardised' figures, it was apparent that the use of the latter would have produced artefactual effects. Similarly, even though the coefficients for women and men on the factors common to both are very similar, unpredictable artefactual effects could have resulted from using different coefficients for each sex. Hence, the reported factors were derived from a sample that was weighted to make the numbers of women and men equal.

3. The juxtapostion of voting and the socialisation index together in a common factor does pose a problem of conceptual interpretation. This result, however, is extremely robust for both sexes, holding for

different types of factor rotation and when different mixes of variables are included in factor analyses. Regression analysis establishes that age is a main determinant of higher rates of voting and of higher scores on the socialisation index. Being married is also a strong predictor of voting, and obviously is strongly associated with having children and thereby being eligible for a score on the socialisation index. Hence, while the 'voting/socialisation' factor may be an artefact of the characteristics of people who both vote and socialise, its presentation with more conceptually interpretable factors has been retained.

4. The maximum possible count that an individual could have received is seven. As in Tables 1-3, to avoid artefactual effects, 'standardised' versions of the factor scores based upon a weighted sample are used.

5. The correlation between the 'assertiveness' and 'women's movement' factors remains non-significant even if its calculation is restricted to the female sample only.

6. The political parties in Northern Ireland do not disclose membership figures.

7. Three men did claim membership in women's groups.

3 Modelling participation

Modelling activity

Besides establishing the variety of forms of political activity in which individuals are engaged, the previous chapter also noted that there is considerable variation both between activities and in the extent of participation within them. The next step is to discover whether these variations can be explained in sociological terms.

Structural causes (cultural capital)

The causes of variance in levels of political activity can be grouped into four broad categories. First, the literature on the causes of political participation identifies a broad category of *structural* characteristics that may have the effect of increasing political activity. The discussion of structural causes is somewhat contradictory, but a common characteristic is a broad hypothesis that political activity is facilitated by the possession or non-ownership of cultural, educational and social capital (Jennings, 1983; Clark and Clark, 1986; Verba, Nie and Kim, 1978, pp. 234-265). As Jennings observes:

> Key institutions in such domains as education, the economy, and the law are configured to deny women the same opportunities, benefits, and protection that are accorded men. The result is that women occupy structural niches that are less conducive to robust political activity. For example, women typically have less advanced education than do men and certainly they often acquire a qualitatively different education even when the years of schooling are equivalent. The female occupational

structure also differs substantially from that of men. (Jennings, 1983, pp. 364-365)

Similarly, the structural effects of higher social/occupational position may be associated with higher levels of public activity. This association can occur either as a result of the extension to other competitive spheres, including politics, of abilities that are necessary for occupational achievement, or they may issue from the opportunities afforded by a higher class position (Goel, 1980). This category of structural features will be termed 'Cultural Capital' in order to differentiate it from a second category of structural features, those relating to social background or location in society. Before discussing this latter type, another group of hypothesised causes of political activity is introduced, *viz. situational* features.

Situational causes

From the situational perspective, sometimes termed the adult socialisation perspective (Sapiro 1983, Andersen 1975), the position of women, particularly those who are married and/or a parent, can be supposed to be more, and differently, affected by marriage and the demands of domestic roles (Christy, 1987; Welch, 1977). Welch (1980, p. 31) encapsulates this explanation thus:

> It has been argued that the traditional women's roles of housewife and mother diminish female interest and opportunity to participate in politics. Because a woman must take care of spouse and children, the argument goes, she has limited opportunity for activities such as political ones that take her outside the home. This can be called the 'situational' explanation.

Jennings (1983, p. 364) echoes this perspective:

> The situational explanation looks to the contemporary characteristics of a woman's life space. Such roles as wife, mother, divorcee, widow, and homemaker are said in one way or another to inhibit political participation. These are held to be confining and isolating roles, roles that do not permit easy access to such political resources as time, money, contacts, organisational life, channels of communication, and the general skill levels that typically accompany high rates of political action. Even when women break out of such traditional roles, it is argued that they must continue to carry the traditional roles along with the new ones, thus imposing a dampening effect. (Jennings, 1983, p. 364)

An alternative means of distinguishing between structural characteristics and situational characteristics is to note that the 'situations' cited by the literature all apply to women in female roles (Welch, 1980). Men should not be affected by situational characteristics, except, that is, negatively by virtue of their non-applicability.

Structural causes (social background)

The second subset of 'structural' features apparent in the literature includes socio-demographic characteristics other than those pertaining directly to education, occupation or class position and which are distinct from the situational variables mentioned above. These characteristics, such as age, geographical location or religion (particularly salient in Northern Ireland), are associated with social background. In effect, these 'Type B - Social Background' characteristics make up a residual category that is neither structural 'Type A' nor 'situational'.

This third category of hypothesised causes of political activity is based upon a socialisation approach: that is, effects that have their origin in the individual's upbringing or the atmosphere in the home during childhood. Clark and Clark (1986, p. 6) summarise the core of the argument thus:

> women do not participate in politics because they are culturally conditioned to accept the world of politics as a male sphere. This perspective assumes that sexual differences in political behaviour stem from sex roles engendered in the socialisation process and that they appear fairly early in childhood.

Jennings (1983, p. 375) also adopts the childhood socialisation thesis to explain the political roles embraced by adults:

> The contention is that pre-adult males and females are not only socialised into different participative roles, but that both boys and girls learn that adult political expression is more of a male than female gender role.... Because these norms are learned early, they also prove resistant to later inducements designed to encourage more female participation. They may even prove resistant to structural and situational reforms that should foster such increases.

Occasionally, the residual that cannot be attributed to structural or situational effects has been (mis)assigned to socialisation. For example, Welch (1980, p. 32): 'Differences in levels of male and female participation that cannot be reduced by controlling for situational and structural factors might be ascribed to the notion that females are encouraged not to participate in politics by the effects of childhood and adult socialisation, or to other causes'.[1] Aside from the flaw in such an argument (the unexplained variance may be validly due to causes other than socialisation, or simply to measurement error in the model), there are real difficulties in operationalizing socialisation. A true test of the concept would require a longitudinal and intergenerational research design that measured the public activity and socialising behaviour of the parents (and other agencies of socialisation) during the childhood of the respondents in order to conceptualise and 'explain' current activities. Our study does have two variables that can be considered to relate, albeit in a non-longitudinal manner, to socialisation: the number of groups to which both the parents and the spouses/partners of respondents belong. One may note, also, that there is overlap between the situational perspective and the socialisation perspective when it is extended to the socialisation of adults. Adult socialisation into a politically active role (or the confirmation when an adult of a politically quiescent role established in childhood) is facilitated by the opportunities available for political activity that are supplied by an individual's context and situation (Dawson, 1980, pp. 87, 97-98).

Personal dynamics

These latter categories lead to a fourth, more innovative, category employed by this study. Qualitative interviews with the active demonstrate that while participation may be facilitated by structure or situation these are neither necessary nor sufficient for explaining higher levels of activity (see Chapter 4). There are, for instance, active individuals who have risen above the limitations imposed by institutional structures and/or by their personal situations. Equally, there is an abundance individuals who both possess a plethora of structural resources and who are situated in ways ostensibly conducive to activity but who are, nevertheless, politically quiescent. The development of a politically active individual may more profitably be seen as an evolution rather than a birth. Significant experiences and significant others can combine with an apparently trivial (or non-trivial) 'key' which unlocks a chain of events that lead an individual towards politically activity. Personal dynamics may therefore underlie political activity and involvement

This study employs a number of quantitative measures relating to personal interactions both within the household and within organisations which concern the incidence of significant experiences in the life histories of respondents and that emerge as precursors of political activity. This proposition will be explored in more detail in Chapter 4 by way of the 'potted' life-histories that were explored during the second qualitative phase. Later in this Chapter we present the findings from the first phase that underline the significance of personal dynamics for the incidence of political participation. First, however, the means of distinguishing among the various levels of explanation for activism are now elaborated.

Operationalising the categories of explanation

In relation to the 'Cultural Capital' explanations for increased activity, a series of indicators of educational experience and occupational/class position are included. The level of educational attainment is represented by an ordinal variable based upon the eleven-category CASMIN scale developed for international comparison (Müller et al, 1988). This corresponds to an educational variant of the structural effects on participation hypothesised by some authors (e.g., Clark and Clark, 1986).

Present occupational/class effects are represented by four variables:
- an ordinal coding of the respondent's own job position, 'SES', adapted from the Nuffield College codings developed for the study of social mobility (Goldthorpe and Hope, 1974);
- a series of employment status dummy variables (full-time employment, part-time employment and unemployed);
- a variable representing the interaction of employment status and level of educational attainment;[2]
- a variable indicating the class of the household.[3]

A series of other 'demographic' variables are included as indicators of 'Social Background' explanations:
- as a test of increasing involvement with age and life experience, age in years;
- two variables to test an hypothesis of a 'peaked' model of involvement, in which activity increases gradually up to middle age only to decline in later life: *viz* a dummy variable of whether respondents were middle-aged or not; and 'age squared' - the square of the difference between the respondent's age and the mean age of the overall sample (Goel, 1980, pp. 118-119);[4]
- two variables relating to marriage and domestic roles are included: whether or not married/with partner; and whether the respondent is the head of household;

- dummy variables for Protestant or Catholic;
- several urban/rural location dummy variables.

The Situational explanation is operationalized by two standard variables common to the literature:
- total number of children;
- number of children under five;

and two additional variables that perhaps more clearly represent the logic underlying the situational explanation:
- an increase in activity for 'family reasons';
- the respondent stating that the presence of children within the household hindered activity.

The Socialisation explanation is operationalized by three variables:
- an adult socialisation effect; i.e., whether or not respondents were 'returners to education';
- the effect of a home background; i.e., whether or not respondents came from politically active families;
- whether the respondents spouses/partners are themselves politically active, represented by the number of 'voluntary or political activities' in which the spouse/partner is involved in.

As stated above, the data also provided the opportunity to develop measures of Personal Dynamics in order to explore their possible effects on political activity. To that end the following variables were included in the model:
- the extent of support from the spouse/partner for the respondent's activities;
- whether the respondent reports that they have been affected significantly in their activities or opinions by another, nameable, individual or event;
- whether the respondent reported being 'asked to do more' on behalf of a particular organisation;
- whether the respondent nominated having more time, more experience or more confidence as reasons for increasing her/his level of activity.

Results

Table 3.1
Regression models of causes of activity[a]

	Polit activism	Charit-able activity	Voting/ Sociali- sation	Asser- tive	Envir- onmen- talist	Wom. move- ment	Religi- ous activist
Female		.088[d]	.074[d]		.069[e]	.096[d]	

Personal dynamics

	Polit activism	Charit-able activity	Voting/ Sociali- sation	Asser- tive	Envir- onmen- talist	Wom. move- ment	Religi- ous activist
Partner support	.132[c]	.314[c]	.103[c]		.140[c]	.101[d]	.317[c]
Important person	.080[d]						
Important event	.162[c]			.070[e]	.084[d]		
Important org./group	.185[c]	.088[d]		.132[c]		.073[e]	.105[c]
Asked to do more							.177[c]
Increased due to more time	.075[d]	.181[c]				.093[d]	
Increased due to experience			.072[d]	.066[e]			
Increased due to confidence	.209[c]			.071[e]			.083[d]

Structural, 'Type A - Cultural Capital'

	Polit activism	Charit-able activity	Voting/ Sociali- sation	Asser- tive	Envir- onmen- talist	Wom. move- ment	Religi- ous activist
Education		.097[d]		.114+			.110[c]
Interaction, SES & Ed	.073[e]				.331[c]	.151[c]	
SES				-.133[c]			
Part-time working				-.111[c]			
Housespouse				-.101[d]			
Number of work groups	.105[c]						.147[c]
Increased due to job					.108[c]		
Household class		.126[c]				.103[d]	

Table 3.1 cont...

Structural, 'Type B - Social Background'

	Polit activism	Charitable activity	Voting/ Socialisation	Assertive	Environmentalist	Wom. movement	Religious activist
Age			$.567^c$	$.105^e$			
Age squared[b]			$.274^c$	$.253^c$	$.101^c$		
Middle-aged	$.063^e$	$.072^e$					
Married			$.096^e$	$.144^c$			
Head of household	$.078+$			$.128^c$			
Belfast resident			$-.107+$	$.109+$			
Protestant						$.109^c$	$.095^d$
Catholic		$.071^e$					
Situational							
Increased due to family						$.071^e$	
Children hinder				$.081^d$	$-.094^d$		
Socialisation							
Return to education	$.117^c$						
Parents active	$.081^d$	$.124^c$					
Spouse active	$.079^d$				$.084^e$		
Adjusted r^2	.349	.252	.336	.191	.241	.112	.255

[a] Variables not included in *any* model are:
- *structural 'Type A'* - part-time employment, unemployed, rural area;
- *situational* - housewife, number of children, number of children under 5;
- *personal dynamics* - decreased due to other interests, decreased due to tension in organisation.

[b] A positive sign indicates age squared is close to the mean age of the overall sample, 42.2 years.

[c] Significant at 0.001 level.

[d] Significant at 0.01 level.

[e] Significant at 0.05 level.

67

Table 3.1 reports the results of these modelling exercises for the seven factors of public activity.[5] The variance in activity that can be explained ranges from 35 per cent for direct involvement in conventional and unconventional politics, the 'Political Activism' factor, to 11 per cent for involvement in the 'Women's Movement' (as can be seen from the bottom (adjusted r^2) row). The amount of variance explained is considerably higher than other multivariate models of participation (e.g., Clark and Clark, 1986, Dalton, 1988, pp. 36-48, Bean, 1991b). The effects are statistically significant and, since previous analyses have shown that high levels of activity are a minority phenomenon, it is to be expected that the models do not explain 100 per cent of the variance in activity.

Given that gross differences exist between the sexes for most of the types of activity, a close inspection of the nature of the effects displayed by the different categories of causal variables proves enlightening. In these multivariate models *the variable of sex does not have a major effect on the level of activity of **any** of the seven activity types*, even for involvement in the women's movement. Neither, however, is the effect of sex excluded entirely from the models. Being female raises the level of activity for four factors: 'Charitable Activity'; 'Voting/Socialisation'; the consumer-oriented 'Environmentalist Activities'; and involvement in the 'Women's Movement'.[6] In these multivariate models, neither women nor men show significantly different levels of activity on any of the factors comprising 'Political Activism', 'Assertiveness' and 'Religious Activist'.

The most intriguing results from this analysis relate to the group of variables that may be defined as the effects of personal dynamics. The most important of these, and the most important single variable overall in the regression models, is the effect of having a spouse/partner who supports the respondent's own activity/involvement. The support of one's spouse has a highly positive effect on six of the seven factors and is the only variable to do so.[7]

The importance of a supportive spouse indicates the significance of social relationships upon activity. The effects of such support are distinct from the rather "mechanical" influences of an individual's demographic and sociological background. This is confirmed by the significant effects exerted by other aspects of personal dynamics: reporting politically significant events[8] or significant others[9] in one's past; the ability to name specific groups or organisations that have exerted important effects upon one's political beliefs; and increasing involvement in groups or organisations either because one has been asked to do more, had more time at one's disposal, gained more experience, or because of a growth in self-confidence. The nature of these 'personal dynamics' effects will be discussed in some detail below.

The effects of the structural variables, either 'Cultural Capital' or 'Social Background', are found to be noteworthy in explaining higher levels of all of the seven activity types. This finding is in common with other prediction models of activity (e.g., Welch, 1980, pp. 32-33). With a larger number of structural variables applied in the regression analyses than is usual, however, one can observe some interesting differences and refinements to the patterns of findings typically noted in the literature. The structural variables (combinations of the respondents' educational experience and/or job status) significantly affect all types of activity with the exception of voting/socialisation - and the effect (with one exception) is in the expected direction: i.e., the higher the respondent's level of educational attainment or employment status, the higher the level of political activity or involvement. The only real departure from this pattern is 'Assertiveness', where SES exerts a negative effect. (But only after a positive effect of higher educational attainment and the negative effects of either being in part-time employment or a housespouse are included.[10])

Individuals in a job of a lower status than is commensurate with their educational attainment might be hypothesised to be more assertive than the norm. In relation to its effects upon level of environmental activism and involvement in the women's movement, however, education only appears in interaction with SES; that is, it is individuals who possess *both* a higher level of education and a higher job status who are the most active. The link between organisational involvement and public activity sometimes noted in the literature appears here. Involvement in groups related to employment is a highly significant predictor of the extent of conventional and unconventional 'Political Activism' and of the 'Religious Activist' factor. Household class has positive effects on 'Charitable Activities' and, somewhat ironically - given that the operationalisation of the 'household class' variable is often a *de facto* proxy for the social status of the husband - upon involvement in the 'Women's Movement' (similar to McDonagh (1982) for the United States).

In relation to the 'Type B' structural category (other sociological/demographic variables), the urban/rural division proves to have relatively few effects on activism: Belfast (urban) residents rank lower on the Voting/Socialisation index and higher on the Assertiveness index. Religion has only three significant effects: an association between a Protestant identity and religious activism;[11] an association between being Protestant and involvement in women's groups;[12] and a weak association between 'Charitable Activity' and a Catholic identity.

The effects of the age of respondents upon the levels of various types of activity, either directly or as middle-aged, are noteworthy: older age has an extremely strong effect upon the 'Voting/Socialisation' factor, while being younger increases the respondents' index of 'Environmental Activism'. The most pronounced affects of age, however, relate to the two measures of being middle-aged - 'age squared' and the middle-aged 'dummy' variable. Proximity to the average (middle) age of the sample associated positively with 'Assertiveness' and 'Environmentalist' activities but not with 'Voting/Socialisation'. The middle-aged also are found to be both slightly more active politically and slightly more involved in 'Charitable Activity' than either the young or the old. Married respondents of both sexes score higher on the 'Voting/Socialisation' and 'Assertiveness' indices while heads of households, not necessarily men, score higher on 'Assertiveness'.

Compared to the structural variables, there is a paucity of causal effects upon political participation that can be attributed to situational variables. In the multivariate models, the variables most commonly defined as situational - housewife status,[13] number of children and number of children under five - have *no* significant effects on any of the seven types of activity. Arguably, the two situational variables that do show significant effects on activity types do so because they tap more directly the underlying logic of situational effects; that there are particular aspects of domestic/familial roles and child-rearing which affect women more than men and limit their activities outside the home. Claiming that children have hindered public activity is weakly associated with 'Assertiveness'. Respondents were asked: **'Over the years, has the amount of time you devote to the organisation (you) mentioned previously. . . Increased; Decreased; Remained about the same; Increased for some organisations and decreased for others?'** Where respondents stated that the amount of time had 'increased' or 'increased for some', they were then asked the reasons for the increase, with 'family reasons' provided as one of the alternatives. An increased involvement for family reasons is found to have a significant positive effect upon the level of participation in the 'Women's Movement'. This finding challenges the assumed dampening of activity occasioned by situational effects and in two ways: first respondents claimed that their level of involvement in the 'Women's Movement' had *increased* for family reasons; and secondly, the claim that children hinder activity is *negatively* associated with 'Environmentalist Activity'

As noted above, the evidence for socialisation effects has often been taken as implied; i.e., the variance that cannot be assigned to structural and situational causes is attributed to socialisation. Here, the model does contain some measures that are arguably less implicit and these proxies for socialisation do show some significant effects. For instance, having returned to education sometime after completion of the normal pattern of full-time education augments conventional and unconventional types of 'Political Activism'. Equally the number of groups in which the parents of respondents were reputed to be involved had positive effects upon the 'Charitable Activity' and 'Political Activism' of the respondents. Similarly, the number of groups in which the respondent's partner is involved also has positive effects both upon the 'Political Activism' of the respondent and upon the respondent's 'Environmentalist Activity'.

By combining the effects of personal dynamics with structural, situational and socialisation influences, profiles of active individuals across the seven factors can be established.[14]

Profiles of activists

Individuals who score highly on the *personal politics* profile tend to have been influenced in the past by the activities of a discrete group/organisation and to have had their views shaped by a significant event and/or a significant other. They enjoy the active support of a spouse/partner who is also politically active, and are likely to come from a family background which included politically active members. Such individuals have also benefited from the increased confidence derived from organisational involvement; they may be adult returnees to formal education; and tend to be the head of the household. Moreover, they are equally likely to be either a woman or a man.

The second profile refers to those engaged in *charitable activities*. Such individuals have a supportive spouse/partner; their involvement has increased because they have more time on their hands; they tend to come from politically active families and to have been subject to influence by early exposure to a significant group/organisation and/or a significant event. Their household tends to be middle class, they are well-educated, may be Catholic and are predominantly female.

The highly active within the third profile - *voting/socialising young politically* - are frequent voters and make active efforts to socialise their offspring; they tend to be older or middle-aged; to have a supportive spouse; and to live outside the Belfast metropolitan area in a rural or other urban area. They commonly display increased activity consequent upon the acquisition of experience gained from organisational involvement and are more likely to be female.

The *assertive*, the fourth profile, are middle-aged, married and/or head of a household, are neither in full-time employment nor a 'housespouse' and were subject to influence by a significant group, organisation or event. They are educated, but are not necessarily of a high socio-economic status, and tend to reside within the Belfast area. Such individuals also claim to have increased confidence as a result of their organisational involvement and can be either female or male.

Those involved in *environmentalist* activities exhibit both high levels of socio-economic status and educational attainment. They have a supportive spouse who is politically active, and are involved in groups related to their employment. Such individuals also claim that their activities are not hindered by the presence of children and to have been influenced in the past by an important event. They are likely to be female.

Those with a high *women's movement* profile also enjoy a high socio-economic status and have achieved a high level of educational attainment. They tend to have a supportive spouse, are Protestant and middle class. Their level of activity has typically increased both because of greater time at their disposal and for family reasons, and they tend to have been influenced in the past by exposure to a group or organisation. Such individuals are more likely to be women.

The final profile is that of the *religious activist*. They have a supportive spouse/partner and tend to have been asked to do more on behalf of their group/organisation. They also are involved with workplace organisations and in their life history acknowledge the influence of a significant group/organisation. Such individuals are educated, their level of confidence has grown as a result of their activities, they are more likely to be Protestant and can be of either sex.

Modelling intensity of political activity

Having identified the profiles of activists, one can now move to reporting the results of these modelling exercises for the measures of level of intensity of public activity (Table 3.2).

The variance in intensity of activity that can be explained ranges from 43.4 per cent for the number of different types of activity to 29 per cent for number of levels of low activity (adjusted r^2). The effects shown are statistically significant. Close inspection of the types of effects displayed by the different categories of causal variables proves enlightening. In these multivariate models, the gender variable has significant effects upon only one of the four measures: women display a significantly greater number of higher levels of activity.[15]

Table 3.2
Regression models of intensity measures of activity[a]

	No. of types of activity	No. of high levels of activity	No. of low levels of activity	Max. extent of org. involvement
Female		.078[d]		
Personal dynamics				
Partner support	.223[c]	.239[c]	-.160[c]	.445[c]
Important person	.086[d]	.062[e]	-.079[e]	
Important event	.117[c]		-.074[e]	
Important organisation/group	.099[c]	.138[c]	-.097[d]	.093[c]
Asked to do more		.060[e]		.121[c]
Increased due to more time	.102[c]	.110[c]		.160[c]
Increased due to job		-.078[d]		
Increased due to experience		.066[e]		.095[c]
Increased due to more confidence		.102[c]		.074[d]
Decreased due to tension				-.065[e]
Structural, 'Cultural Capital'				
Interaction, SES & Education	.138[c]	.081[e]	-.164[c]	.073[d]
Full-time working				.056[e]
Work groups	.109[c]			
Household class	.081[d]		.161[c]	

Table 3.2 cont...

Structural, ' Social Background'

	No. of types of activity	No. of high levels of activity	No. of low levels of activity	Max. extent of org. involvement
Age	.095^d			
Age squared^b	.169^c		-.139^c	
Married	.068^e		-.080^d	
Head of household	.075^d			
Belfast resident	.060^e			
Protestant	.192^c		-.248^c	.100^c
Catholic	.103^d		-.131^d	

Situational

Children hinder activity		-.063^e		
Number of children	.165^c	.072^e		

Socialisation

Returned to education	.101^c	.065^e	-.081^d	
Number of groups parents were in	.092^c	.115^c	-.065^e	.136^c
Number of groups spouse is in		.112^c		
Adjusted r^2	.434	.296	.288	.416

[a] Variables not included in any model are:
  - *structural* - education, SES, part-time employment, unemployed, middle-aged, rural area;
  - *situational* - housewife, number of children under 5, increased due to family reasons;
  - *personal dynamics* - decreased due to other interests, decreased due to tension in organisation.

[b] Positive value indicates proximity to mean age of sample, 42.2 years.

[c] Significant at 0.001 level.

[d] Significant at 0.01 level.

[e] Significant at 0.05 level.

Effects of personal dynamics

Turning first to the effects of 'personal dynamics', the most important of these, and the most important single variable overall in the multivariate models, is the 'partner effect'; i.e., having a spouse or partner who supports one's own activity/involvement. As with the seven types of activity, 'support of spouse' has the strongest positive effect of all variables on all three of the measures of high involvement, and a strongly negative effect upon the number of levels of low activity. Moreover, the partner effect along with the interaction of education and job status and the 'number of parent's groups' are the only variables to significantly affect all four measures. In addition to the presence of a supportive partner, the significance of personal dynamics is confirmed by the importance of: politically significant events; significant others in one's past; the capacity to name groups or organisations that have had an important effect upon political beliefs; and interactional reasons for increased involvement in groups or organisations.

Structural effects

The effects of the structural variables help to explain the variance in two of the measures of intensity of activity: *number of types of different activities* and *the numbers of levels of low activity*.[16] Unlike its effects upon types of activity the level of educational attainment does not exert a significant influence upon intensity of political activity. (Note the contrast with Sapiro (1983), where the effect of education was most important for activities such as contacting public officials, voting and campaigning.) The effects of education upon level of environmental activism and involvement in the women's movement only appears in interaction with SES. The nexus between organisational involvement and public activity noted earlier appears here, with involvement in employment-related organisations[17] emerging as a highly significant predictor of the number of different types of activity.

The urban/rural division exerts some effects on activism, notably in the finding that Belfast (urban) residents rank lower on the measure of low levels of activity and higher on the index of variety of types of activity. This is perhaps a product of differential opportunity, since the range of avenues for involvement are related to the concentration of the population in the Belfast area.[18] Religion has three significant effects: both Protestants and Catholics show a greater variety of types of activity; a higher maximum extent of organisational involvement; and proportionately fewer instances of low levels of activity.[19] The effect of the age of respondents upon the number of types of activity was again quite strong with the proximity variable for middle age, age squared, having a significant positive effect. Similarly, being middle-aged negatively affects the number of unusually low levels of activity. However, consistent with the results from other multivariate models of women's political participation (Clark and Clark, 1986, p. 19), these age effects for the other measures of intensity of involvement (the number of levels of unusually high activity and the maximum extent of organisational involvement), are subsumed within other variables in the multivariate models. Heads of households, not necessarily men, score higher on the index of number of different types of activity.

Situational effects

Compared to the structural variables, there is a paucity of causal effects that can be attributed to situational variables. Housewife status and number of children under five have no significant effects on any of the measures. Furthermore, where significant effects are found, the evidence is contra-indicative for situational effects. For instance, claiming that children hinder activity is negatively associated with the number of levels of high activity, while a higher number of children raises both the number of types of activity and the number of levels of high activity engaged in by a respondent. Hence, congruent with Sapiro (1983) and Welch (1980, pp. 43-44), there is an overall lack of support for a hypothesised link between the burdens imposed by child-rearing responsibilities and a lower level of political activity; that is, being a housewife, as opposed either to paid employment or seeking work outside the home, has little significant dampening effect on activities.

The three proxies for socialisation used in this study do exert significant effects. Returning to education augments activity, particularly in regard to the number of different types of activity. Furthermore, the numbers of groups/organisations in which the parents of respondents are/were involved has positive effects upon each of the measures of activity. Similarly, the number of groups in which a respondent's spouse participates also has a positive effect upon the number of high levels of activity of the respondent.

Profiles of activists

The interactions of personal dynamics with structural, situational and socialisation effects yields four descriptive profiles of activists.

The first, the *hyperactive*, refers to those respondents who are involved in a wide range of different types of activity. They characteristically enjoy the support of a spouse/partner, profess to be either Protestant or Catholic and are well-educated - perhaps having returned to full-time education after the completion of compulsory schooling. They are likely to be in a high status occupation, are middle-class and participate in employment-related groups or organisations. Such individuals are also middle-aged or older, are married, heads of households and are parents. Their life history includes the experience of a seminal event or the influence of a specific group or organisation and/or a significant other.[20] They also tend to have increased their scope and intensity of activity because they have more time at their disposal. Such 'hyperactives' had politically active parents and are equally as likely to be female as male.

The second group, the *superactive*, exhibit unusually high levels of involvement in several activities. They also enjoy the benefit of a supportive spouse/partner, who in turn is also politically active. The influence of a group/organisation and/or a significant other in the past is a common feature, as is the presence of active parents as role models. Their activity level has increased because of the availability of time, the growth of personal confidence and the acquisition of experience (as well as the effect of having been asked to do more of behalf of the groups to which they belong). They too are well-educated, commonly are adult returnees to education and have high status occupations. The superactive are likely to be parents who have been unhindered by the experience of parenthood. Any decrease in the level of their political activity has occurred for employment-related reasons. The superactive are more likely to be women.

The third of the profiles, the *intensive*, displays involvement in at least one type of activity that is at, or close, to the maximum recorded for the sample. They again enjoy the support of a spouse/partner and have increased their level of involvement because of the availability of time and growth in both their confidence and experience. They also had or have politically active parents, are Protestant and were influenced by a specific group or organisation in their past. They are educated, are likely to be employed on a full-time basis in a high status occupation and are equally likely to be female as male.

The final profile, the *somnolent,* exhibit several unusually low levels of activity in comparison with the rest of the sample. They tend to be in low status occupations, have few if any formal educational qualifications and neither profess to have been influenced by any seminal events nor acknowledge the existence of significant others in their lives. They do not have supportive spouses, are not middle-aged, their parents also were inactive and they tend to cleave to neither the Protestant nor the Catholic faiths.

Although the rank ordering of the significant effects and the measure of activity vary, there is a marked similarity among the "high activity" profiles. The low activity profile, however, is sharply different from each of the others: in fact, a negative image of them. Rather than describing this latter group as somnolent, perhaps a more evocative description might be 'isolates' - they enjoy few, if any, of the resources that characterise the active in our midst.

At least three aspects of these results merit further comment. First, in relation to personal dynamics, there is a need to clarify the role of significant others and the effects of important events that underlie involvement. Secondly, the complete absence of evidence supporting situational explanations for public activity and political involvement encourages a sharper focus on the effects of child-rearing upon levels of activity. And thirdly, there is a need to address the motives underlying political activity and involvement.

Significant others and significant events

In terms of the role models identified by respondents clear differences emerged between the sexes. While the same proportions of women and men stated that relatives in their parental home had been involved in voluntary or political activities, a definite gender pattern was evident. While only a minority of the activists came from 'political' families, among those claiming an active family background, women were much more likely to cite only the mother as having been active (38 per cent compared to only 5 per cent of men mentioning active mothers). Among male respondents claiming an active family background, the contrary applied. Two-thirds of men mentioned only an active father, compared to 21 per cent of women.

Similar proportions of women and men (22 per cent overall) named at least one person who had been important in shaping their political beliefs. While for both sexes these significant others were more likely to be male, this was particularly so for men (73 per cent of the significant others named by men were male compared to 59 per cent for the women). To that extent, men emerge as primary agents of socialisation within the context of the family. This finding, derived from those with active backgrounds is, however, somewhat tempered by related results from the wider sample. For instance, parents jointly emerge as having exerted the greatest influence over the views and opinions of all respondents.

Women were more likely than men to mention their parents as significant others (62 per cent compared to 43 per cent for men) but, unlike those with active backgrounds, only just over half of the parents named by both sexes were the fathers. Apart from parents, the other categories of individuals nominated as significant others included politicians, friends, spouses and other family members. Men were, however, more likely than women to name significant others who were not family members.

The identity of the individual agents of political socialisation also reveal certain gender differences. Of the relative proportions of those named as significant others, men were more likely than women to identify politicians (29 per cent of those named by men, compared to 13 per cent of those named by women) or friends (16 per cent for men, eight per cent for women). Politicians, who were the second most popular source of influence were, not surprisingly, more likely to be male, especially among men. While women were more likely to mention their spouses than were men (six per cent and one per cent respectively), the relative weight of any reported influence exerted by one's spouse is extremely modest compared to other agents (See Chapter 5). Few of either sex mentioned siblings, teachers or ministers of religion as significant others. Approximately seven per cent of both sexes did name members of the extended family as having exerted a significant influence upon their political beliefs.

Turning to significant events, respondents were invited to nominate an experience, whether within or without Northern Ireland, personal or impersonal, direct or indirect, that they considered to have had a formative impact upon their political views and opinions. Overall, more of the men (18 per cent compared to 12 per cent of the women) named such an event in their lives. Of these, the overwhelming majority of events named by both sexes related to 'the troubles' in one way or another. Approximately equal proportions of women and men mentioned either: 'the troubles' in general; a specific event experienced indirectly, most commonly through the mass media; or a first-hand encounter with some aspect of the current cycle of violence.[21] A generation effect can be observed for those whose views were formed before and after the advent of 'the troubles'. For instance, one middle-aged Catholic female respondent, the eldest of five children, noted a closer affinity of view with her parents than with her younger siblings, which she explained in terms of their differential experience of 'the troubles':

I think we probably do hold different views on the political situation, but I think it's the troubles, not so much what my parents brought us up to believe, it's the troubles themselves, I think...I mean they [her siblings] weren't here to see the way it was before and to see civil rights, you know, to see the progression, really...The two youngest in our family...they could never get out of it.

Men, especially Protestants, were somewhat more likely to mention events that related directly to the constitutional status of Northern Ireland: the proroguing of the Stormont Parliament and, more recently, the Anglo-Irish Agreement of 1985 were cited frequently as catalytic episodes by Protestant males. Among Catholic women and men, the hunger strikes of the early 1980s recurred as a significant event, as did the emergence of the civil rights movement in the later 1960s. Despite probes, few mentioned personal or local events that were unrelated to 'the troubles'.[22] There was no discernible pattern among the other named events which included the end of the Second World War, the Suez Crisis, famine in Africa, the collapse of the USSR and the end of the Cold War and the assassination of John Kennedy.

That 'the troubles' should bulk so large among those nominating a significant event is not surprising. Less predictable, however, is the finding that only relatively small minorities of the general population chose to identify the pathological aspects of Northern Ireland as exerting a formative influence on their views. The qualitative interviews indicate strongly that, for many, the experience of political violence has engendered neither apathy nor alienation, but rather a sense of resignation among respondents.

Child-rearing effects

Those with children (of whatever age) were asked: **'How much difference has bringing up children made to your opportunities to be involved in political and other voluntary activities?'** The modal response of both women and men was 'No effect'. Moreover, there was no significant difference in the proportions of women and men who reported that having children had either 'hindered' or 'helped' their involvement. When those who had replied 'hindered' were asked to explain the ways in which children had impeded their involvement, women ranked the increased demands of housework as the main hindrance, followed by a need to devote more time to their children and, thirdly, by having to engage in paid employment in order to meet the costs of bringing up a family. Men gave similar responses, but ranked the increased demands of housework third as an obstacle to involvement. Negligible numbers of either sex ranked other hindrances: these included a 'privatised effect'; i.e., the experience of parenthood gave them less of a feeling of social commitment beyond the family; the children actively disapproving of their activities; or the respondent's anxieties about the personal danger to their families occasioned by their own participation in the public realm. These latter obstacles to public participation were more conspicuous by their absence rather than their presence.

Asked in what ways parenthood had aided their involvement in political and other voluntary activities, both sexes ranked the three following reasons, in descending order, as the most important: that parenting gave them a greater feeling of social commitment; that there was a 'spillover' of their children's interests into their own lives which provided a cue to activity; and that the practical problems associated with bringing up a family acted as a spur to participation. A significant number of men, but virtually no women, also mentioned that they were provided with more time to devote to political activities because their children helped with domestic chores.

Motives for involvement

There was both convergence and divergence between the sexes in relation to their stated motives for political involvement. When the general sample was asked about such motives, both women and men ranked personal satisfaction highest, followed by a felt responsibility to future generations. Among the activists who were re-interviewed, however, women nearly always chose personal satisfaction almost as a routine answer, in contrast to virtually none of the re-interviewed men (See Chapter 4). Also, among the wider sample, women elevated both a perceived duty to perform 'socially useful activities' and a 'Christian commitment' above men. The remaining motives were identified by only negligible numbers of either sex: 'civic responsibility'; 'no one else would do it'; 'in order to influence political decisions'; 'because the government can't be expected to take care of everything'; 'to further the aims of the women's movement'; and 'to embarrass the government into fulfilling its public obligations'.

Thus, particularly in the general sample, there is more that unites than divides the sexes in terms of their reasons for political involvement. Expressive, rather than instrumental, motives predominate: personal fulfilment together with a future orientation, dwarf other potential reasons for engaging in the public realm.

Conclusions

These findings supply a corrective to the assumption that gender is a key variable influencing the extent of political participation and activity. Once a multivariate perspective is adopted, there is only weak support for the claim that women are less participative than men. For the three most overtly political of the seven types of activity - the conventional and unconventional behaviours included in the 'Political Activism' factor, 'Assertiveness' in relation to political discussion and debate, and 'Religious Activism' - there is no difference between women and men. For the remaining four factors, while the effect is weak in comparison to other potentially explanatory variables, being a *woman* predisposes one towards *more*, not less, activity.

The exhaustive comparison of the three main hypothetical explanations for gender differences in activity - the structural, the situational and the socialisation explanations - found virtually no support for a hypothesis of situational effects producing women and men with radically different patterns of political activity and involvement. Furthermore, there is only weak and sporadic confirmation of any hypothesis of socialisation into gendered patterns of political activities. The situational explanation is totally eclipsed by other causes. Setting conventional wisdom aside, being a housewife or a parent, even of pre-school children, does not impose universal or direct limitations upon women's political participation. While the presence of children may act as a constraint upon the political activities of, especially, young women, it appears to be only a temporary one. Motherhood is associated most with the deferral of political participation than with its abandonment. Moreover, in common with Clark and Clark (1986), the ostensible division between, on the one hand, the structural features of employment or educational status and, on the other, the situational features within the domestic realm seems overly simplistic: it neglects a complex array of interactions between constraints and opportunities for political activity.

As noted in other multivariate models (e.g., Norris, 1991; Clark and Clark, 1986; Welch, 1980; Verba, Nie and Kim, 1978), the results confirm the inapplicability, or at least the attenuation, of gender effects. In fact, in relation to the number of levels of high activity some of the findings demonstrate a *reversal* of effect, with women emerging as *more* active than men. Taken as a whole, the results indicate that structural features such as social class (the active being middle class) and the interplay of education and employment (those with both educational qualifications *and* a higher level occupation being active) are better predictors of political activity and involvement than gender, situation or socialisation. It is notable that, within the context of Northern Ireland where national and religious identity are the two dominant and mutually reinforcing cleavages, religion - in terms of a division between Catholic and non-Catholic respondents - does *not* appear as a strong predictor of variance in the seven *types* of activity. Conversely, however, religion does appear as a strong predictor of variance in relation to the *intensity* of activity.

For types of activity, those differences that can be attributed to religion are more easily explained by the structural features of church organisation such as the presence of women's groups organised in association with denominations or churches and the influence of (or, for the Catholic Church the absence of) the minister's wife, rather than any aspects of sectarian conflict. The significance of place, however, is not to be discounted. The context of 'the troubles' is salient in patterning and structuring the levels of current political activities.

The above analyses of political activity may be claimed to be innovatory for three reasons. First, because they employ a much more extensive repertoire of variables to test the major hypotheses in relation to gender differences in the level and intensity of activity. Secondly, they deploy a wider selection of modes of political and public activity as dependent variables. Thirdly, they introduce an additional category - personal dynamics - as a cause of variation in activity.

In respect of the latter, the most significant finding is the importance of a supportive spouse or partner for the public activity of both women and men, thereby adding another dimension to the aphorism that the personal is political. Far from the implicitly conflictual view of the situational perspective, the single most robust finding of the multivariate analyses is the salience, for both women and men, of active and willing support from one's partner for a heightened level of public activity - even when partners may possess a divergent partisan identity. This 'supportive spouse' effect, however, is not simple or mechanical, but rather one that works in tandem with other features of domestic arrangements. Some of the in-depth interviews, for instance, reveal more than a hint of ambiguity where the supporting spouse is male. One Alliance Party supporter, for example, stated that while her husband's attitude is 'very positive in encouraging me to do anything I wanted,' also introduced something of a qualifier:

> I do think on the whole, that though I have a very good and very understanding husband who, as I say, would do as much about the house as I would, I mean he's better at housework than I am, but I do think that getting out in the evening is much more difficult for women. The expectation is not so much that you'll stay in but [that] you'll be

the person to find the baby-sitter, ... but really it isn't a big issue, especially now. It might have been when the children were young.

Another female activist, a Unionist Party supporter with three children aged five to sixteen, underlined the significance of the interplay between spousal support and the constraints of child-rearing:

> When they were very small, now, I didn't get out so much. But at the same time now, my husband was very big and I would say he forced me to go out at least once a month to do something, because I think you could become a hermit very quick if you've wee children in the house. But he did, he would have been more supportive and pushed me out rather than me wanting to go out. And then once they started going to school and they didn't need as much attention, I, really, I was going to town there for a while! And now, it's coming to the stage you know where I really feel as if I need a break you know, But it's hard. I'm the sort of person ... I get into so many committees, nobody wants to be on them and I hate people sitting saying, 'No I couldn't do it because' ... and especially a treasurer's job, 'Oh I don't want to touch money at all', you know, 'I don't want to get involved'. And I said, 'Well, if nobody else'll do it, I'll do it' because I hate an argument and it went on and on and on just to try and get one person to do a job. And really, like, once a month; what commitment's that?

The importance of understanding present activity as embodying an 'interactional' component is also apparent from the effects of other personal dynamics associated with respondents' life histories. Seminal events or significant others in the past structure careers of political participation into the present. Key events, significant others or an important group or organisation act as triggers, causing a person to embark upon a 'career' of activity. This is underscored by the finding that the dynamics of personal interaction - whether relatively banal (being asked 'to do more' on behalf of a particular cause or organisation or rather more profound (involvement increasing because of the growth of self-confidence) - are associated positively with a variety of types of public activity.

Hence, while there are some gender differences in this regard, the findings are broadly consistent with those of Norris:

> While age and education influence political activity, the most important factors to emerge ... are attitudinal rather than socio-economic or demographic. This lends further confirmation to what others have found in previous studies: what distinguishes participants from non-participants are primarily motivational factors - political interest, efficacy and partisan loyalties. (Norris, 1991, p. 74)

Norris is correct in stressing the importance of motivation: what we would claim is that the findings provide some strong indications of the source(s) of these motivational factors. Moreover, once embarked upon a 'career' of activism, the dynamic of involvement begins to develop added momentum. Those who are already active are asked to do more, and are prepared to do so partly because they enjoy the resource of time, but also because they acquire both greater experience and enhanced self-esteem: each of these is associated positively with a higher level of political activity in the public realm. In short, the findings tend to confirm the adage 'if you want to get something done, ask a busy person' - provided s/he has a supportive partner. On that note, we now turn to a consideration of these 'busy people': activists.

Notes

1. The unattributed 'other causes' may include factors such as discrimination against women. The latter emerged as a popular explanation within the sample for the underrepresentation of women in the public realm. See Chapters 6 and 7.
2. An interaction variable of occupation level and educational level is employed to test whether the effect of education and occupation considered together could be multiplicative rather that just additive; for example, whether respondents who have both a high level of education and a high level job are more active than the simple effects of education and occupation alone would suggest (or the converse, that education and occupation could cancel each other out to some extent).
3. In the 'household class' variable used by the market research firm contracted to conduct the fieldwork, interviewers assigned each household a 'social class' code based upon the Registrar General's Census Social Class aggregated into four categories (AB, C_1, C_2 and DE). It is an example of the classic sexist method of attributing a class position to a household. The highest occupational position of any male in the household was used; only if no 'economically active' men were present, were the occupations of the women used. While we will not defend this practice, one does end up with a reasonable proxy for husband's/father's job. Its inclusion does allow one to test the hypothesis that a woman's activity is affected more by her 'status' derived from husband's/father's/brother's occupational position (McDonagh, 1982) than her own job.
4. The authors are grateful to Bernie Hayes for this latter suggestion.

5. Table 3.1 displays the results of seven regression models, one for each factor, in which all potential causal variables were entered simultaneously. The advantage of a regression model is that the apparent effects of any individual variable considered on its own could be a statistical artefact that actually results from other, more direct causes. Regression modelling provides a means of removing artefactual effects (at least for the variables included in the modelling process). Any effects that persist, taking due account of errors of measurement, can be considered more robust than a simple two-way association. The coefficients are standardised regression coefficients, hence constrained to a range between +1.00 and -1.00, where a positive figure indicates a positive association and *vice versa*. The absolute size of a coefficient is an indication of the strength of its effect relative to other variables.

6. From Chapter 2, note that, when the effects of other variables are not controlled, men have significantly higher levels of activity on two factors, 'Political Activism' and 'Assertiveness', and women are significantly higher on three, 'Charitable Activity', 'Voting/Socialisation' and 'Women's Movement'. Hence, the perspective of multivariate modelling shows that some of the difference in levels of activity in favour of men can be more correctly attributed to the effects of other variables.

7. Conducting separate regression analyses for each sex separately confirms that the positive effect of having a supportive spouse is important for the activity levels of both sexes.

8. Respondents were asked whether 'any personal experiences or public events in your life have had an important effect upon your political opinions.' Over two-thirds of the events named related to 'the troubles'.

9. Similarly, respondents were asked, 'Many people can think of persons that they have known personally who have been especially important in affecting how they now think and feel about politics. In your case, can you think of people who have been particularly important in forming your political opinions?' If respondents replied positively, they were asked to place these individuals into categories ('father, mother, brothers or sisters, other relatives, male or female friends, teachers, local activists or politicians') and to state whether 'the influence of these people (had been) "positive", such that they encouraged you or you tried to be *like* them, or..."negative", such that they discouraged you or you tried to be *unlike* them.'

10. Being neither in part-time employment nor a 'housespouse' implies full-time employment.

11. Relations between the Roman Catholic Church and Sinn Fein may be described as, at best, ambivalent. The mutually supportive relationship between Protestantism and unionist politics, long-standing and well-documented, may explain the link between a Protestant identity and a high score on the 'Religious Activist' factor. Ian Paisley's leadership of both the Free Presbyterians and the Democratic Unionist Party would be the clearest present example of this phenomenon (Bruce, 1986; Moloney and Pollak, 1986).

12. Upon closer inspection, the explanation is in fact quite straightforward. A large amount of involvement in formal women's groups in Northern Ireland takes places through the auspices of Protestant churches (Morgan and Fraser, 1994).

13. Technically, 'housewife' status should be termed 'housespouse'; but, in reality, only one man claimed to be a 'housespouse'.

14. The ordering of characteristics attempts to follow the relative importance and statistical significance of their effect. Because the models explain only a minority of the variance in any given factor, the 'profiles' should be seen as tentative descriptions rather than as definitive models.

15. Note that when the effects of other variables are not controlled, the simple effects of gender are different; with men engaging in, on average, more types of activity; neither sex showing a significant difference in the number of levels of high or low activity; and women showing a higher level of extensive organisational involvement. Hence, as before, the perspective of multivariate modelling suggests that some of the difference in levels of activity attributed to gender effects can be more correctly assigned to the effects of other variables.

16. There are significant structural effects on the other two measures - the number of high levels of activity and the maximum extent of involvement in any organisation - but the number of significant effects is fewer and generally of lower levels of statistical significance. For number of high levels of activity there are no significant 'social background' effects.

17. 'Employer-related organisations' does not include trade union involvement, which is defined in this study as falling under the broad category of political/public activity.

18. Approximately a quarter of Northern Ireland's population is located within the Belfast city limits and over half of the population resides in the greater Belfast area.

19. Hence, it is those claiming no religious affiliation or non-Christians who show a lower variety of types of activity.

20. The analysis upon which these profiles are based takes into account whether respondents named *any* event, individual or group/organisation that had a significant effect upon their subsequent political views or activities. The identity of the event, individual or organisation did not influence the profiling.

21. The latter included: having one's house seized by paramilitaries intent on ambushing members of the security forces; the destruction of business premises by bombing; the death of a relative or friend at the hands of paramilitary organisations; and the experience of internment and/or being 'lifted' (i.e., detained for questioning by the security forces).

22. Though among the activists who were re-interviewed, women were more likely to cite personal or intimate events (See Chapter 4).

4 Characterizing activists

Introduction

While the results from the study indicate that the general population emerge largely as 'isolates', we can now begin to establish the characteristics of the more active individuals of each sex. Complete data, derived from both phases of the study, is available for 59 women, all but ten of whom are, on our measures, highly participative, whether as 'hyperactives' 'superactives' or 'intensives'.

The individual attributes of the re-interviewees are in part derived from the first phase of the study and include age, level of educational attainment, religious affiliation, party identity, employment status, marital status and the incidence of parenthood. The quantitative survey also supplied us with information concerning the level of support among the activists for the women's movement and whether or not the respondents were self-identified feminists.

The various individual attributes are complemented by situational data, including information concerning the domestic division of labour within the relevant households and the attitudes of the respondent's partner/spouse to political participation. Much of this information emerged during the qualitative phase of the study as did that relating to structural influences upon the respondents. Among these influences, we include their perceptions of women's roles within the wider society, the effects of living in a divided society, their experiences of 'the troubles' and the perceived effects of both significant others and events as determinants of participation. By combining these sources of influence we can establish both their relative significance in differentiating the activists from the wider population and also explore whether there are broadly convergent or divergent patterns of activity and motives for participation between the female and male activists.

Female activists

Among the 49 active women several characteristics are noteworthy. Dividing the sub-set into three age-bands - 17-34 years, 35-54 years and 55 and above - those in their middle years are significantly overrepresented. Within the youngest age-band, seven women were highly active, the same number as in the upper age-band. The remaining 35 women fell into the 35-54 years cohort. The predominance of the middle-aged as activists is underlined by the age profile of the ten inactive women who were reinterviewed. Of these, five were under the age of 34 years, four aged at least 55 years and only one fell into the middle age bracket. Youth is not, among women, associated with political activism any more than is advancing age.

Far from being an impediment to political participation, marriage appears to be virtually a prerequisite of activism. Among the active women, 38 were married, two were divorced, three were widowed and only six were single. By comparison, of the ten 'isolates', two were married, three were widowed while the remainder were single. Though children were not in all cases present within the household, the overwhelming majority of active women (42) were mothers. By itself, motherhood does not emerge as an insurmountable obstacle to political participation: activist women do, however, have to prove adaptive in negotiating the conflicting demands in order to pursue their chosen activities - a task that does not challenge the male activists (see below).

In terms of educational attainment, a professional qualification and/or the possession of a degree is highly correlated with political participation. While ten of the active women, approximately 20 per cent, possessed no formal educational qualification (compared to 65 per cent of Northern Ireland's female population, HMSO, 1992 and 52 per cent of our sample) and nine had achieved 'O' and/or 'A' levels or their equivalent, 30 (60 per cent) of them had either a degree or some professional qualification, primarily in education or health care, compared to six per cent in the wider population (HMSO, 1992) and five per cent of our sample. Educational achievement, especially at a tertiary level, is evidently a key resource of political activism, although it is noticeable that the absence of qualifications is no necessary bar to participation. Among the ten inactive women, however, only one had a professional qualification, five had attained 'O' or 'A' levels or their equivalent while four had no formal qualifications.

Turning to employment status, participation in the labour force is also closely correlated with political activism. More than half of the active women, 26 in all, were employed on a full-time basis. A further ten were in part-time employment and four were retired. The remaining nine women were housewives. Among the inactives, full-time employment also featured prominently. Six of the ten women were in full-time jobs, three were retired and one was a full-time student.

Working women in Northern Ireland are heavily clustered in three occupational sectors (HMSO, 1992): clerical and related (25 per cent); catering, cleaning, hairdressing and other personal services (23 per cent); and education, health and welfare (18 per cent). Among the active employed women, whether in full or part-time jobs, it is this last sector which is overrepresented, mirroring the occupational profile of the region's female councillors (Wilford et al, 1993). Working in the welfare or caring sector is closely associated with political participation within both the general population and among the region's elected female representatives.

In terms of religious affiliation, 17 of the active women were Catholic, 26 were non-Catholic, two were Humanists and four respondents either refused to identify their religious tradition or had no religious affiliation. Among the non-Catholics, 14 of the active women were Presbyterians, nine belonged to the Church of Ireland, and the remaining three were a Free Presbyterian, a Baptist and a Quaker. Of the ten inactive women, two were Catholic, two were Church of Ireland, two were Presbyterians and there was one woman from each of the following denominations: The Brethren, Free Presbyterians and Jehovah's Witnesses. The remaining inactive woman did not disclose her religious affiliation.

The ratio of non-Catholic to Catholic activists (approximately 1.5:1), is broadly consistent with the religious ratio within the wider female population of Northern Ireland: 1.3:1 (HMSO, 1992). This is less the case in relation to party identity. Within the sample population as a whole the party affiliations of the respondents were as follows.

Among the 49 activist women, the party identifiers were as follows: UUP, 11; DUP, 3; Popular Unionist, 1; Conservative, 1; APNI, 10; SDLP, 12; SF, 1; WP, 2; Green Party, 3. Five of them either refused to disclose their voting preference, had no preference or were 'don't knows'. Among the ten inactive women, five were either don't knows, refusers or had no party preference, three were Unionists, one identified with the Green Party and the remaining individual with the SDLP.

Table 4.1
Party affiliations of all respondents (%)*

Party	Women	Men
Ulster Unionist (UUP)	28	26
Democratic Unionist (DUP)	7	11
Other Unionist	1	1
Conservative (Con)	8	6
Alliance (APNI)	10	7
Social Democratic and Labour Party (SDLP)	17	18
Sinn Fein (SF)	3	4
Workers Party (WP)	3	4
Green Party	4	5
Other	1	1
None	6	10
Don't Know	12	7

* The question asked of respondents was: 'If there was a general election tomorrow, which party in Northern Ireland would you vote for?

N: 1174 Female respondents; 325 male respondents.

Note: At the General Election held on 9th April 1992 the proportion of the vote cast for each of the major parties was as follows: UUP - 34.5%; DUP - 13.1%; Con - 5.7%; APNI - 8.7%; SDLP - 23.5%; SF - 10%; WP - 0.6%; Others - 4%. Source: Rick Wilford (1992), 'The 1992 Westminster Election in Northern Ireland', *Irish Political Studies*, Vol.7, pp. 105-110.

One of the noticeable features among the activists is the overrepresentation of the Alliance Party. As a bi-confessional party, stoutly committed to power-sharing and the politics of accommodation, the impressive level of support for the APNI suggests a preference for coalescent politics.

Though feminism in Northern Ireland has been structured by the preoccupation with competing national identities, the broader effects of its resurgence might be conjectured to have both encouraged women to become politically active and to raise expectations about their life chances. Second-wave feminism, however, emerged in the region during the early and mid 1970s, thereby coinciding exactly with the most violent phase of the troubles: not the most auspicious context within which 'sisterhood' might flourish. Yet, among the 49 highly participative women, virtually one-third (15) embrace the feminist label while the remainder disavow it: among the ten inactive women four were self-identified feminists and six rejected the term.

Although a minority, the proportion of self-identified feminists (31 per cent) among the activists is greater than that within the wider sample population (24 per cent). Moreover, while the majority of active women appear uncomfortable with the feminist label, they are less reticent in identifying with the agenda of the women's movement. Overall, on a scale of 1-10, where 1 corresponds with no, and 10 with complete, support for the women's movement, the 49 active women accord it a mean score of 7, as do the ten inactive women. Despite the absence of a coherent women's movement in Northern Ireland, awareness of and support for gender equality policies is clearly diffused widely throughout the sub-sets of both active and inactive women, a point we take up later (see Chapter 8).

Among the active women all but two of the 15 self-identified feminists are aged between 35 and 54 (the exceptions are aged 32 and 83 years). While they are clustered into the middle-aged band, in other respects the activists who are self-ascribed feminists are a diverse group. Five are Catholic, seven are non-Catholic, one is a Humanist and two have no religious affiliation. In terms of party identity, they are widely distributed. Two support either the SDLP, the Workers Party or the Green Party; three endorse the Ulster Unionist Party or the APNI; one supports the DUP; one has no party identity and the remaining individual refused to identify her party affiliation.

The feminist identifiers among the active women are also predominantly working women or have retired from employment. Of the 15, only two are housewives while all but three of the remaining 12 activists work in the health or education sectors and possess either a professional qualification or a university degree.

What is more compelling than the apparent internalisation of the feminist label, however, is the relatively high level of support accorded to a liberal feminist agenda by both active and inactive women. The endorsement of equal employment rights, equal pay and equal opportunities in general suffuses the thinking of the more active women, irrespective of whether they are self-identified feminists.

In terms of their background characteristics, the composite portrait of the politically active woman in Northern Ireland can be summarised thus: she is middle-aged; married with children; an educational achiever; employed, primarily in the health, education or welfare sectors; is not necessarily a self-regarding feminist, but warmly endorses the liberal demands of the women's movement; can be either Catholic or non-Catholic; and is more likely to vote for the SDLP, the UUP or the APNI. While suggestive of the resources - notably level of educational achievement - that enable women to participate in politics, such attributes supply only a part of the configuration of 'political woman'. By conducting in-depth interviews with each of the activists a more complete portrayal of the factors that precipitate participation can be presented. But before we explore the biographies of the female respondents, we turn to the background characteristics of the male activists: are they different from or similar to the female activists?

Male activists

Re-interviews were conducted with 15 men derived from the original sample, ten of whom are activists. In terms of their age-profile, the male activists closely resemble their female counterparts: eight of them are aged between 35 and 54 while the remaining two are aged under 34 years. Marriage and parenthood are, as with the active women, characteristic of the male activists. Eight are married, one is separated from his wife - all of whom have children - and the remaining individual is single. There, however, the similarities between the active men and women begin to dissolve.

In relation to educational attainment, the male activists are less well-qualified. Only two of them possess a degree or professional qualification, six have 'O' or 'A' levels or their equivalent and two have no formal qualifications. All but one of the male activists is in full-time employment, the exception being a full-time student. Their occupational profile also differs from that of the female activists. Three work in the welfare sector, two are blue-collar workers, two are white-collar workers and the remaining two are self-employed as, respectively, a taxi-driver and a publican.

In terms of their religious affiliations, three of the male activists are Catholic, four are non-Catholic (two Methodists and two Presbyterians), one is a Humanist, one has no religious affiliation and one refused to disclose his religious identity. While three refused to identify their party affiliation the remaining seven were less skewed in terms of their preferences than the female activists: two each supported the SDLP, Ulster Unionists and the APNI, and one the Workers Party. The sharpest, and perhaps most predictable, difference between the male and female activists occurs in relation to both the feminist label and support for the women's movement. Only one of the men described himself as a feminist, while their mean score in support of the agenda of the women's movement was five out of ten.

Thus, apart from their ages, marital status and the incidence of parenthood, the male and female activists do differ substantially in terms of their background characteristics. To gain a fuller picture of their pathways to participation we need to delve into their life-histories and thereby explore the extent of convergence or divergence among them.

Significant others

At the reinterviews the respondents were invited to expand on the role of the significant others they had nominated during the initial phase of the research. What was apparent, first, was that only a minority of the female activists (13) were unable to nominate at least one significant other; and secondly, that this individual was typically a family member. In all, 31 of the 49 activists nominated a member of the family as a positive influence, either solely or in combination with another.

Of these 31 activists identifying family members, ten nominated both parents; nine nominated their fathers; seven their husbands; three their mothers and two nominated a grandparent. Beyond the family, men also figured prominently as significant others. These included male politicians (in five cases); a teacher; a community worker; and a minister of religion. Only three of the female activists nominated women as extra-family significant others, two of whom were teachers and the third a local politician. In all, they identified 38 men as significant others as compared with 17 women.

Men were even more conspicuous as formative influences upon the male activists, although family members figured less prominently than among female activists. Only one identified his father in positive terms as a significant other, two mentioned siblings, both brothers and sisters; one perceived his parents as a negative influence; and one other identified his father-in-law in highly positive terms. One of the male activists acknowledged a male teacher as a significant other alongside his maternal aunt. Of the four remaining male activists, one nominated a youth worker as a positive role model, two identified no significant others, while the fourth cited his teachers, Christian Brothers, as having had a profound and negative influence on his beliefs and activities.

The referents for female activists are, therefore, much more likely to occur within the family context than for their male counterparts, while men predominate as significant others for activists of both sexes. Besides the gender of the significant others, we can also establish the ways in which they served as role models for the respondents. Given the preponderance among the female activists in particular of family members as significant others, is there a 'halo effect' at work? That is, do political activists come from within politically active families, as tends to be the case among Northern Ireland's female councillors? (Wilford et al, 1993.)

The 'political' family?

Of the 31 active women who nominated a family member as a significant other, 16 came from families within which there was a record of political activism, in some cases spanning at least two generations. In effect, active women were as likely to come from families with no history of political activity as those with such a record. Consistent with the broad definition of political participation that we employed, the range of activities engaged in by these family members extended from informal, essentially individual modes of participation, *via* church-based and other voluntary or charitable organisations to active membership in political parties, although the incidence of the latter was small. Overall, two-thirds of active women did not come from families that had a history of public involvement in politics.

In those cases where there was a family history of public participation there was some evidence of continuity in the types of activities engaged in. For instance, respondents with a parent, invariably the father, who had been an active trade unionist tended also to be actively involved in union affairs. One woman employed as a community nurse traced her active involvement in her union to her father's influence:

> It was a very working-class family and he was very strong about socialism and the trade union movement. I was always aware that there should be equal things for everybody; that everybody should have the same chance in life. What I got from him was a strong belief in equality for all and the importance of unions in fighting for workers rights.

An even clearer instance of continuity of involvement was supplied by a playgroup worker who explained her active involvement in, among other things, a women's lodge of the Orange Order, the Mother's Union and the UUP in terms of her grandmother's example:

She really believes in leadership ..for want of a better phrase, she really drummed orangeism into us. No matter what you're going to do, no matter how trivial it is, you're wondering "What would granny think of this?".

Induction into specific party-based activities by the family is not the monopoly of the dominant traditions in Northern Ireland. One respondent, an active member of the Alliance Party, explained her involvement through the influence of her father. An active member of the APNI from the first, he had been instrumental in establishing a number of cross-community organisations, a form of activity she too has embraced - as has her husband who also identified her father as a significant other.

Among those with a family background of political activism continuity between generations is most apparent in terms of church-based activities. Respondents whose parents were involved in charitable organisations associated with their respective churches - from the Legion of Mary to the Presbyterian Women's Association - also tended to become involved in such activities. Such activities were, however, seldom apprehended as 'political' by the respondents. A recurrent feature among the activists was the tendency to dissociate charitable and/or church-based activities, whether engaged in by themselves or other family members, from 'politics'.

The propensity to, in effect, 'render unto Caesar' that which is political is common to members of all denominations, whether in relation to themselves, their parents or other family members. One respondent, whose parents were involved in a string of Catholic charitable agencies and a number of voluntary caring associations, described them as 'very apolitical'. Equally, she described her own involvement in like organisations as 'social' rather than political. In this case, as in many others, the effect of the Northern Ireland context upon what is perceived to be 'political' activity is readily apparent. She voiced a common response among the majority of activists by equating politics with sectarianism:

My parents were very apolitical, I think to avoid bigotry. It may be something that you find just in Northern Ireland, but if you've got people who want to avoid bigotry, especially if you grow up in a mixed area as we did, then you tended to play down politics.

The association of politics with sectarianism recurs time and again among the activists, whether or not they come from within families that exhibit a tradition of overt participation in associational activities. Another respondent, a Catholic, state enrolled nurse in her mid-thirties, actively involved in fund-raising activities for the chronically ill, a trade union and a parent-teachers association, eloquently displays the bracketing of politics with sectarianism.

Her brother had survived a murder attempt by gunmen, her parental home had been peppered with bullets and on a subsequent occasion her parents had been coerced into sheltering two PIRA gunmen on the run after the shooting of a police officer. Fearing further threats her parents and her siblings moved to the Republic of Ireland while she remained in the North where she was married shortly after their departure. The legacy of these events left her 'without any politics. I would be very much my own person...I don't believe that this country should be divided between one type of politics and the other: Catholic and Protestant'. While a consistent supporter of the SDLP she defines herself as 'non-political because I'm middle of the road: I'm Irish, but I've got a British passport'. For her 'political' was equated with the mutually reinforcing cleavages of national and religious identity, hence 'politics doesn't come into this house'.

The stated perception among a majority of respondents that politics and sectarianism are linked, and/or that politics is confined to the activities of political parties, eclipsed the view that it was a seamless activity. This idea that politics occurred within a sharply circumscribed public realm is underscored not only by the tendency to interpret their own activities in 'social' terms, but also by the frequency with which their families were presented as moral arbiters rather than as agencies of political socialisation. Female activists were prone to interpret the enduring influence of their parents as a moral rather than a political one.

The elision of morality and politics is articulated by women of all ages, denominations and political affiliations. One fifty-year old, heavily involved in a number of Church of Ireland bodies, the Orange Order and the Boys Brigade, stressed that such activities were 'not political in any way, just Christian', an interpretation she attributed to her father's influence who 'brought us up very straight'. A Presbyterian, also fifty, and active in her professional association, a hostel for the homeless, prison counselling and her local church was at pains to stress that her parents - themselves active in a number of voluntary organisations - 'were not at all political. It wasn't a political home, it was Christian'. Equally, a thirty-eight year old Catholic who understood her activities in a wide variety of environmental groups, third world charities, and among alcoholics as 'social' rather than political, attributed this to the 'strong Catholic influence' of her parents:

> They passed on to us...concern for other people as much as for yourself. You know, politically aware in that sense of always judging life and decisions in life with how they will influence others: that sense of being connected.

Respondents, notably those who came of age amidst 'the troubles', frequently reported that for their parents 'political' meant involvement in paramilitary organisations, whether republican or loyalist and which, in some cases, they were bluntly instructed to avoid: 'They'd say things like "If any of you joins anything" - they meant the IRA - "you needn't be coming back round this house again"'. Occasionally, though, parents emerged as sectarian warriors themselves. One 24 year-old respondent from a farming background and who is actively involved in the Presbyterian Church and the Young Farmers Club, recounted that during her adolescence her mother had been quite explicit about any prospective boyfriends: 'She'd say things like, "You come home with a Roman Catholic and I'll break your back"'. Asked what she would do if, in the future, her own daughter was to bring home a Catholic the respondent was unequivocal: 'I'd kill her...I'd point her in the right direction as to who she should go for and why. I'm quite definite about that'.

Such raw sentiments were, however, very much the exception rather than the rule. The female activists, whether or not they came from publicly active families, were much more likely to indicate that they had been steered away from the extremes by their parents, while those who now have children of their own expressed similar intentions. Epithets such as 'cool', 'level-headed', 'liberal', 'tolerant' and 'open-minded' were frequently ascribed to parents, especially fathers, who emerged in the majority of cases as significant others.

There were, though, cases where the trenchant views of one or another parent acted to deter respondents from dutifully following in their footsteps. One described her mother as an 'unacceptable role model' because she was 'a straight down the line unionist. To discuss politics with my mother was to be disloyal'. This respondent attributed her activities, in particular her support for the APNI, to a conscious rejection of her mother's unreconstructed views and the 'lessons of moderation' she acquired from her father. Similarly, one woman described her rejection of republicanism as the product of her father's self-presentation as 'the great Irishman' while another, actively involved in a number of charitable organisations, stated that she was also put off politics by her father, a member of the Communist Party: 'He talked politics all the time; it was really boring'.

Activism and domestic labour

'Talking politics' with the female respondents led almost inexorably, certainly initially, beyond the front door to the public realm. Less evident was the overt recognition that the 'personal is political'. But while not openly articulated, there was a widespread, if nuanced, understanding among the activist women that the pattern of sexual division of labour within the domestic realm exerts a profound influence upon their opportunities for participation in the public sphere. It was equally characteristic of younger and older activists, of Catholics and non-Catholics, of parents and non-parents, feminists and non-feminists and those both in and out of paid employment.

Though the female activists who were married or involved in a long-term stable relationship cited the expressive support of their partners as a key resource facilitating their participation in the public sphere, most acknowledged that they bore the heavier responsibility for domestic labour. While a few commented somewhat acidly about the attitudes both of their own mothers for meekly accepting 'their lot' within the home, and of their mothers-in-law for 'spoiling their sons', many were themselves resigned to the fact that within their own households the onus was on them to make the time and space in order to participate in the public realm.

There was, in fact, some ambivalence expressed by many of the female activists concerning the dual burden borne by women. While on the one hand sensitive to the constraints that inhibit their external activities, especially those pertaining to motherhood, on the other it was not uncommon for them to endorse the view that mothers with young children *should* devote themselves to their well-being. One respondent, for instance, whilst decrying her mother's 'old-fashioned ideas about a woman's place being in the home', went on to say: 'In a way I agree with her...a few years at home with the children gives them a good basis...there's a kind of security in knowing mummy is at home'. Similarly, it was not uncommon for them to accept the 'responsibility' for housework, a view captured by one particularly active respondent thus:

> It's because if some visitor comes here and things are a bit 'grotty' they're not going to blame my husband, it's going to be my fault, so I do it. He probably wouldn't see certain things - and I don't blame him for that - so I do that bit extra because I feel it's my responsibility: the perception is that it's my responsibility.

The reported incidence of a more or less equal division of household tasks was rare, but where it did apply it was seen to be the product of the relationship - 'a happy partnership' as one woman put it - between the respondent's own parents rather than the result of any external influence, including the women's movement. One female activist who drew inspiration from her mother's example as a working woman, articulated the role strain that this created. Married with two young children and in full-time employment, she expressed the internalised conflict that she felt:

> When I'm at home, I spend all the time with my children that I can...You always have this guilt thing when you work full-time about spending more time with your children. It does restrict you where it wouldn't restrict a man. A man would say "Right, fine, I'm off" - and that's that.

In her own case, her husband 'splits looking after the children 50:50, but' she added, 'he's from a strange family for here. His parents were both professionals - his mother was a headmistress. It's wholly dependent on the mother and the role she plays'.

This respondent's opportunity to both work and pursue a variety of activities outside the home, while informed by the examples of both her mother and her mother-in-law was, however, eased by the employment of a child-minder who also undertook a large share of the household tasks, including washing and ironing: 'without her it would be impossible'. Reliance on a child-minder or 'daily' was, though, uncommon: the overwhelming majority of activist women emerge as extremely capable individuals, juggling the competing demands of home, employment and their other activities in an efficient and effective way. As one respondent put it: 'I think if you look hard enough, you will find ways around the demands of the home even if you work full-time'. Invariably, it is the women themselves who find ways of negotiating such demands, whether deferring the housework until the weekend or late at night, arranging a baby-sitter, or postponing their activities - including employment - until their children are of school-age.

The latter option does not, though, resolve the role conflicts that develop. One of the respondents put her finger on a recurring dilemma:

> If I thought my job was in any way detrimental to my children, I'd give it up tomorrow: they come first. It's this maternal thing - it's more than tradition, it's a maternal instinct. It's something very basic, at the end of the day.

Another respondent, the mother of a two-year old, was more prescriptive: 'My place is in the home. This is the position women should take when they have children'. A third, whose children had left home, was equally forthright: 'Personally, I'm very glad I stayed at home when my children were young. Parents now expect child-minders to be available as a right: I think that's wrong'.

Whether voiced in terms of biological determinism or social construction, the dilemma between public and private activities was uncharacteristic of the male activists: none referred to a sense of 'guilt' about their extra-domestic roles, nor spoke in terms of 'basic paternal instincts'. But instinctive maternalism was itself a minority view among the female activists. More common was the felt weight of cultural expectations about women's roles within the typically 'Irish' or 'Ulster' family, especially where the care of children and elderly relatives is involved. 'I do it all' was a familiar refrain: a social script that some, certainly, sought to rewrite by positively encouraging their children, whether sons or daughters, to undertake chores around the house. One respondent consciously gives her sons 'a hard time' in relation to housework: 'I don't want them to be like their father, he doesn't do a stroke'.

Among the female respondents, there was a keen sense of changed opportunities for women and of the fluidity of gender roles. For instance, they understood the significance of the different expectations harboured by young women in contemporary society and of the expanded opportunities available to them. It is as if the women are living somewhat vicarious lives, casting themselves as interlocutors between the impediments of the past and the promise of the future. One, aged 46, who had left employment when pregnant with her first child - a decision she explained in terms of her mother's example - takes a completely contradictory view towards her pregnant daughter: 'I regret not staying at work: I hope she doesn't make the same mistake.' Similar sentiments were voiced by a 27 year-old. Married with three daughters, she openly acknowledged the influence of feminism upon her aspirations for her children which she understood as a reaction against her mother's 'old-fashioned' beliefs:

> She was biased towards my brothers, she thought they should be educated but not us. We were expected to run around after them, picking up their clothes and shoes. That started off the feminism in us.

The respondent also acknowledged that her husband did little or nothing about the house: 'and when he does it's only to expose me, a stick to beat you with'. The seeming contradiction of this respondent's situation - a self-identified feminist apparently acquiescing to an inequitable division of domestic labour - was in part resolved vicariously through her three daughters: 'My ambition in life would be to get them a good education so that they aren't dependent on any man. I would encourage them not to get married too young and preferably to have no children'.

Autonomy is here perceived as the product of educational attainment and the avoidance, not of marriage, but of motherhood. But in this case, the exercise of autonomy was not merely deferred to her children. Despite the 'total opposition' of her husband, she obtained an elective sterilisation. This followed a two year struggle during which she was pressurised by hospital staff to obtain her husband's consent, which she steadfastly resisted:

> I was appalled at their attitude. They told me that if I didn't get his signature they wouldn't carry out the operation. They'd say things like "What if something happens to your children? What if one of them dies? What if you change your mind?" You just have to show that you're really keen to get it done and be very persistent.

The inequitable division of domestic labour that typifies the households of the activists is not untypical of households in general in Northern Ireland. The study by Turner (1993), for instance, demonstrates the gendered asymmetry of housework and child-rearing in the region. Despite such inequality, by dint of organisation, commitment, the emotional support of their partners and, occasionally, by employing other women to undertake household tasks, the activists emerge as resourceful individuals finding ways and means that enable them to participate in the public realm.

The tacit acceptance of 'responsibility' for housework; for devising means that afford them the opportunity to engage in the public realm; and, in some cases, blaming themselves for not insisting upon an equal division of domestic labour, chimes with Hedlund's (1988) characterisation of the negative side of women's culture. This she portrays as a culture of the suppressed, containing 'elements such as passivity, dependence on men and lack of self-confidence' (p82). Yet the fact that the activists do prove inventive in creating the time and the space to become participants in the wider public arena also demonstrates the more positive dimension of women's culture. Their independence, determination and, as we shall see later, widely shared belief that they can bring a distinctive perspective and set of values to the public realm, discloses the duality of the hypothesised women's culture. Activist women are not self-regarding victims of patriarchy but accomplished strategists.

The fact that activist women are motivated primarily by personal fulfilment (see below) also supplies a glimpse into the positive side of women's culture. There is a link between self and other-directedness among participative women that is revealed by their involvement in caring activities, both in relation to their employment and their political involvements. The duality of this culture demonstrates, as Hedlund suggests, the ability of women to negotiate, if not slough off completely, the slavish effects of patriarchy: women are not wholly oppressed, they are not wholly powerless, but enact values 'that are independent of the male world and not merely compensatory to it' (p82).

While the incidence of publicly political families among the female activists is low, among the male activists it is even rarer. We have already noted that the male activists are much less likely to nominate family members - or anyone else - as significant others. This disinclination among the men to attribute influence to others by itself distinguishes them from the female activists. Moreover, whilst a number of the re-interviewed women nominated their husbands as a significant other, none of the activist men identified their wives or partners in this way. Similarly, while it was noteworthy that some of the women explained their activities as the product of parenthood, this was not mentioned by the male activists as a catalyst for participation.

Whether as the source of a role model, an agency of socialisation for themselves or their children, the site of inequality in relation to unpaid work, or the springboard to particular types of public activities, the family emerges as a key institution among women. Its salience also helps to explain the incidence of 'family feminism' among women in Northern Ireland. (Chapter 8) Whether nuanced or explicit, the linkage between the private and public realms is clear: active women supported by, rather than dependent upon, their spouses conjure up strategies to reconcile the many and conflicting demands upon their time and energy. That they manage to do so suggests a strong motivation on their parts to become involved in political activities.

Motives for participation

We noted in Chapter 2 the possible motives for political participation that were identified by Parry and his colleagues (1992). As we acknowledged, distinguishing among motives is not always a straightforward matter: there may be several reasons for activism which may overlap, thereby obscuring their relative significance. The following table discloses the motives for political participation identified by the sub-set of active respondents.

Among women, the reward of self-fulfilment in pursuit of the interests of others, both in the present and the future, emerges as a compelling motive. The preeminence of personal satisfaction - met through the needs of others - suggests a primarily expressive orientation towards their activities. By comparison, civic duty and more instrumental motives - influencing decisions, embarrassing the government into action, filling gaps left by government inaction - appear as unattractive reasons for public participation. Nor is it the case that women feel impelled to become involved for the simple and negative reason that no-one else does: the motives are more positive and purposive, and imply a dovetailing of self and other-directedness.

Table 4.2
Motives for participation among activists

	Women (N)	Men (N)
My involvement gives me a feeling of personal satisfaction	17	1
One has a responsibility to future generations	15	3
People should devote part of their time to socially useful activities	13	3
As a Christian, I have a duty to help others	11	2
In a democracy, all have a duty to take on civic responsibilities	4	0
To embarrass the government into fulfilling its obligations	3	1
To influence political decisions, individuals must involve themselves in public life	3	1
Because of the women's movement/feminism	1	0
No-one else would do it	1	1
The government cannot be expected to take care of everything	0	0

Note: Respondents were invited to nominate no more than two primary motives for their activities.

Among the male activists it is noteworthy that personal fulfilment is virtually absent as a motive for public participation. However, they also disdain instrumentality and civic duty as motivating factors, inclining towards social utility and concern for the future. But while other-directedness also appears as a reason for activism among the men, it seems unconnected to what might loosely be described as the 'feel-good' factor that characterises the female activists.

To label motives either as 'expressive' or 'instrumental' is, however, a somewhat blunt device: invariably the two merge. The mixed nature of the motives for activism is exemplified by a twenty-two year-old single woman, employed full-time as a social worker, who stated that her activities were undertaken primarily for reasons of personal satisfaction and social usefulness. Her first foray into the public realm was on behalf of a local hospice in which a close relative had died. Raising funds for the hospice led to involvement in a cancer-related charity which was also undertaken as a way of repaying the care that her grandfather had received - or more properly, as an expression of what Titmuss called the 'gift relationship' (Titmuss, 1970). However, her heaviest involvement occurred through her trade union, notably in opposing the introduction of trust status to the health and personal social services. She explained her involvement in dualistic terms:

> It's because of the effects it will have on the quality of client care, community care, acute care, plus the fact that our conditions and pay will be adversely affected...You see, with me it would depend if it affects me enough, which isn't very fair.

Expressive and instrumental motives, while they may elide, are not the only spurs to participation. As Parry et al (1992, pp. 12-13) note, a communitarian motive may also inspire participation. Developing out of 'a concern for the community of which a person is a part' it contends that 'where people are highly integrated into the local community, and where they identify strongly with it, participation would be greater'. Underlying such a view are notions of interdependence, neighbourliness, the awareness of shared, preeminently local, needs that are believed to be typical of small, tightly-knit societies rather than large-scale, atomised ones.

Northern Ireland is, of course, both geographically and in terms of its population, a small society. More pertinently it is a divided society. The renewal of 'the troubles' in the late 1960s fostered a sharper sense of communal identities structured by conflicting national identities and religious beliefs. Under direct rule successive governments have, until recently (Wilford, 1992), adopted public policies in Northern Ireland that, while promoting elite political accommodation, have also consolidated both the physical and psychological barriers between erstwhile communities. Social, educational and residential segregation required, as it were, high fences to accomplish what passed for 'neighbourliness'. Mutual distrust, fear of violence and the uncertainties of the future bound the distinctive communities together, accentuating difference and insularity.

Against a background of chronic and occasionally acute violence, some expressions of arguably communitarian participation have taken a decidedly pathological turn, notably the 'self-policing' of local neighbourhoods by both loyalist and republican paramilitaries. However, it is more normal expressions of the communitarian motive that are apparent among the female activists in our sample.

Communitarian motives and 'the troubles'

The divided nature of Northern Ireland has defined what might be termed 'a sense of community'. The study of women's organisations in rural and semi-rural areas of the province by Morgan and Fraser (1994), for instance, conveys a persuasive picture of parallel realms of activity engaged in by Catholic and non-Catholic women, whose lives rarely intersect. We were interested in exploring the effects of 'the troubles' upon the activities of the more participative of our respondents. Did they, for instance, understand 'community' in inclusive or exclusive terms? To what extent, if any, have the significant events in their lives patterned the types of activities they engage in?

Results from the first stage of our research demonstrated that the significant events most frequently cited by the sample population were related to 'the troubles', whether a single incident or the more generalised aspects of the conflict. Asking the sub-set of activists to explain in more detail the effects of their chosen event(s) assists in illuminating the motives for participation: has inter-communal violence either deterred or promoted particular modes of participation? Is communitarianism expressed within or across communities? Are both women and men equally likely to exhibit a communitarian motive?

Women, communitarianism and inclusiveness

As with the general population, 'the troubles' dominated as the significant event of the activists lives. Each of the male activists cited some aspect of the violence in Northern Ireland as having exerted a profound influence upon them. Among the female activists, however, there was some difference. While 28 of the 49 referred to 'the troubles' as a defining serial event in their life-histories, a significant minority identified a number of other experiences that had shaped their activities. Though not discounting 'the troubles', when re-interviewed they also cited some personal rite of passage - including marriage, childbirth, divorce, widowhood, being 'born-again', illness - as a signal moment in their lives. This more interior catalogue of events was peculiar to the female activists, implying a distinctively gendered way of understanding the relationship between self and 'community.

Experiences of 'the troubles' varied. A number had had a direct and, in some cases, a life-threatening encounter. One woman, now a teacher in a Catholic primary school, had previously helped her husband to run a public house which served a mixed clientele. Having participated in the early civil rights marches, 'straight after our honeymoon', the pub was later bombed and their lives threatened by loyalist paramilitaries. This led them to leave the business, move house and change jobs. While still active, her modes of activity became preeminently intra-communal: mainly involvement in her local church and a neighbourhood environmental group. The withdrawal from a wider public stage she understood as stemming from the insecurity generated by her experience. Having lived on a largely Protestant estate with friends from 'the other side', she and her family retreated into her 'own' community: 'Now I feel uncomfortable in their (Protestant) company. No matter how friendly they are, you do feel uncomfortable if you know they are from the other community'.

Another respondent, a Protestant, cited the murders of friends by republican paramilitaries and the Anglo-Irish Agreement as significant events in her life. These personal and constitutional traumas reinforced both her beleaguered sense of unionism and 'suspicion' of Catholics. In the wake of the murder of one friend she teetered on the verge of becoming involved in paramilitarism: 'If the right person had tapped me on the shoulder then, I might have got involved in something'.

A member of the Orange Order and the UUP, she had withheld rates in protest at the Anglo-Irish Agreement, attended demonstrations opposing the Agreement, ushered her children into the junior lodge of the Orange Order, established a creche at her church, raised funds for the local children's hospital and become an officer in the Girls Brigade. The circumscribed sense of 'community' is also exemplified by her opposition to integrated education and the introduction of 'education for mutual understanding' (EMU) into the schools curriculum, withdrawing her youngest child from its programme of activities because it included a visit to Dublin.

Yet, despite insisting on her Britishness, and stressing her antipathy to cross-community initiatives, there is an inclusive sense of sisterhood lurking beneath the surface. While her own activities were narrowly focused on her neighbourhood, she expressed admiration for 'the strong women' involved in the peace movement and spoke of the unmet needs of women in Northern Ireland. A self-identified feminist, she perceived women as an oppressed group: 'They are hard done by, they're just the lower class. Even in the upper class they are treated as maids and servants. Intelligent women never get the chance'.

A staunch advocate of state-funded child care, she has a clear perception of the shared interests among women who, she believes, are ill-served by the political parties in Northern Ireland, a view shared by a large majority of all women in the province (See Chapter 6). Moreover, she embraced a rather essentialist view of the differences between the sexes, believing women to be more tolerant and balanced than men:

> Women are far more tolerant and it's inbred, it must have something to do with our chromosomes or something! Bringing up children has a lot to do with it because you've got to listen to their tantrums and take both sides and all the rest of it.

A dyed-in-the-wool Unionist, she yet acknowledges a nascent community of interests among women in Northern Ireland: 'There is a sisterhood, just by being a woman even. Women don't ask other women who they are and where they're from, they mix better: men don't'. Such views are echoed by a woman from east Belfast whose entry into the public realm was precipitated by the signing of the Anglo-Irish Agreement in 1985.

Previously home-centred, her 'sense of betrayal' by the British Government led her to attend the demonstrations at Hillsborough Castle, the venue for the signing, and thence to join the DUP. Motivated by the need 'to influence political decisions' and 'to embarrass the Government into fulfilling its public obligations', she subsequently picketed meetings of the Inter-Governmental Conference in Belfast, Dublin and London: 'I am always there with a placard...hounding Ministers and getting the point across'. Undaunted by the later collapse in the numbers of sister and fellow protesters and the diminished support of the DUP leadership, she persisted in her highly public demonstration of opposition to the involvement of the Irish Government in the affairs of Northern Ireland.

Resident in a loyalist heartland area, her sense of identity is narrowly drawn:

> I am proud to be an Ulsterwoman and a Protestant. When the new year comes in the first thing I say is, "God bless Ulster and the Ulster Defence Regiment and thank goodness it is only seven months to the 12th of July!"

Opposed to integrated education and EMU - 'The Agreement is behind all that: we are being pushed together and I object very strongly' - and prepared to fight for the Union - 'I would love to know how to shoot a gun; if it comes to civil war I would want to defend my home and country' - her views and actions appear uncomplicated. Yet, during the course of the interview, it emerged that she had participated in the peace movement during the 1970s: 'I remember walking up the Shankill with them. But it fizzled out because it was labelled as a women's movement. It would take all the community, both men and women to take part'.

While operating with an exclusive sense of national identity - 'I hate to see the Tricolour flown in the North. The South has no claim over us and the sooner they realise that the better' - in other respects she articulates a more inclusive view of 'community':

> If we got rid of the IRA, and the drive for a united Ireland, the ordinary people here could live and work together. We could all fight the same issues - better employment, better housing, better everything. If we got rid of the gunman we could do all these things, as it is we're in a vicious circle. Religious differences don't amount to much, just bits and pieces.

This perspective on community is especially pronounced when filtered through a gendered lens:

> While I say that the South should have no say in running Ulster, we could have a great relationship in the sense that the women's groups there and here could meet and help each other. Both parts of the island could benefit while still keeping their separate governments. I would be very much for that.

This sentiment is typified by her attitude towards Mary Robinson. In 1985, whilst a member of the Irish Senate, Robinson resigned from the Irish Labour Party in protest at the Anglo-Irish Agreement believing it was 'unacceptable to all sections of unionist opinion. I do not', Robinson continued, 'believe it can achieve its objective of securing peace and stability within Northern Ireland or on the island as whole' (Bew and Gillespie, 1994). Whilst the respondent had picketed the visit of *An Taoiseach*, Charles Haughey, to Belfast in April 1990, when Robinson visited the city in February 1992, fifteen months after her election as President, she took a different view: 'I was glad she came. I wouldn't have taken part in a protest because I feel she is a friend'.

'Friendship' or communality is though, conditional upon the maintenance of the Union. This is underscored by her changed view of Margaret Thatcher. While expressing undimmed enthusiasm for her stand during the hunger strikes of 1981, the former Prime Minister's fall from grace occurred with the signing of the AIA: 'She let Ulster and the people of Ulster down'. But beyond, or below, the high ground of the constitutional issue the respondent suggests a shared and unmet feminised agenda while simultaneously rejecting the feminist label and according only a modest level of support to the women's movement. 'Women's attitudes', she insists:

> are different from men's. We're more for running the home, the welfare of our children. The bond between women is stronger than that between men: we stick together and have more in common on social issues.

These views are hardly radical, but that they are aired by a self-regarding loyalist does occasion surprise. Yet, locked into what has become a virtually one-woman campaign of opposition to the Anglo-Irish Agreement, her belief in the existence of communality among women has been subordinated to 'a greater cause': a not unfamiliar experience for women throughout Irish history, whether nationalist or unionist.

Other women, however, seek consciously to transcend the communal divide. One respondent in her early fifties, born in Northern Ireland but who had spent a large part of her life in England, had returned in 1968 to take up a teaching post. Educated in the province until the age of thirteen and the product of a mixed marriage, she recalled the daily playground ritual at her primary school:

> There was a battle each day, the Brits on one side, Irish on the other. The children knew which side they were on, but I didn't really because my mother was a Protestant and my father a Catholic. It was a bit difficult for me, that. Sometimes I was on one side, sometimes the other: I hedged my bets! But it really stuck in my mind.

Those memories were rekindled upon her return to Northern Ireland at the outset of 'the troubles'. Unable to identify with either 'side' - 'I can't have a friend who is firmly entrenched in one camp or another' - she became actively involved in a voluntary, schools-based cross-community project that was opposed by her local town council. It denied the group the use of a "neutral" site for their activities, which served only to galvanise her resolve.

A humanist, committed to promoting 'communication' between children, she has persisted in a variety of cross-community programmes that, since the curricular reforms of 1989, have become an integral part of government educational policy. Similarly her active involvement in the 'Peace People', 'Cooperation North', and the Alliance Party she understands as ways of 'building bridges in what is, after all, a small community'. In particular, she believes women are naturally better equipped than men to engage in cross-community activities:

I think it's because women are more conciliatory, more people orientated than men. Women have a "live and let live" attitude...it's a pity that the more sort of caring attitude women have, which is probably biological, isn't utilised more.

Belief in an apparent female essentialism is mirrored by her views about men: 'It's very important for men to be seen as powerful by other men, it's part of their nature...it's where their self esteem lies.' Women, by comparison, besides being more 'people-oriented', are motivated 'to actually handle issues and [are] less aware of themselves in doing so.' Here, then, there is a sense of difference between the sexes that, while veering towards biological determinism, associates an inclusive vision of community with women.

A similar view is expressed by a Catholic woman born and bred in west Belfast, now married with six children and living in the north of the city. Employed part-time as a social work assistant, she works in an exclusively Protestant area of west Belfast. An SDLP supporter, her entry into politics was through the civil rights movement:

There was nothing dubious about it, everything was good about it. You felt you should be out there, you should be doing something about it, getting equal rights and seeing that people got jobs...we were doing something to right a wrong; you felt you were fighting for a place.

Motivated by personal satisfaction and the desire to be socially useful, she is a founding member of a support group for a hospice in which her father had died; a member, through a friend who had lost a baby, of a cot-death association; is involved in the girl guides - 'which my daughter roped me into' - and an active trade unionist. Like a number of the female respondents, her more recent activities were deferred until her children reached school-age: the trigger was returning to paid employment:

When you go out to work there's a lot more opportunities to be involved in things, you want to be involved. If I was at home I wouldn't get the chance...looking after the children you lose your confidence because you're at home all day. [Before I went back to work] if we were out with friends I would talk about babies and more babies! When you go out to work you feel a lot more confident, you discuss a lot more things, you feel able to express an opinion.

For her, working in a Protestant context is unthreatening and unproblematic, not a view shared by her mother or her seven siblings, all of whom still live in west Belfast. She recalls Northern Ireland before 'the troubles', an experience which she believes distinguishes her from her brothers and sisters: 'They could never get out of the area, they didn't know what it was like outside the Falls'. Whilst at school, she had worked on Saturday mornings on both the Shankill Road and in Sandy Row, predominantly Protestant areas, while her father had been among the minority of Catholics who were employed in the docks.

Those experiences, together with the latitude provided by her parents - 'They never said "Don't go there, that's a Protestant area"...there was never a distinction between Protestants and Catholics, that stood by me when I grew up and the troubles did start' - have enabled her to engage in a variety of cross-community organisations. In addition, her children attend a Protestant grammar school while she endorses fully both integrated education and EMU. Though not a feminist and only moderately supportive of the women's movement, she too subscribes to the idea of a transcendent sisterhood in Northern Ireland, while at the same time rejecting the notion of an equivalent fraternity:

> The women have the most experience of the troubles, the effects of the troubles and probably have the solution to its problems. Men have dominated here for so long and have one-track minds on politics. I think women would be more open about it, they're more peaceful because of the maternal thing. The troubles unite women, they come off worse because they are the ones that have to worry, to go through the grief, the bereavements and cope with everybody else. Women can identify with the other side whereas men can only see their own side, one faction against another. The sisterhood isn't political like brotherhood is with men: it's to do with grief, bereavement and children.

This is an instructive extract, encapsulating a set of perceptions which conveys the duality of an implied women's culture. One aspect of this culture is portrayed in terms of the romantic, even wistful, image of a keening 'mother Ireland', dutifully shouldering the burdens inflicted by patriarchal violence. The other aspect is more positive. Women are believed, somewhat paradoxically, to possess a clearer vision of 'the solution', one focused by their oppression and their shared experience of maternity. Apolitical women, it seems, have the potential to overcome the divisions created and sustained by political men.

This is a comforting portrayal of a dual system of cultural values she believes to be monopolised by women. It is, for instance, precisely because of her sex that the respondent believes she can work in a Protestant area whereas a Catholic man could not: 'There's a suspicion about men, but not about women. If I thought my husband was to work where I work, I'd tear my hair out. I'd be saying "Please don't, you're better off on the dole"'.

Like the overwhelming majority of women in the survey, whether active or inactive, this respondent does not regard 'the troubles' as exerting a deterrent effect upon involvement in the public realm of politics. Female identity is, in fact, widely believed by the activist women to confer the advantage of relative physical safety upon them, although not a badge of immunity from violence. Moreover, among the wider female sample the reasons for the conspicuous absence of women from the more orthodox spheres of political activity are understood in what, within the context of Northern Ireland, may seem more prosaic terms than fear of injury or death to either themselves or their families. (See Chapters 7 and 8.)

Nor is bitterness an emotion that characterises activist women, even those who have been intimately affected by violence. One respondent, whose father was shot and severely disabled by the PIRA shortly after his retirement from the security forces, stated that the experience merely reinforced her concern for others, of whatever religion or political persuasion. A humanist, she engages in a variety of activities on behalf of the homeless, the mentally disabled and environmental organisations, besides working full-time in a residential centre for the physically and mentally handicapped. For her, like the majority of female activists, 'community' is understood in terms of the needs of others, irrespective of their religious or national identity.

Male activists

Among the male activists an inclusive sense of community is much less apparent. While each of them cited 'the troubles' as a significant influence, in most cases it was understood as having reinforced divisions rather than acting as a spur to activities that breached them. There are exceptions, notably in the case of two respondents who are very actively involved in the bi-confessional Alliance Party. One, self-employed in the transport business, is an interesting departure from the norm.

The product of a broken home in east Belfast and an only child, he left school with no qualifications at the age of fifteen to care for his invalided mother. When the violence flared in the late 1960s and members of his extended family gravitated towards loyalist paramilitarism, the need to look after his mother, both materially and physically, deterred him from involvement 'with the hard-men...I had too much on my plate. Looking after her was a sort of insurance policy. I was encouraged to join the UDA

[Ulster Defence Association, the leading loyalist paramilitary organisation], but I was worried about my mother'.

Alarmed by the mounting 'hatred and bigotry', he joined the Alliance Party in 1971 shortly after its formation. The decision was triggered by an attack, led by women, on a local Catholic-owned shop:

> It sickened me. I thought it was very wrong and felt I had to do something. I suppose I was a bit of an idealist, wanting to bring about change, the working-class "Prod" out to revolutionise the world! I suppose I was a bit naive really.

Whether or not this was an ingenuous decision it was, in the circumstances, an unusual one. By now married to an unreconstructed loyalist and with some of his cousins involved in the UDA, he not only joined Alliance but was later to serve in an elected capacity on its behalf, although not in his local area: 'that would have been too close for comfort'. His motivation was to 'do something for the underdog, for the working-class of whatever background. The interests of the working class are the same everywhere'.

No longer an elected representative, he has retained his membership in the party and has more recently become an active member of his trade association: 'I love to influence people, but I don't know why. Perhaps it's because I always want to argue for the underdog, having been one. I've had to be a survivor because of my background'. For this respondent a combination of civic duty and a desire to influence decisions were the underlying reasons for his activities: what unified them was the ambition to forge links among the working-class, although he rejected any socialist alternatives, believing them to be tainted either by their association with violence or their 'bureaucratic tendencies'.

The background of the other member of the APNI is very different. A senior professional in the health sector, his active introduction to the party came through his future wife's family, particularly her father. From a middle-class family, whose parents were members of an exclusive religious sect and 'apolitical', he had not encountered Catholics until he entered university: 'I remember the very first lecture, there were Roman Catholics there. It came to me that they were just the same as me. I'd never had Roman Catholic friends before'. Initially a supporter of the Northern Ireland Labour Party - 'at the time, politics for me was about class' - he switched allegiance in the early 1970s believing that there was no alternative to the APNI as a means of 'changing people's attitudes'.

The formative experience for him was not a specific event, but rather his time at university from the mid 1960s until the early 1970s, in particular the fact that his intake year at university, about one-third of whom were

115

Catholic, were mutually supportive and free of sectarianism. This, he believes, was crucial in convincing him of the need for consensual politics in Northern Ireland, prompting him to vote for the APNI before he met his future wife. Thereafter, he has become integrally involved in all aspects of work on the party's behalf, short of running for office.

There is a missionary zeal about his commitment to Alliance's agenda which he believes is the only means of combating intolerance and division:

> This business of seeing people as different because of where they come from, what church they attend, is unhealthy and divisive. We must see them as people: I feel very strongly about it. We must stop this labelling!

Like the previous respondent, he is an enthusiastic exponent of integrated education and of education for mutual understanding:

> Little but good can come out of them. There can't be enough of children growing up together, of being educated together: it's the only way we'll learn to understand our differences and create a tolerant society.

The aspiration to generate tolerance and a wider community of interests is, for both, expressed primarily by their commitment to the APNI, although in one case it is refracted through a class lens and in the other by the celebration of cultural pluralism. While neither is deterred by any potential risks to themselves or their families that may result from their activities, both are keenly aware that their security is in part afforded by the fact that, as the first of them observed, 'the Alliance Party poses no real threat to the diehards'.

Men and exclusiveness

Their politics of coalescence is, however, the exception among the male activists. Each of the others, most of whom have been personally affected by 'the troubles', operate with a more exclusive notion of community. Two of the respondents, for instance, from radically different ideological backgrounds, have been imprisoned because of their paramilitary activities.

One, a former and senior member of the Ulster Defence Association, now a shop steward in a manufacturing company - a role he acknowledges he occupies partly because of his past 'activities' and his reputation for being 'a good organiser' - eloquently expresses the exclusive understanding of community. Operating in the context of a religiously mixed workforce, he presents himself consciously as a mediator between Protestants and Catholics: 'Sometimes feelings run high and the shop stewards have to step in to cool it off, to keep politics' (i.e. sectarianism) 'out of the shop floor and to keep management out of it'. The respondent conveys a vivid picture of a potentially eruptive workforce and of the shop stewards acting as neutral arbiters negotiating a fragile order in the factory:

> There's people that are there for the divide and who want to keep it from being healed. You know that there are nationalists that are activists, and nationalists know that there are Protestants that are activists, so that's where I try to forget about politics on the shop-floor because it's dynamite. My job is to make sure it doesn't go off and that means watching people.

Asked whether Catholic workers were aware of his paramilitary background, the exclusive sense of community becomes apparent: 'Oh yes: *we* know *them* and *they* know *us*' (respondent's emphasis). Treading the line and keeping the peace was, however, understood as an instrumental necessity: 'It's a question of your bread and butter, of paying your mortgage, of whether the place stays open or closes'. The honest broker role is also effected by ensuring that flags and emblems of both traditions are kept out of the workplace. Beyond the factory gates, though, the insularity is explicit:

> Here it's close-knit communities. They, the nationalist people, are a close-knit community and we, the Protestants, are a close-knit community. Where I live, it's like a family - that's how the Ulster people are.

While recognising the need for 'harmony' at work, 'once we're out of the factory everyone puts the shutters down. You don't associate with an enemy'.

This vocabulary of difference and division excludes a wider communitarian motive. But such divisions also occur on an intra-communal basis as is evidenced by the other former internee. An active member of the Workers Party, he was imprisoned in the early 1970s for activities associated with the 'Republican Clubs' (a forerunner of the Workers Party), whose origins lay in the Official IRA. Committed to socialism, his is a vision of class unity which was encouraged initially by a youth worker who established a cross-community folk club in the respondent's neighbourhood which he joined while still at school.

A Catholic, many of the members of his peer group during adolescence were Protestants, friendships that were reinforced for him by the blatant sectarianism he witnessed at the week-long 'missions' to which primary school children were sent to be 'harangued by fire and brimstone priests'. He recalls one priest 'preaching about "bad company", children who didn't have the chance to be good kids because they weren't Catholics and how we should avoid non-Catholics'. This only consolidated his relationships with his Protestant friends and made him 'suspicious of religion'.

Unqualified, he left school at fifteen to work in the family business and was recruited to the now defunct NI Labour Party (NILP) by the youth worker. This caused a rift both with his mother, a devout Catholic, who interpreted the NILP as 'a godless band of communists' and with his father whose family boasted active members of the old IRA and who were bitterly anti-Protestant: 'They tried to instil nationalism into me, but it never really stuck'. Having participated in the civil rights movement and a self-professed pacifist, it was the forced move of Catholics from North Belfast in 1969 when their houses were deliberately set on fire, that began to change his views. Shortly afterwards a fellow employee was shot dead at work and, in 1972, his home was bombed by loyalist paramilitaries. He and his family, including his first child - then six months old - were lucky to escape from the ensuing blaze. This was the catalyst for his conversion to 'defensive violence'.

Refusing to regard the Protestant community as his 'enemy', he became attracted to the Official IRA:

> With the provos and the loyalists running riot, I thought, "who do they see as their enemy?" I began to equate the provos and the loyalists as people with the same thinking: both were my enemy. The Officials were opposed to the politics and tactics of the provos. They struck me as reasonable people who persuaded me of the necessity of defensive violence. They asked me if it was morally correct to sit back and do nothing if a neighbour was attacked. It wasn't, so I took the decision to learn how to use a weapon. I thought that if there are people out there who are prepared to use guns indiscriminately, I'd better learn how to use them and make them available as a defensive mechanism.

Having survived five attempts on his life - by the Ulster Volunteer Force (UVF), PIRA and the Irish National Liberation Army (INLA) - he has remained an active member of the Workers Party, although he has not run for public office because of the potential danger it would entail: 'My wife doesn't like me being up front. We've got five kids now, the risks are too great'. What has sustained him is an unwavering commitment to socialism in the midst of both inter-communal violence and internecine warfare within his own community:

> I feel duty-bound to help to try and change an unbalanced world, it's a moral thing really. I just can't accept things as they are, international capital is the real enemy. People here are not ready for real politics.

Of the remaining six male activists, all bar one tend to confine themselves to activities within their own communities. The exception, a socialist, is an active trade unionist and a voluntary worker with alcoholics in his area. But the remainder, chastened by troubles-related experiences, have adopted insular lifestyles and political activities. One, a young full-time Catholic student and SDLP supporter living in a rural area involves himself in a number of church-related charitable activities and studiously avoids contact with republicans in his neighbourhood. Though he has Protestant friends at his college and does discuss politics with them, he does not socialise with them in his own locality for fear of reprisals. He also has a Protestant girl-friend, a born-again Christian, although he has not told his family, fearing their disapproval. Another, a middle-aged Catholic teacher living in an isolated rural area, restricts his activities to his trade union: 'We're too exposed here to do anything else. If I lived in Britain, or even in Belfast, I'd probably do more, but I fear for my family out here'.

Summary

A sense of risk is more acutely felt among the male activists, partly as a result of experience and partly because of their place of residence. Unlike many of the female activists who subscribe to some sense of 'sisterhood', albeit an essentially maternalist one, male activists are much more diffident about even a skeletal sense of fraternity. They also tend to agree that women in Northern Ireland have more in common with one another than men do, both within and across communities. Though the commonalities they ascribe to women are invariably couched in traditional, if not patriarchal terms, 'brotherhood', even for active trade unionists, tends to have only a narrow instrumental meaning: it rarely extends beyond the workplace, as the shop steward graphically related.

The extended interviews with the activists suggest that an inclusive communitarian motive is both more evident among women than men and is also perceived by both sexes to be the preserve largely of women. While socialists of both sexes are inspired by a belief in class as a unifying factor, among female activists of differing religious and political affiliations, there is a sense of shared interests among women *qua* women. This should not, though, be overstated. Often, 'sisterhood' is expressed in aspirational rather than behavioural terms: only one of the activist women is, for instance, involved in an expressly feminist group, although a significant minority do claim a feminist identity.

There are inherent problems involved in suggesting that the communitarian motive is feminised. Its association with locality, sharing, interdependence, cooperation, mutuality, connectedness, caring and concern, suggests an affinity with ideas concerning female essentialism. Yet, standpoint and eco-feminists, 'maternal revivalists', exponents of welfare feminism and a women's culture not only accept but celebrate such linkages and the conflation of self and other-directedness they imply. The preeminence among activist women of personal satisfaction as a motive for political activity and its pursuit through meeting the needs of others, does indicate a difference between the sexes that carries implications for the more orthodox modes of political participation.

The significant level of support among women for increased female representation in elected office and the buoyant belief that more of them would 'make a difference' if elected, topics that we discuss elsewhere (see Chapters 7 and 8), does provide food for thought. Previously marginalised by the violence of 'the troubles', an established peace may create the space for women to enter the public realm of politics through more orthodox routes, notably *via* the parties. Imbued with other-directed motives and, in the case of female politicians, as we see in Chapter 7, ascribed with distinctive characteristics, there is a belief within the wider population that if elected in sufficient numbers women have the capacity to change matters in Northern Ireland for the better. The evidence of the positive aspects of a women's culture denoted by Hedlund (1988) apparent from the behaviour and opinions of the female activists tends to reinforce this view.

In Chapter 6 we take up the issue of the relationship between women and the region's political parties, both in terms of the extent to which they are perceived to represent the interests of women and the strategies they have adopted as means of increasing the proportion of women in elected office. Before that, in Chapter 5 we turn our attention to the domestic arena as a site of political behaviour by exploring, in particular, the reciprocal effects of the activities and opinions of spouses/partners.

5 The personal dynamics of participation

As discussed in earlier chapters, political activity can occur during one's everyday interactions and discussions with family, friends and workmates. The propensity to discuss politics and current events, to attempt to mould the opinions of others, the types of persons with whom these discussions and arguments take place and the individual's perception of their own efficacy in debate all fall within the dimensions of political activity as conceived by this study. Previous chapters have also demonstrated the importance of the spouse and other family members as 'significant others', especially among the most active, who affect the level and scope of public participation engaged in by the individual. For these reasons, the balance of views within couples and the congruence/incongruence of their political viewpoints are important areas that deserve investigation.

Talking politics

As part of the study's focus on a broad conception of political activity, respondents were asked a series of questions relating to their willingness to discuss political issues and, in the event of a disagreement, whether they saw themselves as able to influence or alter the opinions of others, thereby providing measures of self-perceived efficacy. These questions related both to 'others' generally and to the spouses of those who had ever been married or who had cohabited. Table 5.1 reports the responses to three questions directed at the extent to which female and male respondents indicated a likelihood to discuss political issues; in effect they are measures of 'political interest' as adopted, for instance, by Inglehart (1981).

Table 5.1
Political discussion: women and men

	Political discussion with someone in last two weeks[a]			
	Yes	No	Total	(N)
Women	19.9	80.1	100.0	(999)
Men	27.3	72.7	100.0	(272)

	Likely to talk about a news story the next day[b]				
	Often	Sometimes	Seldom	Never	Total
Women	39.9	41.5	11.2	7.4	100.0
Men	40.1	42.6	10.7	6.6	100.0

	Would introduce politics as a topic of conversation[c]				
	Often	Sometimes	Seldom	Never	Total
Women	2.0	17.1	30.0	51.0	100.0
Men	5.9	26.5	35.3	32.4	100.0

[a] Differences between sexes significant at $p < 0.01$.
[b] Differences between sexes not significant.
[c] Differences between sexes significant at $p < 0.001$.

While a majority of both sexes stated that they had not engaged in a political discussion with someone else during the preceding two weeks, significantly more men than women did claim to have done so. Similarly, although majorities of both sexes said that they seldom or never introduce politics into a conversation, more men claimed to do so 'often' or 'sometimes', whereas over half of the female respondents stated that they never bring politics into a conversation. Hence, men are more likely to claim that they have initiated or have engaged in political discussions and to that extent they appear to exhibit higher levels of political interest.

The responses to these questions, however, contrast markedly with that to the following: **'If a news story in the paper or on television or radio had interested you, would you be likely to talk about it with someone the next day?'** Over 80 percent of respondents said they would do so often or at least sometimes, with no significant difference between women or men. As discovered in the qualitative interviewing, one defensive mechanism employed by people in Northern Ireland to cope with the political situation is to avoid discussing politics, particularly when the opinions of others are unknown or are presumed to be at variance with one's own. The reason for this taboo is often given as 'Not wanting to offend' and seems to be a strategy that is employed somewhat more often by women than by men. This is illustrated in the following extract, from an interview with a female Catholic teacher:

> I might avoid discussing politics at work. We have a couple of non-Catholic colleagues at my school and, what with the situation being what it is in Northern Ireland, we do tend to avoid discussing politics because of that.

The respondents appear to draw a distinction between commenting on news stories and participating in a discussion about them: referring to a news item is regarded as carrying less risk than the direct discussion of politics. In that respect, women emerge as being more disposed toward conflict avoidance than men.[1]

Those who had engaged in a political discussion in the previous two weeks were asked to identify their 'fellow' discussant(s). Only one person mentioned a conversation with a politician. Three-quarters of the discussants nominated by the male respondents were of their own sex, compared to half of those nominated by the female respondents (Table 5.2a).

Table 5.2a
Sex of political discussant by sex of respondent

Sex of respondent	Sex of discussant	
	Female	Male
Female	48.5	23.6
Male	51.5	76.4
Total	100.0	100.0

Women were more likely than men to name discussants who were family relations or spouses, whereas the majority of men mentioned non-related friends or workmates (Table 5.2b). As in general for all discussants, the sex of co-discussants who were other family members or friends/workmates that were named by women were equally likely to be of either sex. In contrast, the other family members and friends/workmates named by men were much more likely also to be male. So, while men behave as if discussing politics is a 'male only' pastime, women are equally likely to discuss politics with either sex.

Table 5.2b
Relationship of political discussant to female and male respondents

	Sex of respondent	
Discussant	Female	Male
Mother	3.5	2.0
Father	4.8	1.2
Sister	3.4	2.4
Brother	4.3	2.4
Spouse	20.0	12.7
Other family, female	6.6	1.4
Other family, male	8.7	11.3
Friend/Workmate, fem.	22.6	8.8
Friend/Workmate, male	23.6	56.3
Politician/Activist, fem	0.0	0.0
Politician/Activist, male	0.3	0.0
Others, female	0.6	0.0
Others, male	1.0	1.6
Total	100.0	100.0

An interesting expression of the dynamics of both sides of this phenomenon can be seen in an extract from an interview with one of our activist respondents, a Catholic SDLP supporter whose husband had formerly supported Sinn Fein. Though from similar backgrounds, she explained her husband's earlier support for republicanism in terms of the influence of his former workmates:

> It was because if he was chatting with the boys down there you had to be seen to be with them And now that he doesn't go there anymore, he doesn't associate with,...you know...I would say because he's out of that...environment that his politics has changed...And you see I was

124

never out in the pub with him…in that pub…It wasn't that he was more Sinn Fein, it was because…it was all around him.

In addition to being questioned about whether they engage in political discussion, the respondents were asked to judge their political efficacy, that is, in the event of a disagreement, the extent to which they believe their own views or opinions will prevail.(See Table 5.3) First, respondents were asked a general question, **'When you hold a deep conviction, are you able to persuade your friends, companions or acquaintances to adopt this conviction?'** While neither sex claimed to be overly persuasive, half of the women, as opposed to a third of men, believed that they could never persuade others. Men in fact emerged with a higher regard for their powers of persuasion: almost 40 percent believing they could persuade others either often or at least sometimes.

Table 5.3
Ability to persuade others in political discussion: women and men*

| | *Able to persuade others to adopt your view (%)* | | | | |
	Often	Sometimes	Seldom	Never	Total
Women	2.7	23.0	24.9	49.4	100.0
Men	4.8	33.8	28.7	32.7	100.0

| | *Likely course of action if disagreement (%)* | | | | |
	Say nothing	Change subject	Would discuss	Would argue	Total
Women	25.1	10.2	47.4	17.4	100.0
Men	17.8	9.7	43.1	29.4	100.0

| | *Whose views would prevail? (%)* | | | | |
	Mine	Other person	Would vary	Agree to disagree	Total
Women	11.5	9.8	39.2	39.6	100.0
Men	18.9	3.2	40.0	37.9	100.0

* Differences between sexes are all significant at p < 0.001.
Note: The third question, *'Whose views would prevail?',* was asked only of those who would *discuss* or *argue:* 634 women and 190 men.

125

Asked what they would do if a member of their family expressed a political opinion with which they disagreed, the modal response for both sexes was to discuss the issue. Significantly more of the women, however, stated they would say nothing, while more of the men claimed they would argue. This apparently more deferential stance by women extended to judgements concerning personal efficacy; i.e., who would 'win' the discussion or argument. Among those prepared to engage in discussion and/or argument, while most said either that the winner would vary or that they 'would agree to disagree', significantly more of the women conceded that they thought the views of the other person would prevail. Men, by contrast, were more likely to claim that they would 'win' the argument and thus appear not only to be more interested in politics, but also emerge with higher levels of self-confidence or assertiveness than women.[2] The apparent lack of confidence among women is exemplified by the self-deprecating view expressed by the following respondent: 'I don't like to get into an argument. I hardly think I would win. There'd always be someone brighter than me who would put me down.' Another female respondent seems to grant the right of expression to everyone except herself:

> I would tend not to say too much because I wouldn't want to offend my husband or anyone else. People are entitled to their own views whoever they are. I'm aware of that and I don't say what I would like to say, even to my husband. If there are things that are going to cause an upset or a row, I just avoid the issue.

Spousal influence

This latter strategy of conflict avoidance leads to the discussion of reciprocal influence and efficacy within couples. If women regard themselves as less influential beyond the domestic arena, is this also the case within the household?

Table 5.4
Importance of spouse for political views: women and men

	Likely course of action if in disagreement with spouse[a] (%)				
	Say nothing	Change subject	Would discuss	Would argue	Total
Women	19.5	5.5	47.1	27.9	100.0
Men	15.5	6.1	50.2	28.2	100.0

Table 5.4 cont...

Whose views would prevail?[b] (%)

	Mine	Spouse	Would vary	Agree to disagree	Total (N)
Women	11.7	21.0	27.0	40.2	100.0 (781)
Men	17.9	8.8	31.7	41.7	100.0 (247)

Importance of spouse's viewpoint[a] (%)

	Very	Fairly	Not very	Not at all	Total
Women	8.7	26.6	32.7	31.9	100.0
Men	6.1	22.3	34.4	37.1	100.0

If spouse supports different candidate in an election[a] (%)

	Say nothing and vote for:			Disagree and vote for:		
	their pref	my pref.	Not vote	their pref	my pref.	Total
Women	4.1	37.7	4.8	2.1	51.3	100.0
Men	2.9	33.7	5.3	0.4	57.6	100.0

Couples who intend to marry should agree about politics[a] (%)

	Strongly agree	Agree	Neither	Disagree	Strongly disagree	Total
Single:						
women	4.4	30.0	18.5	40.7	6.4	100.0
men	3.7	29.4	23.9	36.7	6.4	100.0
Ever married:						
women	4.0	23.8	22.7	38.8	10.7	100.0
men	6.2	27.6	19.6	34.9	11.6	100.0

[a] Difference between sexes is not statistically significant.
[b] Difference between sexes is significant at $p < 0.001$.

First, respondents were asked what would be their likely course of action if their spouse expressed a political opinion with which they disagreed. The modal response again was that they would discuss the disagreement. In contrast to the responses concerning disagreement within the family in general, however, women did not adopt a less assertive position than men - female respondents were no more likely than males to claim that they would opt for saying nothing, while male respondents were no more likely than female respondents to take the more extreme option of arguing. In effect, women seem rather more likely to allow themselves to express disagreement within the family if the person disagreed with is their spouse.[3] In the event of an argument or discussion, however, the pattern resembles that for the family generally. Most 'agree to disagree' or state that the outcome 'would vary'; yet significantly more women state that their spouse's opinion would prevail, and significantly more men assert that they would dominate any dispute. Such acquiescence is exemplified by the following respondent: 'I don't have differences of opinion with my husband, he knows more than I do, he's more political. Whatever he says, I agree with. He has time to read the papers and watch TV, so he knows more.'

The frequency of the 'agreeing to disagree' strategy becomes rather more apparent when one investigates the salience of the spouse's political opinions for the respondent's own viewpoint. Two-thirds of both women and men say that their spouse's political opinions are not at all or not very important in shaping their own beliefs. Similarly, when asked **'If your spouse/partner supported one candidate in an election and you favoured another'**, nine out of ten of both sexes said they would vote for their own preference. A Catholic SDLP supporter provides a representative response to this question:

My husband is opposite to me politically...but we never argue about it, because as far as I was concerned, it was, in this house, it was closed shop. He had his opinions and I had mine, and that was the way it was, the way it is. You see, because there's no argument about it. I go my way whenever I'm voting. He knows who I'm going to vote for anyway. He knows that. And, like, I knew what he used to do...we just went down to the voting together and he went in and I went in. But I never asked him what he did - because it was his business. And I would say it's the only thing we never really discuss...because we never feel the need to discuss it.

Both 'ever married' and single respondents were also asked whether couples who intend to marry should be in broad agreement about politics. Less than a third concurred with the proposition, with no significant difference between the 'ever married' or 'singles' of either sex. This is surprising when one considers the salience of local politics for life in

Northern Ireland. However, the qualitative interviews provided evidence to the contrary, as for instance, in the following case:

> It's very important for couples to think similarly on politics. A difference in political opinions could be one of the biggest threats to marriage. In a marriage you can argue or reason with, say, if a husband or a wife is having an affair, you can argue or reason. Or if one of them has a drink, drugs or gambling problem, you can argue. But if they're of a different, really deep, political persuasion, you haven't a chance!

This was put rather more succinctly by a Church of Ireland Ulster Unionist Party supporter:

> You can't live with somebody that you don't agree with. If you're going to have that in the back of your mind, there's bound to be a certain amount of distrust.

A likely explanation is that couples, as well as 'self-selecting' each other at an early stage on religious grounds,[4] also rule out potential partners on the basis of incompatible political views. As a middle-aged Church of Ireland activist stated:

> ...there must be some point at which, you know, you find somebody that everything works nicely with and the relationship progresses. I don't mean that there aren't other things like initial attraction and all that sort of thing, but I think perhaps, you know, a relationship progresses when you do find that you think the same way over a lot of things.

A Catholic SDLP supporter articulated a similar view:

> When I was in my mid-twenties and at the stage of looking for a partner, I didn't want to become involved with someone who wouldn't be accepted at home - whether on religious grounds or political grounds. I remember one boyfriend - there was a shooting and he didn't show up that weekend. I hoped to God he wasn't involved. I didn't want any more hassle so I chose someone with similar, moderate views.

In other words, politics appears so salient that, long before marriage is contemplated, those with conflicting political views are ruled out of the equation.

Regression analysis

Crosstabulating the responses to given questions by gender, interesting though it may be, does not permit an analysis of the possible causes and correlates of a willingness to discuss politics or to be assertive in exerting one's opinions, either in general or within the more specific family context, especially *vis a vis* one's partner. Furthermore, the response to any single question is dependent upon its exact content and wording.[5] In order to address these issues, composite indices were constructed by combining the responses to the individual questions cited above, with the highest weight placed upon the more extreme responses. Three indices were produced: one of political discussion based upon the responses to the questions in Table 5.1; one of persuasion, based upon the responses to questions in Table 5.3; and a variable of influence within marriage, based upon the responses displayed in Table 5.4. Regression analyses were then conducted to establish the characteristics that influence propensities to discuss politics or to exert influence.

The independent, causal, variables can be grouped into two types: structural variables that relate to concrete social status or position (above the dotted line in Table 5.5); and interactional variables that relate to experiences, involvement or attitudes (those below the dotted line). The single most important determinant of all three composite indices (individual's level of discussion, their perceived efficacy at persuasion and influence over spouse) is the number of different types of political activity - a *variety* of types of activity is associated with higher levels of discussion, persuasion and influence over one's spouse. In effect, the more one is involved, the more there is to discuss.

Younger respondents, those with a higher level of educational qualification, or those with a higher occupational position than their spouse are more likely to discuss political issues, as are respondents who answered positively to the following question, **'In your case, can you think of people who have been particularly important in forming your political opinions?'** Among the other structural variables, those who lived in Belfast were more likely to discuss political matters than those living elsewhere and, once the effects of education and higher status relative to the spouse had been taken into account, residing in a lower class household had the effect of reducing the likelihood of discussing political matters.

Table 5.5

Table 5.5
Regression models of discussion, persuasion and influence within marriage

	Discussion	Persuasion	Influence
Sex[a]		-0.086^g	
Age	-0.112^f	-0.199^f	-0.148^f
Not middle-aged[b]		0.089^g	
Education	0.110^f		
Returned to education		0.061^h	
Job status			-0.091^h
Household class	0.080^g		
Job status relative to spouse[c]	0.113^f		0.137^f
Belfast resident	0.101^f		0.073^h
Number of types of activity	0.380^f	0.492^f	0.220^f
Number of organisations	-0.074^g	-0.152^f	
Influential person in background	0.117^f	0.072^h	0.101^g
Influential event in past		0.095^f	
Views influenced by an organisation	0.063^h		
DUP supporter			0.105^g
SDLP supporter	0.084^g		
Sinn Fein supporter	0.071^g	0.064^h	
Green Party supporter			0.071^h
Left/Right views[d]	-0.065^h		
Anti-sex discrimination views	-0.081^g		
Agree with women's movement		-0.059^h	
Anti positive discrimination			0.131^f
r^2	0.336	0.283	0.150
(Weighted N)	(993)	(993)	$(700)^e$

[a] Dummy variable: male $= 0$, female $= 1$.

[b] Squared difference from mean age (42.2).

[c] Positive value indicates job status is higher than spouse's job status.

[d] 'Left-wing' opinion scored higher.

[e] Single respondents excluded from analysis.

[f] Statistically significant at $p < 0.001$.

[g] Statistically significant at $p < 0.01$.

[h] Statistically significant at $p < 0.05$.

Note: In addition to the above variables, the effects of a large number of other independent variables were tested which were not significant for any of the three dependent variables. These included: direct socio-economic status; interaction between socio-economic status and level of education; whether R was in fulltime employment, part-time employment or unemployed; whether R was a housespouse; marital status; Protestant or Roman Catholic; number of children and number of children under 5;

rural location; joint or exclusive control of household finances; membership of NI political parties other than those listed in the table.

Among the experience/attitude factors affecting the likelihood of discussing politics, respondents who could nominate a specific group or organisation that had affected their opinions were more likely to be political discussants, as were supporters of the SDLP or Sinn Fein. The *variety* of types of activities, rather than the gross amount of a single kind of activity, is more important as a cause of the propensity to engage in political discussion. Once the effect of number of types of political activity is taken into account, the intensity of involvement in any single organisation had no effect; while belonging to a greater number of organisations than average had a dampening effect upon the likelihood of discussing politics. Interestingly, in the multivariate model, holding left-wing or anti-sex discrimination views are both also found to have weak depressive effects upon likelihood to participate in political discussion. About one third of the variance in the 'discussion index' could be explained by the regression model.

For the perceived ability to persuade others, the most significant effects, after types of activity, are that older respondents regard themselves as less able to do so. This may simply be an effect of age - as people move into old age, physical decline and falls in economic and social standing can cause disengagement from everyday life and a consequent loss of confidence. The lower level of persuasiveness reported by the older respondents may also reflect a cohort effect. They would have entered adulthood in the 1940s and 1950s at a time when a measure of reserve in public, especially perhaps among women, was considered more acceptable behaviour.[6]

As with discussing politics, the number of organisational memberships has a negative effect upon self-perceived efficacy. Women present themselves as less persuasive than men. Being able to name some personal experiences or public events that have had an important effect on one's political opinions, as well as being able to name an influential person in one's background, is positively associated with persuasiveness.[7] Returning to education after completing full-time study, being a Sinn Fein supporter and not supporting the women's movement, all have independent, though weak, effects upon judgements concerning one's powers of persuasion.

Perhaps reflecting the general picture of indifference to the opinions of one's partner noted above, there is a generally less deterministic picture from the analysis of influence on the spouse within marriage. The number of different types of activity continues to have the strongest effect on influence, but at a lower level. Older respondents of both sexes also claim to exert less influence on the opinions of their spouses. Having a higher occupational status than one's spouse indicates an increased level of influence on the opinions of the relevant partner. This implies that men exert more influence in marriage since a disproportionate number of husbands have higher occupational statuses than their wives. Respondents with lower job statuses claim a higher level of influence on the opinions of their spouses. Living in Belfast, opposition to positive discrimination for women, being a supporter of either the DUP or the Green Party, are also associated with the stated ability to exert more influence upon one's spouse.[8]

Discussion

In general, the results portray women's propensity to discuss political matters and their ability to persuade or influence others as significantly below that of men. Women report less political discussion than men and state that they are less likely to initiate discussions of politics. They are more likely to name men as the persons with whom they would discuss political matters; more likely than men to name family members or spouses as the co-discussants; while men are most likely to mention non-related friends or workmates. Female respondents were less likely to believe that they could ever persuade others to adopt their own views, even if they were strongly held. If a disagreement did develop, they were more likely than men to say nothing and less likely to argue. In the event of their participating in a discussion or argument, they were again more likely than men to feel that the other person's views, rather than their own, would prevail. Such findings conjure up a stereotype of women as lacking in both confidence and assertiveness.

This image can, however, be viewed from other angles. While the results reveal women, (by and large) to be less involved and more passive than men, it does not follow that the male respondents themselves present a completely contrasting image. While the responses of women and men differ significantly, they resemble each other more than they diverge. Most people, regardless of gender, claimed not to have had a political discussion with anyone in the previous two weeks and stated that they seldom or never introduce politics into a conversation. Despite claiming to talk about politics less often, one should note that women were as likely to nominate another woman as a man as the individual with whom they had discussed politics. Furthermore, the emergence of the family as the primary site of political discussion among women simply may reflect their lower levels of economic activity. By the same token, the preponderance of workmates and friends as men's discussants may merely reflect their higher level of participation in the workforce. Among working men, for instance, over 70 percent of political discussants are friends or workmates; by contrast, for economically inactive men, this proportion drops to 47 percent. Similarly, with regard to persuasiveness, the clear majority of both sexes believe that they can seldom or never get others to adopt their views and clearly preferred, rather than argument, the option of discussion.

Men do tend to extend their discussion of politics into spheres outside the family, whereas women, who are more likely to engage in intra-family discussions, may feel more constrained to adopt less confrontational, more conciliatory roles.[9] Women may in effect adopt a self-effacing role of mediator in order to maintain harmony within the family.

This hypothetical explanation for the more diffident strategies adopted by women does not appear to apply to disagreement with one's spouse. There is no significant difference between the sexes in the response to the question concerning their likely course of action if they disagree with their partner. The explanation for this is not a change in the male pattern of response (which remains virtually identical), but is rather due both to more women stating they would be willing to argue with their spouse and the fact that fewer women state that they would say nothing (though more women still say they would eventually defer to their husband's views). While it may only reflect the low salience of politics for many couples,[10] the general lack of importance attached to the spouse's political views by both sexes is noteworthy. Any assumption that women slavishly emulate the views of their partners does not appear to be substantiated by these results.

The multivariate analyses, however, disclose the relatively minor significance of sex in comparison to other factors: the variety of types of activity, and age, are clearly of more significance than one's sex in determining the level of political discussion, persuasiveness or influence within marriage. Such results provide a cautionary tale about the perils of adopting an over-gendered conception of personal political behaviour.

Household finances

Whether afflicted by the effects of public or private patriarchy, or a combination of both (Walby, 1990), the position of women in the labour market has historically been weak and vulnerable. Subjected to both horizontal and vertical occupational segregation (Hakim, 1979), the 'family wage' tradition (Land, 1980) and the patriarchal ideological assumptions of the welfare state (Williams, 1993), women have been exposed to a lack of economic and political autonomy which has made them the principal victims of poverty (Glendinning and Millar, 1992). While some feminists have advocated 'wages for housework' as a strategy both for ending their financial dependency and as a means of politicising women (Dalla Costa and James, 1972), this prescription has attracted much criticism from within the wider women's movement on the ground that, *inter alia,* it merely institutionalises the sexual division of labour within the domestic arena.

Whatever the combination of causes, the relationship between the relative earning power of women and men raises the question of the allocation and management of household finances; more particularly, the issue of whether, within the home, 'money is power'. Given higher rates of economic activity among men and their higher wage levels, it might be hypothesised that within the domestic realm this skews personal politics to their advantage. Men, being more likely to work in the formal economy and to bring in a higher wage in comparison to their economically active partners, do hold the financial 'high ground'. A countervailing argument has been that some women at least exercise control over the household finances as part of the 'woman's domain' of hearth and home. To this end, respondents were asked how they and their partners organise the family finances. The respondents were given five options:

- 'common pot' - partners pool all their money and each takes out what is needed;
- 'allowance' - one spouse/partner manages all the money and gives the other an allowance/share;
- 'allowance' - the respondent manages all the money and gives her/his spouse an allowance/share;
- 'partial pool' - partners pool some of their money and keep the rest for themselves;
- 'independent' - each partner maintains financial autonomy.

The majority of respondents, almost two-thirds, report an equal sharing of household finances, the 'common pot' option. For the rest, approximately equal proportions either give or receive allowances, a smaller number report a partial pooling of finances, and only a small proportion claim complete independence from their spouse in financial matters.

If men have a higher level of financial power in the household, one might anticipate differences between the type of financial arrangements reported by male and female respondents, men perhaps being more likely report allocating allowances to their wives, or to claim complete financial independence for themselves. There are, of course, other competing explanations for a more or less egalitarian distribution of money within households. One could suppose, with the rise of 'second-wave' feminism and a general trend in society towards more equality between the sexes, that younger respondents would report more equal financial arrangements. Households with a higher socio-economic status, which is highly correlated with a higher level of education among the family generally, may also be more egalitarian. Conversely, education does impart power to individuals, which in this case might be used to justify the management of household finances. Educated men may use their possession of qualifications as a justification for inequitable financial arrangements within the household, while female respondents with a higher level of education might claim a more equal distribution of household finances. Making a direct financial contribution to the household *via* an income from the formal economy could also of, course, be used as a justification for a dominant, or at least a participatory, role in household finances.

In order to establish which of these competing hypotheses for more or less equal household arrangements was supported, a logit analysis was conducted in which the effects of sex, age, educational level and employment status upon reported household financial arrangements were tested.

Table 5.6a
'Family finances' by educational level of respondent

	No qual.	Some qual.	A-level or higher	Total*
'Common pot'	62.0	65.4	67.7	63.7
Receives allowance	12.0	10.8	6.5	11.0
Gives allowance	14.4	11.2	3.8	12.1
Partial pooling	7.0	11.0	15.4	9.2
Independent finances	4.6	1.6	6.6	4.0
Total	100.0	100.0	100.0	100.0
(N)	(576)	(290)	(123)	(990)

* Weighted to give equal numbers of men and women.

The most parsimonious model with an adequate fit to the data was one in which neither gender nor age has a direct effect upon household financial arrangements; their effects can be considered artefactual - subsumed within relationships between household financial arrangements and both educational level and employment status.[11]

The effects of education point generally towards a weak association between high educational level and more egalitarian arrangements.(Table 5.6a) Those with qualifications equivalent to A-level or higher are more likely to claim 'partial pooling' or 'common pot' finances and less likely to report giving or receiving allowances in comparison to the others, particularly those with no formal educational qualifications.

Table 5.6b
'Family finances' by employment status

	F-T emp.	P-T emp.	Unem-ployed	Retired	House spouse	Other
'Common pot'	64.5	68.1	65.3	71.6	57.4	62.5
Receives allowance	8.5	9.0	23.0	7.6	14.5	12.8
Gives allowance	7.7	10.6	4.7	8.7	20.6	8.1
Partial pooling	15.0	9.5	4.7	4.1	4.3	16.6
Ind. finances	4.3	2.8	2.3	8.1	3.2	0.0
Total	100.0	100.0	100.0	100.0	100.0	100.0
(N)	(350)	(158)	(38)	(114)	(305)	(23)

One can see evidence (Table 5.6b) that some of the effects of gender and age upon household financial arrangements are subsumed within employment status. For instance, retired people are the most likely to report both a 'common pot' and complete financial independence from their partner[12] - a result contrary to that which would be expected if there was a trend towards less egalitarian arrangements with older age. Those in full-time employment report a higher than overall proportion of 'partial pooling', while the unemployed are the group most likely to say they are allocated an allowance by their spouse. 'Housespouses', virtually all women,[13] report higher than average proportions of both receiving an allowance (when their husband was in full-time employment) *and giving* allowances (particularly when their husband was unemployed). Thus, while the status of working without pay in the home can be linked to unequal financial arrangements, with some 'housewives' being financially dependent upon their husbands, in those instances where the husband is out of work, wives who are 'housespouses' - i.e., not in the formal economy - are likely to control the finances and dole out allowances to their partners. It seems to be the case that the more straitened the financial circumstances the more likely it is that women assume the role of household managers.

Socialisation

One of the functions remaining to families is that of primary socialisation of the young - involving the transmission of basic notions of social justice, identity and morality. Hence families, either consciously or unconsciously, are central to defining the parameters within which an individual's political identity will evolve, adapt and change over the course of decades. While these parameters are not impervious to change, whether their sources are the influence of external events, the gains and losses of social mobility, or the force of political argument and persuasion, a person's basic outlook on the world formed in childhood can be assumed to have a permanence that can defy the machinations of manipulators of political opinion. Consequently, socialisation can be seen as an activity with profound political consequences; even when the socialisation itself is not directly oriented to the communication of political views. Arguably, the mundane activities of child-rearing can have fundamental consequences for political evolution. The analyses of the underlying causes of public and political activity in Chapter 3 found that 'significant others' were a prime determinant of higher levels of involvement and that a large proportion of these significant others were parents.

For these reasons, the study was concerned to evaluate socialisation practices as they relate to the development or acquisition of attitudes and views that have political implications whether directly or undirectly. The results below report the findings of the quantitative survey for those questions that related to socialisation and other practices and that can be viewed as attempts to influence the attitudes and behaviour adopted by the respondents' children.[14]

To introduce these results, a regression model (Table 5.7) is presented of the characteristics of respondents with children who were ranked on a composite index of behaviours that could have an effect upon their offspring's views and behaviours.[15] About 20 per cent of the variance of the composite index can be explained by four (really three) variables. Older respondents and those in middle age report more behaviour-forming activity

138

directed at their children. To a lesser extent, female respondents and those with less, or no educational attainment report more attitude and behaviour-forming activities.

Table 5.7
Regression model of attempts to influence children

Sex[a]	0.095[d]
Age	0.453[c]
Not middle-aged[b]	-0.235[c]
Education	-0.074[d]
r^2	0.206

[a] Dummy variable: male = 0, female = 1.
[b] Squared difference from mean age (42.2).
[c] Statistically significant at $p < 0.001$.
[d] Statistically significant at $p < 0.05$.

As with many of the regression results, variables that do not appear in the final model excite as much interest as those that do. Apart from an indication of more directive socialisation from those with lower levels of education, neither socio-economic status nor class of household seem to affect the model. Similarly, neither broad religious identity (Protestant or Catholic), employment status or working solely within the home, place of residence (urban or rural location), the number of children or their sex (whether they were solely girls or boys or both sexes) has a unique or significant effect upon the socialisation index.

These results can be fleshed out by examining some of the responses to the questions that comprised the index (Table 5.8a). Respondents were asked if they regularly send or take their children to church or religious services. The high level of past and present religious practice in Northern Ireland is reflected in the answers. Well over half claim to take their children to religious services with the majority of the balance saying they send their children. Only small numbers admit to neither alternative. Fewer of those who admit to neither taking nor sending their children to church are men. This is the only instance where men state a significantly higher level of involvement in socialisation practices than women.

Over three-quarters of parents report encouraging their children to join youth groups, party organisations for young people or other similar organisations. By contrast, only small proportions report being themselves currently involved with any groups or organisations associated with schools attended by their offspring.

Table 5.8a
Measures of socialisation activities: female and male parents

Taking children to church*(%)

	Female	Male
Take	53.1	58.4
Send	33.7	36.5
Neither	13.2	5.1

Encouraging children to join youth groups, school societies, party organisations for young people etc (%)

Female	Male
82.0	79.3

Involvement with groups associated with child's school (%)

Female	Male
12.9	10.8

Mean number of school-based activities currently involved in as parent

Female	Male
0.12	0.11

* Statistically significant at $p < 0.01$.

As a means of discovering the extent to which parents attempted to exercise control over the influences to which their children are exposed, a series of questions were asked about the age at which respondents would allow their children to view television programmes with certain types of content.(Table 5.8b) The most restrictive responses given by respondents were to programmes or films with an 'adult' content. Well over three-quarters of parents felt that children had to be in at least their mid-teens before they were allowed to view such programmes, with over 20 per cent saying they were unsuitable at any age. The response was almost as restrictive for programmes with a violent content. Most parents did not censor the viewing of news programmes, with fathers tending to be significantly less restrictive in this case. However, the majority of respondents did not wish very young children to have unrestricted access to the news. Pre-testing and some of the qualitative interviews established that this was due primarily to parents' fears about the effects upon their children of the reporting of violent events. This misgiving is particularly salient in Northern Ireland where the reporting of violence may show locations with which young children are familiar, and where a regular feature of the aftermath of killings is footage of grieving relatives, including the children of victims.

Table 5.8b
Censorship of media: female and male parents

At age:	Polit.bias[a]		News[a]		Violence		'Adult'	
	F	M	F	M	F	M	F	M
0 to 3	5.5	9.8	32.1	44.5	1.7	4.2	0.9	1.9
4 to 7	3.1	7.0	29.6	24.8	1.6	2.3	0.2	0.9
8 to 10	7.6	6.5	19.9	18.8	4.2	5.1	1.8	0.9
11 to 13	17.5	20.9	10.7	7.8	14.7	13.4	4.6	7.4
14 to 16	29.1	23.3	3.8	2.3	29.1	32.9	23.0	25.9
17 or over	19.5	17.7	1.4	1.4	27.5	22.7	46.0	42.6
Not at any age	17.8	14.9	2.5	0.5	21.1	19.4	23.6	20.4

Allow child to watch television programmes containing:

[a] Statistically significant difference between female and male respondents at $p < 0.01$.

In relation to programmes with a perceived political bias, the response falls somewhere between those for news viewing and programmes with a violent or 'adult' content. Men are significantly more liberal in terms of the age at which they would allow their children to view programmes which they themselves considered to be politically-biased. The modal response for both sexes is the mid-teens, with over a third wishing either to restrict the viewing of such programmes to those over seventeen or considering them unsuitable at any age.[16]

Parents were also asked about the extent to which they had attempted to persuade their children to share their views on religion, sexual equality, sexual behaviour and politics (Table 5.8c). The respondents were most directive in their attempts to get their children to adopt their religious opinions, with almost a third of mothers and a quarter of fathers stating they had tried 'very much' to do so. This was followed closely by attempts to inculcate views on sexual behaviour. By contrast, their efforts to influence views on equality between the sexes and politics generally was much lower, with well over half of respondents stating they had never tried to get their children to share their views on sexual equality, and well over two-thirds claiming no attempt to persuade their children to adopt their own political views.

Table 5.8c

Attempts by parents to persuade their children to adopt their views on religion, sex equality, politics and sexual behaviour

	Religion[a]		Sex equality[b]		Politics		Sex. behav[a]	
	F	M	F	M	F	M	F	M
Very much	30.5	25.1	12.3	8.7	5.2	6.9	28.9	21.7
A little	40.5	34.7	31.5	26.6	23.9	26.1	34.6	30.9
Never tried	29.0	40.2	56.2	64.7	70.9	67.0	36.5	47.5
Total	100.0	100.0	100.0	100.0	100.0	100.0	100.0	100.0

[a] Statistically significant difference between female and male respondents at $p < 0.01$.
[b] Statistically significant difference at $p < 0.05$.

Within these broad parameters, women were somewhat more directive in the moral socialisation of their children. Significantly more mothers than fathers reported having tried to some extent to get their children to share their views on religion and sexual behaviour. Women also were more likely to report attempting to influence their children's views on sexual equality, but to a lesser degree of statistical significance. There was no significant difference between the sexes in the extent to which they sought to influence their children's political views.

Even the most directive of parents must recognise that, as their children grow older, the relative influence of the home will dwindle in comparison to agencies outside the family - in particular to the influences of schooling and peer group. One of the ways that parents can attempt to continue to influence the socialisation of their children outside of the home is through the choice of school. In order to assess the reasons underlying the choice of schools by parents, respondents were asked '**If you were choosing a school today for a girl/boy child of your own who was entering secondary[17] education, which would be the two most important characteristics that**

142

you would look for in a school?' Respondents were asked to give the first and second most important characteristics from a list of ten alternatives (Table 5.8d).

Table 5.8d
Ranking* of most important reasons for choosing a secondary school:
female (F) and male (M) parents

Reason	For daughter		For son	
	F	M	F	M
Training for a good job	0.50	0.49	0.58	0.59
Emphasis on acad. achievement	0.46	0.52	0.46	0.48
Sound moral education	0.47	0.52	0.41	0.51
Strong discipline in school	0.45	0.40	0.59	0.50
Caters to special needs of the child	0.31	0.24	0.25	0.17
Convenient location	0.17	0.18	0.14	0.17
Mixed by religion	0.23	0.19	0.23	0.18
Mixed by sex	0.17	0.13	0.15	0.12
Mixed by social class	0.10	0.15	0.09	0.12
Relaxed atmosphere	0.12	0.14	0.08	0.12

* Respondents gave the two most important reasons for selecting a school. The most important was scored '2', the second most important '1' and those not mentioned '0'. The rank in the Table is the arithmetic mean of these scores.

By and large, responses favouring the practical considerations of training for work and academic achievement, followed closely by responses emphasising the inculcation of morality and strict discipline, eclipse those that would be congruent with a desire to use the school to promote 'liberal' views. Even the 'liberal' response with the highest adherence, choosing a school that 'caters to the special needs of the child', shows a practical bent. The responses which can be interpreted as more explicit promotions of sets of attitudes, i.e., mixed by religion, sex or social class, receive only a minority of choices.[18 19] While schools may be of potential importance for infusing social/political attitudes into their pupils, parents adopt more practical and career-oriented reasons in making their selections, favouring the more predictable attributes of hard work and academic application.

Congruence of political behaviour within couples

A generally low level of political activity among the samples of both women and men already has been established. Also, the presence of a supportive spouse has been found to be of consistent importance for those of both sexes who show high levels of involvement in each of the different types of activity encompassed by the study. Two opposing models of the dynamics of activity within couples can then be proposed. Spouses may support the respondent's public and political activities by themselves taking a 'backseat' role. This may be facilitated through the assumption of responsibility for either domestic chores and/or wage-earning. In each case, the spouse supplies the respondent with the resources of time and energy that make political activity feasible. In effect, the spouses perform complementary roles. Alternatively, the spouses may actively support each other in both their public and political activities: a model of mutuality whereby each takes on both domestic and outside public responsibilities.

Table 5.9
Measures of activity of respondent by whether their spouse is a member of organisations: all respondents

	No	Yes	Signif.
Number of types of activity	5.5	7.7	0.001
Number of organisational memberships	1.3	2.2	0.001
Voted in last three elections	2.3	2.3	N.S.
Political party 'helper'	0.2	0.7	0.001
Informal political activities	1.1	2.5	0.001
Trade union activity	0.8	1.0	N.S.
Consumer activism scale	3.2	3.8	0.05
Charitable activities scale	1.0	1.6	0.001
(N)	(954)	(85)	

The interview schedules questioned respondents at length about their own activities, but asked only limited information about the activities of spouses or partners. After they had been questioned about their organisational membership at length, respondents were asked to state whether their spouses participated in any of the same types of organisations. A limited number of spouses had done so. Table 5.9 displays a range of measures of

144

activity with respondents divided into two groups: those who did, and those who did not, have a spouse who was reported as being a member of at least one organisation.

The results are clearly congruent with the model of mutuality. For most measures of participation, respondents whose spouse is a member of at least one organisation show a higher level of activity. This result is most pronounced for those activities that are the more comprehensive measures of participation: such as number of types of activity; number of organisational memberships; and the measures of more clearly overt political behaviour, including the index of informal political activity and activism on behalf of a political party. The instances where there is no significant difference, voting and trade union activism, can be seen, respectively, as behaviours common to practically everyone and only a small minority.

Congruence of political behaviour within couples: 'matched' couples

The results of the above and preceding sections provide some insights into intra-couple behaviour. All of the information about the spouse's behaviour or attitudes reported above, however, is indirect, in the sense that the respondent is reporting on their partner.[20] In order to conduct analyses limited to actual couples, the survey design included the opportunity to deliberately sample both members of a random subset of couples. In these cases, both spouses were given full interviews, normally with their partner not present. This yielded 184 'matched pairs' of interviews allowing direct comparisons of the responses given by each partner.[21]

Table 5.10 shows the coefficients obtained when a variety of indicators of activity, knowledge and behaviour are correlated. The difference from the preceding analyses is that here the measures are direct; the levels of activity of each respondent is being compared explicitly with those of their spouse. As before, there is overall support for an hypothesis of 'mutuality'. The typical correlation of an activity or opinion between spouses is of the range 0.40 to 0.50, highly significant at the 0.001 level. Significant, positive correlations exist for both the most composite measures of activity (number of types of activity and number of organisational memberships) and the most overtly political measures of activity (informal political activity and extent of political party activism). As before, trade union activism is not highly correlated between spouses, due probably to its generally low incidence in the sample.

145

Table 5.10
Within-couple correlations of measures of activity

	r	Signif.
Number of types of activity	0.51	0.001
Number of organisational memberships	0.52	0.001
Accuracy of knowledge of local councillors' names	0.49	0.001
Accuracy of estimate of number of female MPs	0.43	0.001
Informal political activity	0.40	0.001
Political party 'helper'	0.62	0.001
Trade union activity	0.16	0.05
Charitable activities scale	0.50	0.001
Consumer activism scale	0.65	0.001
Feminist attitudes scale	0.36	0.001
Discusses politics scale	0.48	0.001
Persuades others scale	0.20	0.01
Influences spouse scale	0.29	0.001
Support for spouse's activities	0.37	0.001

Note: Spearman's rank-order correlations yield the same substantive results.

Political knowledge, as indicated by accuracy of knowledge of local councillors and the number of female MPs, is positively associated between spouses.[22] The less overtly political measures of activity, the scales of consumer activism and charitable activities, also show a highly significant level of agreement between spouses.

Spouses also agree in their scoring on a scale of feminist attitudes and there is a positive correlation concerning the extent to which they discuss politics. The mutual 'supportiveness' of couples is further confirmed by the positive correlation of influence on spouse - if one partner feels that they have influence on the other's opinions, this perception is reciprocated. Evidently having influence on one's partner is not a zero sum game, but rather a variable sum affair. The most direct measure of mutual support is provided by the positive correlation between the spouses' responses to the direct query concerning the extent of each spouse's support of the other's involvement in organisations and groups. The only contra-indication to an hypothesis of 'mutuality' comes from couples' scorings on the persuasion of others index. While persuasiveness is positively correlated between couples, the correlation is less significant than that for level of political discussion. This may indicate, however, that the assertiveness of the individuals concerned differ, rather than that the couples themselves disagree.

Partners were also asked about their extent of political knowledge; more precisely, whether they knew the name of their local Member of Parliament, the name of their local electoral ward, and the names of their local councillors. Perhaps the most striking result is the relatively poor level of knowledge. About 60 per cent of all respondents could name their MP, but fewer than 15 per cent knew the name of their local electoral ward, while almost none could name all their local councillors and only six per cent could identify more than half of their local councillors.

Within couples, there was high agreement in the level of knowledge, whether high or low. If one's spouse could, or could not, name the local MP or electoral ward, the respondent's modal response would be congruent, whether correct (or incorrect). For instance, when asked to identify the local MP, if one spouse knew the MP's name, their partner was also likely to know it: *both* the husband *and* the wife in 48.5 per cent of the couples could name their MP correctly. Similarly, the modal response of knowledge (or ignorance) about the identity of local councillors was for each spouse to know some, but less than half. Political knowledge (or ignorance) seems shared within couples.[23] Though these measures are limited, the extent to which the responses 'match' is compelling. On the basis of these indicators, it does not seem that 'opposites attract'.

There was also extensive agreement between spouses in relation to voting preferences and this extent of agreement was of equal strength for the main Unionist and Nationalist parties, the minority parties and the Alliance Party. Also, within the main Unionist and Nationalist blocs, couples were jointly supportive of the same Unionist or Nationalist party, rather than other members of each party 'family'. For instance, households where one spouse supports the Ulster Unionist Party while the other supports the Democratic Unionist Party were rare. Again, perhaps reflecting political endogamy at the stage of choosing a partner, while respondents claim both that their spouses have little effect upon their own political views and that couples who intend to marry do not need to agree on politics, the *actual level* of broad political agreement within couples was very high.

Response to a question on hypothetical support for British political parties lends support to this observation. For those who said they would vote for either the Conservative or the Labour Party in Britain, the modal response of the spouse was to support the same party. Similarly, there was agreement between spouses if one said they would not support any British party or where one partner chose a minority party in Britain. Hypothetical support for the Liberal Democratic Party does not show this association within couples, but this may be due to voters being unclear about its policies towards Northern Ireland or, more generally, its location along a 'left/right' continuum.

Table 5.11
Agreement between spouses on British political party support*

Husband	Conserv.	Wife Liberal Dem	Labour	Other/None
Conservative	68.7	31.3	2.6	23.4
Liberal Dem	9.6	18.8	2.6	8.5
Labour	10.8	25.0	71.1	17.0
Other or None	10.8	25.0	23.7	51.1
Total	100.0	100.0	100.0	100.0
(N)	(83)	(16)	(38)	(47)

* Significant at $p < 0.001$

The results of crosstabulating the responses of each couple to the questions on political discussion, disagreement and influence appear in Table 5.12. In reply to the question as to whether respondents had discussed politics with their spouse in the previous two weeks there is considerable agreement: the large majority, over 90 per cent of both sexes, answered 'No'. Among those who answered positively, the significant point is that more spouses did not remember any political discussion. In particular, of the 8.2 per cent of the wives who recalled a political discussion, two-thirds of their husbands did not. The low salience of political discussion between spouses, a finding noted generally in the quantitative results, seems to hold even when one spouse claims that political discussion has taken place.

A similar level of divergence appears in relation to the likely course of action when disagreement occurs. The passivity of the individuals who would 'say nothing' appears to be confirmed in an offhand manner by their spouses, more than half of whom, in the event of disagreeing with their partner's opinion, give the more assertive answers of readiness to argue or at least to discuss. That aside, there is a (statistically) significant level of agreement in as much as a majority of those of both sexes who anticipate discussions or arguments exact a mutually combative response from their spouses.

Table 5.12
Importance of spouse for political views: matched couples*

Discussed politics with spouse in last two weeks

| Husband's response | Wife's response | |
	Yes	No
Yes	2.9	1.2
No	5.3	90.6

Likely course of action if in disagreement with spouse

| Husband's response | Wife's response | | | |
	Say nothing	Change subject	Would discuss	Would argue
Say nothing	4.2	0.6	6.5	1.2
Change subject	0.0	1.8	3.0	1.8
Would discuss	7.1	1.2	31.0	9.5
Would argue	6.0	1.8	10.1	14.3

* Per cents are total percentages of those in each table.

Note: The Chi-square association between the responses of spouses is significant at $p < 0.001$.

Interestingly, many of both sexes of those who say they 'would discuss' have spouses who select the more passive option of 'saying nothing'. There is also some disagreement within couples about when discussion or argument takes place: while 14.3 per cent of all couples agree they would argue, many of the spouses of the 'arguers' choose the less conflictive option of discussion (and almost as many wives of male 'arguers' say they would 'say nothing').

As to whose views would prevail in an argument or discussion, (Table 5.13) husbands who expect their opinion to win have this expectation somewhat limply confirmed - marginally more than half their spouses are more likely to agree with that option than with any other. This is not confirmed for women who think their views would win out; the modal response from their husbands is that they 'would agree to disagree'. For both sexes, there is agreement amongst those who anticipate that they will

149

'agree to disagree' (23.5 per cent of all couples) or that the 'winner' 'would vary'(12.3 per cent of all couples), particularly if one combines these categories, which are rather equivalent in terms of their assertiveness.

Table 5.13
Whose views would prevail: matched couples*

Husband's response	Wife's response			
	Mine	Spouse	Would vary	Agree to disagree
Mine	3.1	11.1	1.9	4.3
Spouse	3.7	1.9	2.5	1.2
Would vary	1.9	3.7	12.3	10.5
Agree to disagree	4.9	8.6	4.9	23.5

* Per cents are total percentages of those in each table.
Note: The Chi-square association between the responses of spouses is significant at $p < 0.001$.

The greatest source of disagreement between couples occurs amongst those who expect the husband's opinion to prevail. Male and female respondents had very different expectations about whether the husband's views would win an argument. Men who believe their views will dominate are likely to have this belief confirmed by their wives. By contrast, among those women who believe their spouse's opinion will prevail, the husbands are almost as likely to claim that the couple will 'agree to disagree' as to state that they would win. A significant minority of men who believe that the atmosphere of political discourse within marriage is one of give and take do not have this perception confirmed by their spouses:

> I wouldn't discuss politics with anyone except my husband - well, he would discuss and I would listen. We don't have differences of opinion because I follow whatever he says - he's older than I am and I look up to him because he is more knowledgeable than I am. It is important for couples to agree and think similarly. If he started thinking differently I probably wouldn't be with him.

In response to the question, **'How important are the political opinions of your spouse/partner for determining what you think?'**, (Table 5.14) there is moderate but statistically significant agreement between partners on the relative importance of their spouse's viewpoint. This is particularly true of those for whom the viewpoint of their spouse is 'fairly important' (15.4 per cent of all couples) or 'not at all important' (19.5 per cent of all couples). One should note, however, that both sexes have instances at the extremes; i.e., where one spouse feels their partner's views are important while the other does not reciprocate this feeling.

Table 5.14
Importance of spouse's viewpoint: matched couples*

Husband's response	Wife's response			
	Very	Fairly	Not very	Not at all
Very important	2.4	2.4	3.0	0.6
Fairly important	1.2	15.4	4.1	2.4
Not very important	3.0	8.9	11.8	8.9
Not important at all	1.2	4.7	10.7	19.5

* Per cents are total percentages of those in each table.
Note: The Chi-square association between the responses of spouses is significant at $p < 0.001$.

Table 5.15
Action if spouse supports a different electoral candidate*

Husband's response	Wife's response				
	Say nothing & vote for:		Not vote	Disagree & vote for:	
	their pref.	my pref.		their pref.	my pref.
Say nothing & vote for:					
their preference	1.2	1.2	0.6	0.0	1.2
my preference	0.6	22.9	0.6	0.6	6.0
Not vote	0.0	1.2	2.4	0.0	0.6
Disagree & vote for:					
their preference	0.0	0.0	0.0	0.0	0.6
my preference	1.8	18.7	0.0	1.2	38.6

* Per cents are total percentages of those in each table.
Note: The Chi-square association between the responses of spouses is significant at $p < 0.001$.

Concerning support for different candidates (Table 5.15), the couples are often at variance about whether they would voice disagreement or remain

151

silent, with a greater proportion of women saying they would 'not say anything'. The majority of both sexes agree, however, that they would vote for their own preference rather than that of their spouse.

Discussion

In making sense of these results, one is compelled to question the extent to which political activity, even broadly conceived, can be stretched to include 'the personal'. As earlier analyses have established, it is a small minority of both women and men that can be typed among the politically active. This conclusion applies even when very broadly conceived conceptions of political participation are tested. When the politically active are subjected to in-depth interviews, they too tend to understand political participation in terms of extra-domestic activity in the public realm. The majority of activists, whether women or men, comprehend the essence of political participation to be its 'publicity': party activism, voting and, to some extent, pressure group activity are commonly regarded as the prime *loci* of politics. As one respondent stated when questioned about what politics meant to her:

> I see my family as outside of official politics, as socially aware rather than politically aware. I always think of politics in a more formal way, belonging to a party, being interested in who gets elected, canvassing, that sort of thing.

One can argue that political activity does have a broader compass, an argument that the underlying premise of our study does make, but one should still take into account the perceptions of the practitioners themselves. While support within the family was found to be mutual between spouses and to be of significant importance for political activity, the overall impression gained from the quantitative analyses and the in-depth interviews is not one of personal relationships themselves forming a nexus for political activity. Rather, the family and the support located within it, can be seen as a springboard to activity elsewhere; i.e., in the external public arena. The familiar axiom, 'the personal is political' does not seem consciously to inform the views and attitudes of the majority of women and men in Northern Ireland.

A countervailing argument can also be made, however. The inhibition that our respondents harbour about discussing politics beyond the family may, paradoxically, be seen as an indication of the true salience of political issues for people in the province. In Northern Ireland, the political really is personal; almost all, if not directly touched themselves, have family members, friends or acquaintances who have been affected by the political situation in the province - either as members of the security forces, as paramilitaries, prisoners or victims. Even the least affected will, at a minimum, have been subject to the daily routines of security screening and the accompanying inconveniences and anxieties. The following comments proffered by two respondents asked about politics at their workplaces are illustrative of the pervasiveness of 'the troubles':

> I only discuss politics at home. There are women at work with sons in prison. Whenever they express opinions, I walk away. To nod your head is to agree with them, to shake your head is to disagree, so I just walk by and go on with my work.

> I wouldn't discuss politics at work. The workforce is mixed and anyway it's a good place to escape from politics. My boss doesn't allow sensitive issues like politics or religion to be discussed and I think that's a good thing. Anyway, a discussion about politics would always get onto religion or *vice versa* and it's always possible to find somebody who would disagree. It's better to avoid these things altogether in order to maintain good workplace relations.

Not engaging in political discourse outside of a close circle of family and trusted friends, the reluctance to view everyday activities as perhaps having a political dimension, even the politically endogamous choice of a life partner, can all be seen as signs of the ways in which the personal has been politicised. It is the very salience, and sometimes deadly nature, of politics in Northern Ireland that inhibits the public expression of political belief. The significance of place is captured by one female activist who insisted that in Northern Ireland, agreement on political issues with one's partner was essential:

> ...because of the present situation we are living in, in the North of Ireland. I mean, it might be different if you are living outside Northern Ireland in Australia or somewhere and have different political beliefs...you can discuss them, row over them and then forget about them. But if you are actually living in the situation, I think you need a bit of harmony, you know!

Notes

1. Such news stories may, of course, have nothing to do with the Northern Ireland context.

2. This is broadly congruent with the findings concerning the underrepresentation of women in the public realm. Female respondents are more likely to support the proposition that women lack the confidence to enter politics. (See Chapter 7)

3. Though unlikely, it is conceivable that the respondents who gave 'passive' answers (would *say nothing* or *change the subject* or *other person/spouse* would win an argument) concerning disagreements with family members could have given 'assertive' answers (*discuss, argue* or *me* winning a dispute) in relation to disagreements with their spouses. In fact, there is a high level of agreement between the responses given for disagreements with one's spouse and with other family members. In all instances, the modal response for the 'family' questions is the same as the 'spouse' version of the same question. For instance, 70.5 per cent of those who would argue with other family members would also argue with their spouse.

4. Religious endogamy in marriage in Northern Ireland is remarkably high. Lee (1994) reports census tabulations that give a two per cent rate of Catholic/Protestant intermarriage. He then considers in depth the extent to which this could be an underestimate but concludes: 'On the basis of scattered additional evidence, however, it is unlikely that the number of "mixed" couples "hidden" by these factors [religious conversion, emigration and non-response to voluntary questions on the Census and surveys] is very considerable.' (p. 119)

5. As is the case with three of the four items in Table 5.4, where there are indications that women give somewhat more 'deferential' answers, the general pattern of responses may be of interest even though the response to individual items does not reach statistical significance.

6. For a discussion of another society (Germany) where cohort effects on the level of political activism are pronounced see Kolinsky (1993).

7. The majority of events named by people relate to 'the troubles'.

8. The reason these three apparently disparate variables all exert a positive effect on "influence upon spouse" is that they each share the holding of stronger (than average) views. As such, respondents may be motivated to proselytise these views.

9. There may be more political agreement within families than there is between members of the population generally; even within the same ethnic segments of the population.

10. It is possible of course that couples may select each other for reasons of political endogamy.

11. The best fitting model ($X^2 = 221$, df $= 227$, p $= 0.607$) was: Household financial arrangement (HFA); Sex; Age Category; HFA

with Educational level; HFA with Employment status. The age categories used were: less than 30; aged 30 to 50; over 50. The categories of household financial arrangement, educational level, and employment status are as shown in Tables 6a and 6b.

12. Only those currently living with a spouse or partner were asked the household finance questions; the retired, widows and widowers are not included in this analysis. Separated and divorced respondents are also excluded. Only six respondents reported living with another person in a common-law arrangement.

13. Only one man claimed to be a 'housespouse'.

14. The responses to the questions reported here often relate only obliquely to socialisation practices. In the absence of questions already developed elsewhere, considerable effort was directed towards the construction of quantitative measures of 'political' socialisation practices during the pretesting and piloting stages of the interview schedule - particularly towards the values and attitudes that respondents may attempt to inculcate into their offspring and the means that they might use to do so. Many of these measures could not be included in the final schedule due to problems of reliability and respondent recall that could not be resolved. The items reported here are those that survived evaluation during the pretesting and piloting phases.

15. This index is a prime component of one of the measures of respondents' activity described in Chapter 3.

16. The bias of such programmes is that with which respondents disagree.

17. The choice of secondary rather than primary school was decided upon since parents are likely to send their children to the closest primary school of the appropriate religious denomination. The transfer to secondary education is governed by a highly selective procedure, pupils being subjected to a series of 'qualifying' examinations which, if passed, allow them access to an elite grammar school stream. Prior to the examination results, parents must consciously choose a grammar school or a second-tier secondary modern school.

18. One could argue that for reasons of congruence, parents also should have been given the options of school *not* mixed by religion, sex or social class. Realistically, however, in Northern Ireland very few schools are formally mixed by religion or social class while the proportion not mixed by sex, particularly amongst the grammar schools, is high.

19. These school choice results also throw light on a conundrum. Surveys in Northern Ireland routinely find a large proportion or a majority of the population favouring religiously integrated education whereas only

155

a small proportion of children (less than 2%) attend such schools: active support for integrated education, while vociferous, is strictly a minority affair. The results here show that while parents may favour integrated education, the majority will attach more significance to choosing schools that will benefit their children in the concrete areas of job skills and academic achievement. Even choosing a school because of its convenient location emerges as more important. (One of the reasons advanced for the low take-up of religiously integrated education however is its lack of local provision in most areas.) One should also note that a significant reason why many parents send their children to religiously integrated secondary schools is that they provide a 'comprehensive' alternative to the grammar and secondary schools. One final point worth noting in this context is that some schools in the state (Protestant) system do have a significant informal religious mix.

20. The field-workers were asked to conduct interviews whenever possible with the spouse or partner out of the room.

21. Respondents were asked to provide information about the occupation of their spouse. A comparison of the codings for the respondents own employment status and socio-economic grouping code of their job with those derived from their occupation as reported by their spouse showed an extremely high level of agreement..

22. This is reinforced by a number of cross-tabulations of categorical questions of political knowledge that are not shown here. These cross-tabulations also displayed a highly significant agreement between spouses in their level of knowledge.

23. Fieldworkers were instructed to interview each spouse of a 'matched couple' separately. Sometimes, however, this was not possible. Also, on some occasions interviewers conducted the interviews separately but on different dates. To the extent that the other spouse may have been present during an interview, or that the first-interviewed spouse may have discussed the content of their interview with their partner before the second interview took place, there may have been some 'cross-contamination'.

6 Parties, partisans and participation

Introduction

In this chapter the focus turns to the attitudes of party identifiers towards the region's political parties, notably the extent to which the parties are perceived to represent the interests of women[1]. It also discusses the policies of the parties concerning gender equality and the 'fit' between those policies and the attitudes of voters in Northern Ireland, as well as the strategies adopted by the major parties in selecting their candidates. In the latter respect we deploy the three-fold model of party strategies delineated by Lovenduski (1993): *viz* whether they adopt 'rhetorical', 'positive action' or 'positive discrimination' strategies in selecting female candidates. That is, whether the parties merely encourage women to enter the public realm of representative politics by making, as Lovenduski puts it, 'frequent reference to the importance of getting more women into office'; whether they implement special measures such as training seminars or provide financial support to enable women to put themselves forward as candidates; or by reserving places for women on candidate lists through the use of gender quotas.

There are a variety of reasons for focusing on Northern Ireland's parties, not least the fact that majorities of both female and male respondents agree that they fail to give women 'the opportunity to enter politics'. Moreover, the respondents to the survey deprecate the chronic absence of women from elected office: almost two-thirds of all female respondents (62 per cent) endorse an increase of women representatives at national level, as do 50 per cent of all male respondents. Furthermore, 64 per cent of women support an increase in the proportion of female councillors, a view shared by half of the men in the sample population.

Explanations for the underrepresentation of women in public office commonly embrace an array of factors that, according to Norris (1993), operate at three levels: the systemic level, including factors such as political culture, the electoral system, the party system and legislative competition; the party level, that is those factors, including ideology and organisation, that govern a party's strategies and procedures concerning the selection of candidates; and the individual level, notably the motivation and resources that aspiring candidates themselves are able to summon up in seeking selection, as well as the attributes deemed by 'selectorates' to define an eligible candidate. Thus, at the individual level both supply and demand-side factors operate: the former influencing whether potential candidates come forward and the latter influencing whether they are chosen. Together, the factors operating at each level interact to structure the recruitment process.

Before exploring these issues we can rehearse, briefly, the arguments in favour of an increase in female representation. (Pitkin, 1967; Phillips, 1991 and 1993). They include, first, the claim that it is simply unfair and unjust that at least half of the population is not mirrored in the public realms of politics; secondly, an argument based on social utility, *viz* that the virtual male monopoly of public office effectively deprives society of the talent, skills and resources possessed by women; and thirdly, that the failure to recruit women biases the perception of political role-models in a male-centred direction, thereby bolstering the perception that politics is an 'unnatural practice' for women and effectively deterring them from seeking entry into office.

A related, and more contentious, argument is that an increase in representation by women would generate a different, even a better, 'politics' - a position adopted by a plurality of women in Northern Ireland, 45 per cent of whom agree that in general things would improve if there were more women in public office. (See below and Chapter 7). Whether rooted in notions of female essentialism (Bjornsdottir and Kristmundsdottir, 1995) or an awareness of the social construction of gender roles, the belief in 'difference' tends to portray women as agents of change (Kelly, 1991; Thomas and Welch, 1991; Welch, 1984). Asserted, among other things, to be more disposed to compromise and consensus than men they, the argument runs, are not only equipped to alter the style of political discourse but also, because they are concerned with issues that are often overlooked or neglected by male politicians, the substance of policy (Norderval, 1985; Skjeie, 1993). Whether adopted by conservative (Ruddick, 1980) or radical (Daly, 1978) exponents of feminism this perspective, in adopting the view that only women can speak for women, either implies or explicates a belief in interest rather than merely numerical representation (Sapiro, 1981).

However the arguments about representation are couched, there has been a recent and growing demand for more women to enter formal political arenas, itself signalling something of a change in the agenda of the broadly-defined women's movement (Lovenduski and Randall, 1993). Whereas in the early phase of second-wave feminism mainstream politics tended to be discounted in favour of more informal methods of political engagement, concerted efforts to lever women into formal public office have become increasingly widespread. Such attempts, while sensitive to the need to change the rules by which candidates are chosen, are equally attentive to the influence of systemic factors.

We noted in Chapter 1 the culturally conservative context of Northern Ireland that, in combination with the martial character of its politics, has tended to disadvantage women (Opsahl, 1993; Hinds, 1995). Such a context, which has contributed to patterns of inequality in the employment process as well as in the realms of political office, need not, however, prove conclusive. In other culturally conservative political systems women have been advancing steadily in terms of political representation, notably in Germany (Kolinsky, 1993) and, to a lesser extent, in the Republic of Ireland (Galligan, 1993). Such instances suggest the influence of other factors that intervene to counter social conservatism regarding the public roles considered appropriate for women (Darcy et al, 1994; Norris, 1985; Rule, 1981, 1987; Rule and Zimmerman, 1992).

The effects of the wider social and political system do, though, percolate to the individual level, influencing the availability of women as potential candidates. Subject to cultural expectations about women's 'proper' role that may usher them away from the public into the private realm, women can become tied to the hearth by, for instance, the effects of related situational constraints such as inadequate levels of state-funded child-care provision (Gustafsson, 1994). Privatised in this way, women may be deprived of the resources deemed appropriate for an aspiring politician: educational attainment; occupational status; time; and access to the financial support that candidates require in order to compete for selection. The corresponding policy changes to tackle such obstacles include widespread and affordable child-care measures, the entry of women into 'eligibility-enhancing professions' and campaign funding earmarked for women seeking candidacy *via* initiatives like 'EMILY's List' (Carney, 1994)[2].

Perceptions of women's interests

This latter point relates to the structure of opportunities and constraints available to women within political parties, notably the ways in which each organises its candidate selection procedures. These matters are discussed below, but perhaps the first point to make is that the eligibility pool in Northern Ireland, as measured by the extent of party membership, is narrowly drawn. Results from the survey demonstrate that only 1.6 per cent of women and 2.1 per cent of men in the general population are members of a political party (which probably helps to explain why none publish actual membership figures!) The low level of party membership does not, however, deter voters from expressing their views about the extent to which the parties are perceived to represent 'women's interests'.

Table 6.1
'Which party in Northern Ireland best
represents the interests of women?' (%)

Party Identity	UUP		DUP		APNI		SDLP		SF		ALL	
	F	M	F	M	F	M	F	M	F	M	F	M
Own Party	27	28	22	26	37	39	33	33	11	31	14	15
Other Party	14	25	19	22	9	33	15	37	31	30	36	28
No Party	59	48	59	52	55	28	52	30	58	39	50	57

Figures are rounded.

Only a minority of both female and male identifiers state that their own party best represents the interests of women, while a majority of women (and half of all men) of all political persuasions believe that all parties effectively fail women. Such findings amount to a swinging criticism of the parties. Women identifying with the DUP, for instance, are almost as likely to nominate some other party as their own, but the most sweeping indictment emerges from within the republican electorate. Women who support Sinn Fein are almost three times as likely to choose another party as their own: while 10 per cent nominated the SDLP, 18 per cent identified the then Workers Party[3] as that which best represented women's interests.

The collective verdict of failure among female partisans is somewhat less sharply evident within the male electorates. Yet, even among men a majority of DUP supporters and pluralities aligned with the UUP and Sinn Fein believe that no party best represents women's interests, while a plurality of SDLP supporters are more likely to nominate another party,

160

notably the WP. Though male partisans are more likely than their female counterparts to nominate their own party, they are almost as likely to state that some other party best represents women's interests. Among men, only APNI supporters express a plural vote of confidence that their party best serves women's interests: hardly a ringing endorsement. The most compelling gender gap emerges among Sinn Fein identifiers: male supporters are significantly more likely than are their female counterparts to nominate the party, although unlike women they reject the Worker's Party as the single most 'woman-friendly' alternative, according it an equivalent level of support (eight per cent) as both the SDLP and, more surprisingly, the NI Conservative Party.

The judgement about the representation of women's interests is, though, contestable since the substance of those interests are left unstated. Elsewhere in the survey, however, a number of both more general and more specific questions were posed that help to indicate the perception of women's interests and which may help to explain the perceived failure of parties among their respective electorates.

Table 6.2
'Attempts to provide equal opportunities
for women have gone too far' (%)

	UUP		DUP		APNI		SDLP		SF		ALL	
	F	M	F	M	F	M	F	M	F	M	F	M
Agree/strongly agree	24	33	22	50	18	25	13	26	28	28	19	30
Neither	12	14	12	14	8	17	12	14	7	14	12	14
Disagree/strongly disagree	65	53	66	36	75	58	75	59	66	57	69	56

Women supporting each of the parties are, with the exception of Sinn Fein, less likely than their male equivalents to agree that equal opportunities have exceeded the limits of acceptability. The gender gap is most pronounced among DUP supporters: only a little over a third of its male identifiers disagree that gender equality has 'gone too far', compared to two-thirds of their female counterparts. Among women, the level of disagreement with the statement applies within and across the parties, suggesting the existence of an unmet and perhaps submerged agenda shared among women of all party affiliations. Women who support Sinn Fein, for instance, share much common ground with those who identify with the two major unionist parties

161

in terms of the level of disagreement with the proposition. The DUP apart, a majority of male identifiers also disagree that equal opportunities have gone too far, implying that men as well as women would support attempts to propel gender equality issues further up their respective party agendas.

The broad levels of support within female electorates for maintaining, if not extending, equality of opportunity policy are leant substance by their responses to a further series of questions, themselves shaped by the intensity of support for the women's movement. Respondents were invited to locate themselves on a ten-point scale, where 1 indicated 'no support' and 10 'complete support' for the perceived agenda of the women's movement.

Table 6.3
Intensity of support for the women's
movement among voters* (%)

	UUP		DUP		APNI		SDLP		SF		ALL	
	F	M	F	M	F	M	F	M	F	M	F	M
Low	14	28	19	27	13	17	13	12	4	0	13	20
Medium	66	54	61	61	69	58	59	65	54	80	63	61
High	20	18	20	12	18	25	30	23	41	20	24	19

* 'Low' is the aggregate of points 1-4 on the ten-point scale; 'Medium' the aggregate of points 5-7; and 'High' the aggregate of points 8-10.

Among both sexes, unionist voters are much less likely to accord virtually unqualified support for the women's movement than those identifying with either the SDLP or, more especially, Sinn Fein. Alone among male voters, those who support the Alliance Party identify more fully with the women's movement than their female counterparts. The most complete endorsement, however, emerges from among Sinn Fein supporters: 25 per cent and 13 per cent of, respectively, its female and male voters accord the women's movement a maximum score of ten, compared to 12 per cent of women and nine per cent of men in the general population.

The relative strengths of identity with the women's movement by partisans of both sexes is generally consolidated by other results. For instance, women who support either the SDLP or Sinn Fein are more likely to agree (71 per cent and 80 per cent respectively) that women suffer from discrimination in the job market than the UUP's female voters (59 per cent), whereas those supporting the DUP tend to converge with nationalist electorates (69 per cent) as do APNI women (71 per cent). Male voters, with exception of the APNI - 75 per cent of whom agree that women are disadvantaged by sex discrimination at work - are less likely to concur with this proposition. Those supporting the SDLP (51 per cent) and Sinn Fein (60 per cent) are most likely to agree that women suffer discrimination in the job market, whereas UUP and DUP voters are least likely to do so (47 and 45 per cent, respectively). Again the attitudinal gender gap is most pronounced in the DUP: a majority of its male supporters (53 per cent) disagree that women suffer employment discrimination compared to 19 per cent of its women voters.

With the exception of Alliance identifiers, there is a higher perception among female than male voters of the generalised incidence of sex discrimination at work: however, its salience is comparatively low as the following results indicate. Respondents were invited to state whether discrimination on the grounds of sex, religion, age, class and disability was a 'major problem' in Northern Ireland.

Table 6.4
Voters agreeing that various forms of
discrimination are a major problem in Northern Ireland (%)

Discrimination type	UUP F	UUP M	DUP F	DUP M	APNI F	APNI M	SDLP F	SDLP M	SF F	SF M	ALL F	ALL M
Sex	8	10	13	3	14	17	13	7	26	8	13	8
Religion	30	28	36	44	34	39	43	41	59	73	38	39
Age	19	27	20	31	30	17	19	20	22	7	21	22
Class	6	11	6	3	11	17	11	11	21	13	10	12
Disability	41	43	33	34	48	39	37	48	54	29	40	42

Note: Columns will not add up to 100 since the percentage in each cell is those identifying each form of discrimination as a 'major problem': respondents could identify more than one form of discrimination as a 'major problem'.

The results from among voters are consistent with the views of both women and men within the general population who rank sex discrimination in fourth place behind, in descending order, disability, religion and age and only marginally ahead of class-based discrimination. The highest ranking it receives from voters (a poor third) is among women who support Sinn Fein. Despite the widespread recognition of its incidence, the low rating of sex discrimination as a 'major problem' suggests that political parties may be justified in according it a relatively low priority in their policy documents and manifestos: a point that we take up later.

However, the fact that it enjoys only a modest ranking does not mean that the population believes the government should do little or nothing to tackle sex discrimination. Respondents were asked where they would place themselves on a ten point scale where '1' meant the government should 'do nothing' to improve the social and economic position of women and '10' that it should 'do everything possible'.

Within the general population more than one-third of women (34 per cent) endorsed the maximal position, compared to 21 per cent of men. Among female party identifiers, those aligned with the DUP (42 per cent), Sinn Fein and the SDLP (both 43 per cent) were wholly in favour of the government doing 'everything possible', followed by UUP (32 per cent) and APNI (29 per cent) voters. The proportion of maximisers among male voters was lower in each case: Sinn Fein (27 per cent); SDLP (25 per cent); DUP (20 per cent); UUP (19 per cent); and APNI (17 per cent). Women voters are much more favourably inclined than men to intervention by government to tackle the problems of disadvantage that are perceived to confront them.

Endorsing a maximal strategy by government may be hypothesised to include support for a programme of positive discrimination by way of gender quotas. A further item tested the level of endorsement for this muscular form of affirmative action.

Table 6.5
'If women are underrepresented at a place of work, they should be appointed or promoted in preference to men' (%)

| | UUP | | DUP | | APNI | | SDLP | | SF | | ALL | |
	F	M	F	M	F	M	F	M	F	M	F	M
Agree/strongly agree	27	22	25	17	24	0	37	20	31	36	28	21
Neither	22	13	29	8	20	13	21	19	21	36	23	17
Disagree/strongly disagree	51	65	47	75	56	88	42	62	49	28	49	63

Clearly there are limits to the maximal position among party supporters. Moreover, within the general population while 28 per cent of women and 21 per cent of men endorse positive discrimination, 49 per cent and 63 per cent, respectively, reject it. Though nationalists are more likely than unionists to sanction preferential treatment, a plurality of women who support the SDLP and virtually half of Sinn Fein female voters are opposed to gender quotas. Men, with the exception of Sinn Fein supporters who emerge as the most equivocal group, are strongly against such a measure. By extension, this implies that the adoption of positive discrimination strategies by the parties in selecting their candidates is unlikely to find favour within their respective electorates.

Opposition to gender quotas in employment does not, though, extend to support for negative discrimination against women. Respondents were asked: **'If there are lay-offs at work, women should be made redundant before married men'**. Women in the general population were opposed to this proposition by a ratio of almost 2:1, 56 per cent disagreeing and 30 per cent agreeing with the statement. Although the ratio among all men was much lower, the balance of opinion was against such a discriminatory act: 48 per cent disagreed compared to the 38 per cent who agreed. Among partisans of both sexes (Table 6.6) there were clear communal and gender differences in response to this item.

Table 6.6
'If there are lay-offs at work, women
should be made redundant before married men'

	UUP		DUP		APNI		SDLP		SF		ALL	
	F	M	F	M	F	M	F	M	F	M	F	M
Agree/strongly agree	40	40	42	49	21	29	29	43	15	33	30	38
Neither	15	18	3	16	14	0	14	9	18	20	14	15
Disagree/strong agree	45	42	55	35	65	71	58	48	68	47	56	48

With the exception of UUP voters, a majority of women identifiers are opposed to the proposal, a view shared only by male supporters of the Alliance Party. Men who identify with the DUP are the only group to express plurality support for the option of making women redundant before married men. In terms of the differential between agreement and disagreement, women who support the major unionist parties appear to be more traditional or deferential in their attitude on this item, and Alliance and especially Sinn Fein supporters the least. In terms of agreement with the proposition, women unionists appear to have more in common not just with their fellow voters but also with men who support both the SDLP and

165

Sinn Fein, leaving the views of nationalist and republican women somewhat exposed.

Underpinning the differential attitudes among women and men towards the scope of equal opportunities, support for preferential treatment, the extent of agreement with the women's movement and the priority accorded to sex discrimination as a source of disadvantage, there may lurk deep-seated views that turn on the familiar nature/nurture axis. This issue was probed by the following question: **'Women are by nature happiest when making a home and caring for children'**. Within the general population a small majority of men (51 per cent) agreed with the statement, 34 per cent disagreed while the remainder (15 per cent) were undecided. Women were more equivocal: while 46 per cent did not agree that they are most fulfilled within the domestic sphere, 41 per cent did, with 13 per cent neither agreeing nor disagreeing. Opinion among partisans (Table 6.7) revealed some sharp differences of view.

Table 6.7
'Women are by nature happiest when making
a home and caring for children' (%)

	UUP		DUP		APNI		SDLP		SF		ALL	
	F	M	F	M	F	M	F	M	F	M	F	M
Agree/strongly agree	51	57	51	71	27	26	40	55	36	64	41	51
Neither	13	18	15	5	15	30	13	7	9	14	14	16
Disagree/strongly disagree	36	26	34	25	58	43	47	39	55	21	46	34

Among women voters, there is a clear division of opinion. Despite the blandishments of Marian devotion, it is a majority of those supporting the unionist rather than the nationalist parties who agree that women's happiness is essentially hearth-shaped. While a majority of female Sinn Fein voters and a plurality of SDLP supporters disagree that their natural place is in the home, it is women aligned with the Alliance Party who most firmly reject the equation between contentment and domesticity: and among men only Alliance Party voters express views that are broadly consistent with their sister supporters. A majority of men aligned to each of the other parties believe that women are naturally disposed to find happiness within the private realm, a view that is especially pronounced among DUP and Sinn Fein supporters.

The resilent belief that nature is destiny, while by no means overwhelming, does create an obstacle for women seeking to expand their horizons into the public realm. It can also supply a rationalisation for the parties, all of which in Northern Ireland are male-dominated, to concentrate their policy proposals for women on the basis that they belong within the narrow confines of home and family. Such an easy assumption is, however, tempered by the existence of widespread and strong support for the provision by employers, in both the public and private sectors, of child-care facilities. Overall, 81 per cent of women and 73 per cent of men agree that employers should provide child-care for their female employees. Among party identifiers support is equally impressive.

Table 6.8
Support for employer-provided child-care facilities

	UUP		DUP		APNI		SDLP		SF		ALL	
	F	M	F	M	F	M	F	M	F	M	F	M
Agree/strongly agree	81	61	83	65	78	71	86	81	84	80	81	73
Neither	5	11	5	14	10	17	6	5	7	13	7	9
Disagree/strongly disagree	14	28	13	21	12	13	7	15	9	7	12	18

While unionist men lend the lowest levels of support, it is clear that there is a strong coalescence of opinion on this issue, both between the sexes and across voting blocs. The implied demand for the alleviation of the double-burden shouldered by working women is evident, especially amongst female respondents.

What emerges from these findings is support for an equal opportunities strategy for women, especially among both women within the general population and female party identifiers. Irrespective of their party identity, a majority of women disagree that the existing scope of equal opportunities can be extended no further, a view shared by male partisans with the exception of those who support the DUP. Moreover, the clustering of women and men in the middle range of support for the women's movement (the mean position for all women on the 10 point scale was 6.2, and for all men 5.8) does indicate that a moderate rather than a radical approach to the disadvantages confronting women finds favour in Northern Ireland.

While there is widespread recognition of the incidence of sex discrimination its status as a major problem is, however, relatively low compared to other perceived forms of discrimination. Its more lowly position might, on the one hand, be claimed to compromise the decision taken in 1986 by the Equal Opportunities Commission in Northern Ireland (EOCNI), to campaign against the then Government's proposal to create a multi-functional agency with a remit to tackle all forms of discrimination in the province (HMSO, 1986). Had the proposal come to fruition the issue of sex discrimination would, the EOCNI (1986) argued, have been eclipsed by the agency's likely preoccupation with religious discrimination in the province. In the light of the 'Cinderella' status of sex discrimination, the Commission's successful fight to maintain its autonomy could, therefore, be argued to have backfired. On the other hand, however, had the EOCNI been merged into such a multi-purpose agency, the perception of sex discrimination as a major problem may have fallen further from view.

That there are agreed boundaries to the means considered legitimate in dealing with sex discrimination is clear from the lack of support accorded to preferential treatment: maximal government action does not, in the public's view, extend to positive discrimination. It does, however, include support for the widespread provision of child-care, thereby remedying if not solving a key situational impediment to women's participation in the public sphere. At the same time, however, there are extraordinarily high levels of support for a strategy of self-reliance on the part of women. Asked whether **'Women should themselves make a special effort to overcome sex discrimination'**, 86 per cent of all female respondents and 82 per cent of all male respondents agreed.

Across the five major parties there was overwhelming support between the sexes for the assertion of autonomy by women in tackling sex-based discrimination. This does not imply that men consider this an issue for women alone, although they are more likely to see the domestic arena as the 'natural' domain for women. The findings suggest, rather, that both men and, especially, women desire a more level playing-field upon which the numerical majority of Northern Ireland's population can enjoy equal rights and opportunities. To borrow Lorde's (1984), and mix our own, metaphor, women in Northern Ireland do appear to believe that 'the master's tools' can be used to redesign, if not 'dismantle the master's house'.

Women, the parties and representation

Earlier the support within the wider population for an increase of representation by women, both at national and local level, was noted.

Closer analysis demonstrates that among party supporters a majority of women aligned with the Alliance Party (69 per cent), the UUP (55 per cent), the SDLP (66 per cent) and Sinn Fein (77 per cent) each endorse an increase of women in national tiers of representation, as do virtually half (49 per cent) of the DUP's female supporters. Among male partisans, however, support is less buoyant. Only those identifying with the Alliance Party and the DUP express majority support for an increase of women at national level (67 and 51 per cent respectively); 47 per cent of SDLP supporters favour an increase compared to 49 per cent who endorse the status quo, while Sinn Fein voters are evenly divided between these two options: 47 per cent supporting each alternative. Male supporters of the UUP, however, favour the status quo: 59 per cent endorse this option, compared to 39 per cent who wish to see an increase.

Gender differences are also apparent in relation to the election of local councillors, although they are somewhat less starkly drawn. Among men all, with the exception of UUP supporters (at 43 per cent), lend majority support to the increased presence of women in local government. The highest level of support comes from men aligned with the Alliance Party (63 per cent), followed by the SDLP (55 per cent), Sinn Fein (53 per cent) and the DUP (51 per cent). The balance of view among men suggests that women's place in elected office is perceived to lie within the disempowered realm of Northern Ireland's local councils rather than at national level. Among women, support for an increase broadly matches that accorded to the Parliamentary tier. However aligned, a majority support an increase in female councillors ranging from 80 per cent of Sinn Fein voters to 54 per cent of DUP supporters.

The existence of a gender gap in relation to support for increased representation by women seems to be only partly explained by the extent of confidence female politicians inspire among partisans. Asked whether they would have more confidence in a man or a woman to represent their interests in a national assembly, women who support either the UUP or the DUP are more likely to choose a man (31 and 34 per cent respectively) than a woman (16 and 12 per cent respectively), although 54 per cent of women aligned with UUP and 53 per cent with the DUP state that the sex of an MP would make no difference to the level of confidence s/he enjoyed. By comparison, 21 per cent of women who identify with the SDLP and 23 per cent of those who support Sinn Fein express a preference for a male MP, while 14 per cent of the SDLP's female voters and 29 per cent of those aligned with Sinn Fein express more confidence in a female representative, with 66 per cent and 48 per cent respectively stating that the sex of an MP is irrelevant to the confidence s/he would enjoy. Female supporters of the Alliance party emerge as the staunchest gender neutrals on this issue: 79 per cent state that the sex of an MP does not affect the level of confidence, while 10 per cent express more confidence in a woman and 11 per cent in a man.

Among the APNI's male supporters gender neutrality is even more pronounced: 92 per cent dissociate confidence from the sex of an MP, while four per cent each express more confidence in either a man or a woman. In general, though, and irrespective of their party preferences, men do emerge as possessing less confidence in a woman as a national representative. Yet, with the exception of those aligned with the DUP, men are heavily disposed to state that the sex of an MP makes no difference to the level of confidence entrusted to a politician: 80 per cent of SDLP supporters, 73 per cent of Sinn Fein supporters and 64 per cent of UUP supporters adopt this view, which is shared by a plurality of DUP voters (46 per cent). Four out of ten of the latter do express more confidence in a man, compared to 32 per cent of the UUP's male voters: only three per cent of the latter express more confidence in a woman, as do 14 per cent of DUP identifiers. SDLP supporters split their preferences equally, 10 per cent each favouring a man or a woman, a split that is almost exactly matched among Sinn Fein supporters: 13 per cent each express more confidence in either a woman or a man.

The belief that representatives are capable of being trusted to enact policy commitments, especially on matters of constitutional policy, is at a premium in a divided society where zero-sum politics tend to prevail. While there is something of a preference for men as national representatives, at the same time the modal position of partisans of both sexes - the DUP excepted - is that the level of confidence invested in a candidate is unconnected to a representative's sex. In that respect, and despite the absence of indigenous role-models in Northern Ireland, women candidates do not appear to be hindered by the level of confidence they, *qua* women, inspire in voters. On the other hand, are they helped by their biological identity?

We noted earlier that a significant minority of women in the general population (45 per cent) agreed that the political situation would improve if there were more women in politics, a view shared by 32 per cent of male respondents. Among female partisans, significant proportions supporting the Alliance party (48 per cent), the SDLP (45 per cent), the Ulster Unionist Party (44 per cent) and, to a lesser extent, the DUP (37 per cent) agree that more women would lead to a general improvement in Northern Ireland; a proposition endorsed by a majority (57 per cent) of Sinn Fein female voters.

170

Table 6.9
'In general, things would improve
if there were more women in politics' (%)

	UUP F	UUP M	DUP F	DUP M	APNI F	APNI M	SDLP F	SDLP M	SF F	SF M	ALL F	ALL M
Agree/ Strongly Agree	44	31	37	19	48	55	45	32	57	40	45	32
Neither	29	39	32	27	32	29	30	33	13	33	29	35
Disagree/ Strongly Disagree	23	26	28	40	16	8	19	22	26	27	19	25
Don't Know	5	4	3	14	4	8	6	12	5	0	7	8

Male voters, with the exception of those aligned with the Alliance Party and to a lesser extent Sinn Fein supporters, are somewhat less persuaded by the proposition, especially DUP identifiers. On the other hand, male voters - DUP apart - are, in general, no more likely than their female counterparts to believe that an increase of women's involvement would lead to a deterioration in politics.

The rather negative connotations of this last remark, together with the existence of significant minorities who neither agree nor disagree that more women would improve the situation, hardly amount to a clamant demand for an increase in female representatives. However, the widespread support for enhanced equal opportunities for women, together with support for an increase of women's presence in elected office, whether at national or local level, suggests a recognition of the unfairness, even injustice, of their absence from the public realm. In effect, voters appear to cleave to a belief in numeric rather than interest representation, although a plurality of women do endorse the latter position.

Further evidence from the survey indicates that majorities of female supporters of each of the major parties disagree that women lack the interest, the experience or the confidence to become involved in the public realm of politics. Equally, majorities of male supporters also disagree that women are too inexperienced to enter formal politics. Moreover, a majority of men aligned with the APNI, UUP, DUP and the SDLP disagree that women are uninterested in politics, a view shared by a plurality of Sinn Fein's male voters. While a narrow majority of the latter believe that women lack the confidence to become involved in politics, they are the exception: a majority of men who support each of the other four parties disagree that women suffer from a shortage of confidence. In fact, female supporters of the two unionist parties and the Alliance Party are as, if not

171

more, likely to impute a lack of confidence to women than their fellow party supporters: in these three cases women appear as more self-questioning than they are doubted by men.

With the exception of those aligned with Sinn Fein, women are also more likely to believe that female candidates lose votes than are their male counterparts, a view that seems informed by the belief that women are generally discriminated against in public life.

Table 6.10
Explanations for the underrepresentation of women (%)

	UUP		DUP		APNI		SDLP		SF		ALL	
	F	M	F	M	F	M	F	M	F	M	F	M
(a)	66	51	68	37	74	59	72	54	71	43	69	54
(b)	42	33	49	39	33	25	35	26	34	43	37	33
(c)	63	46	62	49	65	39	64	65	73	47	62	51
(d)	72	72	65	72	64	63	66	62	56	54	65	62

Proportions of voters **agreeing** with the following propositions:

(a) 'In general, there is discrimination against women in public life';
(b) 'A woman candidate will lose votes';
(c) 'Political parties do not give women the opportunity to enter politics';
(d) 'The hours and the working conditions of political institutions suit men and not women'.

Female respondents, irrespective of their party alignment, are much more likely to agree that women face generalised discrimination in the public realm and, with the exception of SDLP supporters, are more inclined than male respondents to agree that the parties fail to provide adequate opportunities for women to become involved in politics. The gender gaps on these two items do, however, dissolve in relation to the working arrangements of political institutions (option 'd' in Table 6.10): there is a concurring majority among and between all voters on this explanation. But, with the exception of the latter, men are less disposed to perceive systemic or structural obstacles in the paths of women seeking entry into political roles. Women, on the other hand, perceive there to be a combination of, if not an interaction between, factors operating at both the systemic and party levels.

The uniformity among female voters in relation to each of these possible explanations for the underrepresentation of women is arresting: including, with the exception of Sinn Fein supporters, their greater readiness to accept the proposition that women will encounter voter hostility. Moreover, across all parties there is also a broad convergence among respondents of each sex in relation to supply-side factors that are construed to operate at the individual level. Significant majorities agree, for instance, that **'Women do not come forward to be considered as candidates'**. The proportions of female voters who concur with this statement are as follows (corresponding figures for male voters in brackets): UUP - 82 per cent (81 per cent); DUP - 79 per cent (78 per cent); Alliance Party - 86 per cent (67 per cent); SDLP - 85 per cent (81 per cent); Sinn Fein - 73 per cent (67 per cent). Equally, voters of each sex also agree that **'Women put their families above a career in politics'**. The respective proportions of women (and men) voters who endorse this possible explanation are: UUP - 67 per cent (62 per cent); DUP - 68 per cent (74 per cent); Alliance Party - 67 per cent (58 per cent); SDLP - 72 per cent (79 per cent); Sinn Fein - 58 per cent (79 per cent).

The interrelationships among the three levels of explanation for the underrepresentation of women (Norris, 1993) apparent among the total sample population are explored in more detail in Chapter 7. Here, attention turns to the parties themselves.

Women, party offices and candidacies

The political parties, or more accurately their selectorates, play a key role in controlling access to the public realms. At this point we examine their selection procedures, the roles occupied by women within party structures and the broader policies they adopt in relation to gender issues. This enables us to ascertain the grounds upon which the widely shared perception of the parties' failure to represent women's interests may be based.

The extent of party membership within the general population is, as noted earlier, extremely low. Evidence from the survey also demonstrates that the proportions of both sexes who have contested, or even considered running for, either a party or a public office is equally modest. While the perceived risks to personal safety incurred by entering Northern Ireland's public realm may be hypothesised to deter potential office-seekers, there is little from the research to suggest that this is the case. Certainly the fact that women have become an increasing presence in the region's nominated bodies, a number of which deal with highly contentious issues, indicates that they are not unduly put off by the pathologies of the province.

Equally, the study of female councillors showed that fear of violence, either to themselves or their families, was a relatively minor consideration among those who had decided or been persuaded to stand for election (Wilford et al, 1993). For the most part what was apparent among the councillors was the fact that very few had contemplated a public role until they were asked, invariably by a man, to seek office: a finding that is fully consistent with the majority of partisans who agree that women are reluctant to present themselves as potential candidates. What then are the strategies of the parties in selecting their candidates?

Table 6.11
Female membership of political parties in Northern Ireland 1995 (%)

Party	%
Alliance Party (APNI)	50
Ulster Unionist (UUP)	42
Social Democratic and Labour (SDLP)	47
Sinn Fein (SF)	33

Note: Figures supplied by the parties. The Democratic Unionist Party (DUP) failed to respond to requests for information.

With the exception of the Alliance Party, women are a numerical minority in each of the parties from which data was obtained, which might be construed to place them at something of a disadvantage. However, this apparent weakness can be offset by the procedures each adopts for the process of selecting party officers, the strategies employed to recruit election candidates, and their internal structures, including whether they have created an organisational base for their female members in the shape of a 'woman's section'.

The existence of such a base is no guarantee that women will be better able to lobby either for increased representation or the inclusion of gender-proofed policies in the party's manifestos: rather than a route to empowerment within a party, the existence of such a section could become a *cul de sac* into which 'women's issues' can be sidelined. All of the major parties from which information was obtained, with the exception of the Alliance Party which has a spokesperson on women's issues, do include a dedicated women's section. The oldest of these is the UUP's Ulster Women's Unionist Council (UWUC), established in 1911.

The UWUC is organised on a constituency basis, delegating members to the party's plenary body, the Ulster Unionist Council (UUC), which has approximately 800 members. The key policy-making agency within the UUC is its 120 strong Executive Committee (elected by members of the party's 17 constituency associations) which, in 1995, included 18 women, equivalent to 15 per cent of the total. There are 120 constituency offices within the UUP, 27 of which (22.5 per cent) are held by women, including two constituency association chairmen (*sic*): all of the party's 14 full-time party officers are men.

Alliance is one of two parties (the other is the SDLP) which has previously been chaired by a woman. In 1995, four women sat on its 12 member Executive, including the Vice-Chair of the party. Six of its 23 local associations (based on district electoral areas rather than parliamentary constituencies) are chaired by women, and ten each of the treasurers and secretaries of the associations are female. The SDLP has six full-time party officers, one of whom (the party's administrator) is female. There are six women on its 15 strong Executive, including the Chair of its 'Women's Group' which was reorganised in 1994. Sinn Fein's 24 member National Executive (*Ard Comhairle*) includes nine women, one of whom is the party's General Secretary. Internally, Sinn Fein is organised into nine 'Departments'[4], six of which have women as 'Directors', while its five person team that has participated in discussions with the NIO in the wake of the ceasefires has included two women throughout. Additionally, women constitute half of Sinn Fein's eight delegates/alternates to the Dublin-based 'Forum for Peace and Reconciliation' established by the former *An Taoiseach*, Albert Reynolds, following the Downing Street Declaration of December 1993.

Until 1995, Sinn Fein was the only major party to exercise positive discrimination on behalf of women in the form of a 40 per cent quota for its National Executive, although this has clearly been exceeded at the level of its Departmental heads. The only other party to embrace internal quotas is its nationalist rival, the SDLP. Following a campaign led by women within the party, at its 1994 Annual Conference SDLP delegates backed the following motion: 'Conference endorses the positive contribution of women in the Party and calls on the Party to adopt an affirmative action programme with the goal of women filling 50 per cent of all levels in the Party'. A working group was then established to bring forward recommendations consistent with the motion and these were debated at a special delegate conference held in June of the following year. The outcome was agreement to guarantee 40 per cent of places on the Party Executive to women and to reserve at least two places for women councillors on a new 'General Council' which will be responsible for developing and implementing party policy.

Gender quotas have, though, been restricted to party offices within the nationalist party family: neither Sinn Fein nor the SDLP has extended the strategy of positive discrimination to the selection of female candidates. The Ulster Unionist Party relies exclusively upon an exhortatory strategy in relation to the recruitment of women, while the Alliance Party, Sinn Fein and the SDLP have each adopted positive action measures, in the form of training and development courses, designed to encourage women to stand for both party and elected offices. Sinn Fein, according to the Director of its Women's Department[5], has discussed the question of adopting women-only shortlists modelled on the procedures adopted by the British Labour Party, although it has yet to step over the line that demarcates positive action from positive discrimination.

The apparent reluctance of the parties to stray beyond a positive action strategy in relation to candidate selection is consistent with the attitudes of both the general population and partisans (see Table 6.5) towards gender quotas, at least in relation to the employment (and promotion) of women. Both issues could, however, become entangled in the future. Under the statutory review of the Fair Employment Act (NI), 1989, which is due to report in 1996, it is not implausible that the measures adopted by the Government to eradicate religious and political discrimination could be extended to include Catholic job quotas. If the legislation is amended to include preferential treatment in this way it could, in turn, stimulate demands for its application to both women's employment and, by extension, to the recruitment of party candidates. In particular, such a change of strategy might appeal to SDLP and Sinn Fein voters: one third of their female supporters already endorse positive discrimination for women in the job market, as do 36 per cent of Sinn Fein's male voters.

To the extent that there has been growth in representation by women in elected office, it has been confined to the local government tier (Table 6.12). Since 1977 when reliable candidate data first became available, the proportion of women who have contested district council elections has risen from 9.5 per cent to 14.1 per cent in 1993. During the same period the proportion of successful female candidates has risen from 7.2 per cent to 12 per cent.

Table 6.12
District council elections 1977-1993:
female candidates and women elected (%)

Year	Total Seats (N)	Candidates (N)	Women Candidates (N)	Women Candidates (%)	Women Elected (N)	Women Elected (%)
1977	526	1002	95	9.5	38	7.2
1981	526	982	107	10.9	42	8.0
1985	566	994	109	11.0	55	9.7
1989	566	905	128	14.1	64	11.3
1993	582	933	132	14.1	70	12.0

Calculated from data supplied by Dr. Sydney Elliott, Politics Department, Queen's University, Belfast.

These increases are, in part, explained by the reluctance of men to come forward, at least according to the 1989 intake of women councillors (Wilford et al, 1993). Yet it is noteworthy that the parties in which women constitute the largest proportion of councillors are those which have adopted positive action strategies. At the 1993 elections, women constituted 25 per cent of the APNI's successful candidates and 16 per cent of both the SDLP's and Sinn Fein's councillors, compared to 11 per cent of those elected on behalf of the UUP and 7 per cent for the DUP. The Alliance Party also fielded the largest proportion of female candidates (31 per cent), double that of its nearest rival, the SDLP (16 per cent) followed by the UUP (14 per cent) and Sinn Fein (12 per cent).

The upward trend in representation by women is consistent with the desire on the part of the wider population for a greater female presence in local government. But if the rate of growth in successful candidacies achieved between 1977 and 1993 is sustained, it will be the year 2119 before women achieve parity with men in the province's council chambers. Moreover, the continuing absence of women from the Parliamentary tier sits very uneasily with the desire for an increase of female representatives at the national level (See Chapter 7). The persistent underrepresentation by women does seem to supply part of the explanation for the widespread disaffection with the parties, especially among women. However, in terms of policy preferences there is a broad affinity between the voters and their respective parties. The support for an equal rights/equal opportunities platform detectable within the voting blocs is consistent with the stated manifesto commitments of their respective parties.

Party policies on gender issues

The finding that sex discrimination has low salience as a 'major problem' as compared to that based on religion, age or disability, does little to discourage the parties from the relatively thin treatment given to gender issues in the past. While the parties do tend to converge around an equal rights/equal opportunities platform, the attention that is devoted to it has been dwarfed by high policy questions. In effect, the historically unhappy marriages between feminism and both unionism and nationalism noted in Chapter 1 have been sustained. Of the five major parties, only the Alliance Party and Sinn Fein have produced expansive proposals in relation to women, although in the latter case women in the party are less than sanguine that their rights are an integral part of the wider republican project.

The tension between feminism and republicanism is apparent in a document published in 1994 by the Women's Department of Sinn Fein, commemorating women's contribution to 'the struggle for national liberation' (Sinn Fein, 1994). One contributor observes that while women in the republican movement 'have always fought alongside our brothers without preconditions, men's support for women's demands has always been conditional. If we don't move together', she declares, 'we won't move forward at all' (McCrory, 1994). These views are echoed by another activist who, while acknowledging that the end to partition is the key priority of republicanism, insists that 'gender-based inequality must be fought against now. We must recognise that the struggle for women's liberation is an integral part of the overall struggle against oppression' (Gillespie, 1994).

Such statements, reflecting clear doubts about the status of women within the republican movement, were also voiced by one Sinn Fein activist whom we re-interviewed. She observed that within the party 'women are always at the bottom of the pile', and commented on the generally patronising attitude of men towards women's issues, while another resented the relative neglect of female republican prisoners by the wider movement. Equally, a Sinn Fein councillor expressed her frustration with the neglect of issues of particular concern to women by her own party: 'The issues that affect women are buried [and] aren't dealt with because men think they are women's problems' (Wilford et al, 1993). Thus, despite the adoption by

Sinn Fein of gender quotas for party offices and its publication of a lengthy policy document on women (see below), there is no evidence of complacency among its female supporters. The unreflective faith of an earlier nationalist leader, Countess Markievicz - 'fix your minds on the idea of Ireland free, with her women enjoying the full rights of citizenship in their own nation' (Beale, 1986) - is not shared by women in the contemporary republican movement. As one activist puts it: 'Equality within our republican communities is still something that politically active women have yet to achieve' (Gillespie, 1994).

Although the SDLP has also moved to embrace internal gender quotas, its record on women's issues is less than inspiring. The party has not published a discrete policy document addressed to women since 1976, preferring to include a few lines or paragraphs in its election literature reconfirming its commitment to an equal rights strategy. The SDLP's manifesto for the Euro-election of 1994, for instance, subsumed its appeal to women within a short statement concerned with 'equality', identifying itself with its membership of the 'Parliamentary Group of the Party of European Socialists' (PES) and the group's commitment to pursue equal rights for women[6].

The attachment to an equal rights strategy does, though, beg the question of whether this is sufficient to overcome the disadvantages that have a differential effect upon women (Pateman, 1992; Rhode, 1992). At root, this approach sanctions the values crafted by and for men that apply in the public sphere. To enjoy equal rights women must, in effect, behave like men and conform with those prevailing values. Chapman (1993) summarises the dilemma for women thus: 'A man can be a person and a parent, active in the world and yet enjoying the comforts and companionship of marriage and the family'. However, 'for a woman it is otherwise: the price of entry to the wider sphere is to put at risk her role in reproduction and everything that goes with it'. (p. 147) Women, on this view are caught between a rock and a hard place: either they campaign to be treated like men, or they do not, instead choosing or being compelled to choose, a more traditionally gendered role within the domestic realm: '[T]hey cannot', as Chapman puts it, ' behave like men without ceasing to behave like women. Conversely, they cannot behave like women without undermining their "right" to behave like men' (p. 146).

Though the SDLP does sanction equality of opportunity in education, training and work for women, thereby moving beyond a formal equal rights strategy, equality of outcomes for women is absent from its agenda. It is by no means alone in pursuing this more limited approach. Each of the major parties endorses equal rights for women, though only the APNI and Sinn

Fein have produced policy documents of any length and substance that are devoted to 'women's issues'. The DUP's manifesto for the 1992 Westminster Election, for instance, contained an 86 word statement on women which, in some respects, seemed radical. Acknowledging that 'women are a majority and should no longer be treated as a minority', it called for the creation of a 'Ministry for Women', with a remit that was to include equal pay reform, equal pension ages, maternity rights, a parental leave scheme and childcare policy including workplace creches and after school care facilitated by tax relief. However, this amounted to little more than a series of slogans rather than a carefully reasoned set of proposals and needs to be set against its equally prominent call for 'the fight for family and moral values'. At the time of the election this rallying cry should be placed within the context of the DUP's (failed) campaign to prevent the opening of a Brook Advisory Centre in Belfast on the ground that it would 'undermine parental authority and family values'.[7]

The UUP has also published little on women. Its 'Policy Statement on Women's Issues' produced for the 1992 General Election was less than two pages long. This affirmed its support for existing sex discrimination legislation and endorsed equal pay for equal work as well as the statutory provision of pregnancy and maternity rights consistent with Article 119 of the Treaty of Rome. Like the DUP it proposed the extension of tax concessions to encourage childcare and nursery facilities at the workplace and in addition called for the expansion of public spending on preschool education and equality of opportunity and access in education 'with encouragement for girls to achieve in areas which have traditionally been male-dominated'. The document also recognised the problem of domestic violence and urged that the government should simplify arrest, charge and prosecution procedures in such cases as well as supplying better aftercare for the victims of such abuse. On health matters, it called for the provision of adequate resources for maternity units and, on the preventive front, extra public spending on screening programmes for women. These preferences, which appear consistent with the views of its electorate, are couched in terms of its belief in 'a society of equal opportunity' and its explicit rejection of positive discrimination .

The Alliance Party bases its most recent policy document, 'Women's Issues', on a more developed equality of opportunity perspective, especially in relation to education and employment. It too supports the expansion of nursery and childcare provision while at the same time insisting that 'proper value and respect should be given to those who work in the home', and sails close to the wages for housework argument in stating that 'parents who choose to stay in the home to raise children or as carers should be valued and their economic worth recognised and respected'. Supporting equal pay for equal work, it sets its face against positive discrimination but, as within its own party structure, supports a variety of positive action measures designed to encourage women to compete for training and employment opportunities. Though it endorses dismantling traditional views about women's and men's work, it believes this is best achieved by attitudinal shifts rather than financial incentives to employers to employ either sex in non-traditional sectors of employment.

Alone of the parties, Alliance also addresses at some length the question of women's absence from the public realm of politics, but in so doing betrays a certain ambiguity as to its causes. While acknowledging that 'politics is a male-defined agenda' it tends towards the portrayal of women as the authors of their own misfortune, asserting that they lack self-belief as credible political actors and acquiesce to men. To overcome this combination of self doubt and deference, the document recommends a mix of self-examination, exhortation, social utility and an appeal to interest representation. Thus, women are encouraged to: 'question their attitudes and assumptions'; 'take their place in leadership positions'; 'assess what the lack of female input to public bodies has created...a great loss of ability, talent and energy'; and to recognise that the male monopoly of Parliamentary seats means 'that over half the population in Northern Ireland is not adequately represented'.

The party with the most developed set of policy proposals for women is Sinn Fein (Sinn Fein, 1993). The length and complexity of its policy document, is explained by the fact that it is addressed to both parts of the island and therefore has to contemplate the situation of women in two different jurisdictions. The discourse of the document is woman-centred, although it inclines to a maternalist perspective: 'Present economic and social structures' it states, 'are built around the life-cycles of men. Women's life-cycles are different; changes will have to reflect the needs of women as mothers, within the family, as well as their right to participate in all...aspects of society'. The proposals, which refer to family law, employment, social welfare, reproductive policy, violence against women, health and education, are sustained both by a concern to empower women in the public and private realms and the recognition that 'gender and social class are the two most important determinants of a person's life-chances'.

Within the family context, it proposes the introduction of no-fault divorce legislation funded by free legal aid, women's right to an income and an equal share of marital property within marriage and argues that the custody of children under 12 years should automatically rest with the mother, 'unless she waives that right or is proven to be unfit'. In the field of employment it calls for the introduction of a statutory minimum wage, equal pay for work of equal value, the abolition of mandatory retirement ages, the extension of maternity leave on full pay, the provision of free comprehensive childcare and the introduction of positive action programmes 'to enable women to get access to education and retraining especially in non-traditional occupations'. In terms of social policy it argues that income-maintenance programmes must be 'restructured to remove the concept of the dependent adult', and in particular to reject the definition of women in terms of their marital status or relationship to a man. Instead, welfare citizenship should be understood in terms of the need to 'deal with poverty, irrespective of its cause'.

Such wide-ranging proposals are, however, uncosted and in that respect take on the appearance of a wish-list rather than a reasoned set of expenditure commitments. Similarly, its proposals to increase spending on women's health, whether by way of education, prevention or treatment, does not carry a price-tag, nor is there any indication of the relative priority each of these programmes should be accorded. In relation to violence against women, it calls for the state-funding of refuges for victims of domestic violence and, in the north, because of distrust of the RUC and the criminal justice system, vigilant and supportive action by local community workers in addressing the needs of battered women. In respect of the offence of rape it proposes: a widening of its definition; the introduction of strict sentencing guidelines; the inadmissibility of a woman's sexual history as evidence in court; the preservation of a complainant's anonymity; that rape and sexual assault cases should be held in camera; and that there 'should be an objective test of consent in rape cases and that submission should never be seen as consent'. Moreover, the document also argues for an expansive definition of pornography which has as its motive the protection of women: the production, distribution and sale of such material would be banned.

In the tricky area of reproductive policy, Sinn Fein treads somewhat carefully, especially in relation to abortion. In Northern Ireland, while women are not confronted by a constitutional prohibition as they are in the Republic, access to a termination is much more narrowly defined than in Great Britain. The 1967 Abortion Act, even as amended, does not apply in the province; access is instead governed by the Infant Life Preservation Act, which was extended to Northern Ireland in 1945, some sixteen years after its application in Britain. While supporting the right to information on abortion services available in Britain, Sinn Fein rejects an unqualified right to choose, but does accept the need for a termination in cases of rape and child abuse as well as in those cases where a woman's life is at risk or in grave danger.

The sensitivity of all parties to the vexed issue of abortion rights is, though, consistent with the general population's less liberal attitude on this matter (Montgomery and Davis, 1991). Women in Northern Ireland are much more conservative than their British cohorts about the grounds on which a termination should be available. None of the parties support the extension of the 1967 Act to the province: it is one of the relatively few issues upon which they are able to agree.

Summary

In general terms, there does seem to be congruence or 'fit' between the major parties and the preferred agenda of their respective electorates. To adopt the typology devised by Chamberlayne (1993, pp. 173-4), both the parties and their supporters by recognising the 'particular obstacles impeding women's equality' tend towards the endorsement of a 'gender recognition' approach, rather than a wholly 'gender-neutral' one which takes almost no account of 'the specificity of women's position'. A third approach delineated by Chamberlayne, that of 'gender reconstruction', stresses the need to change men's roles, 'primarily by increasing their involvement in reproductive activities'. This is much less evident in Northern Ireland, although the support for a parental leave scheme by the DUP, the concern to dismantle prevailing beliefs about what constitutes women's and men's work by the UUP and the Alliance Party, the latter's insistence that men should be encouraged to share family responsibilities on a fair and equal basis, are all nods in the direction of reconstituting men's perception of their 'proper' roles.

While there is a clear tilt towards gender recognition among the parties, there is also lingering evidence of what Chamberlayne terms the 'gender reinforcement' approach. This, as she explains, has two dimensions. It can either 'mark out the terrain of radical separatists by virtue of its emphasis on the different social space occupied by women'; or, conversely, 'reaffirm the traditional female roles and values associated with conservatism' (p. 174). Evidence of the first of these, articulated by the radical separatist exponents of cultural or lifestyle feminism (Randall, 1991; Tong, 1989), is not apparent in the platforms of the parties. However, the more conservative variation, which is also espoused by pro-family or maternalist feminists, does inform the programmes of both the parties and their respective electorates.

Pro-familism has proven to be highly divisive within the broader feminist movement. Critics like Stacey (1986) for instance claim that its celebration of the compatibility of motherhood with feminism, merely recreates a patriarchal snare for women by legitimising traditional female values both within the public and private realms. Though the parties do not frame their policy prescriptions within the terms of 'maternal revivalism', their common emphasis on maternity rights, Alliance's stress on 'value and respect for those who work in the home', the UUP's insistence that 'considerable emphasis be given to value of the family unit in society', the DUP's trenchant defence of 'family values', together with more than a hint of mother-centredness evident in Sinn Fein's policy proposals, are each symptomatic of a more conservative, pro-family view of women's role. Equally, the disposition among unionist women and men of all political persuasions, other than those who support the Alliance Party, to agree that women are most fulfilled in their roles as wives and mothers discloses the tenacity of traditional views about their 'place' within the wider society.

The parties and their electorates appear in effect to manifest a preference for gender recognition policies, tempered by the more conservative gender-reinforcement strategy, which is more evident on the unionist side of the equation, especially among men who support the DUP. But in broad terms there is an alignment between the parties and their electorates in favour of gender recognition. This though creates a paradox: if there is such a rough symmetry, why do majorities of women voters perceive that their preferred party fails to represent their interests? The answer appears to lie partly in relation to gender policy questions and partly in terms of the seeming incapacity of the parties to broker a political and constitutional settlement.

At the time that the first phase of the fieldwork was undertaken there was no apparent sign that 'the troubles' were to be arrested. Indeed, the indications were to the contrary (Bew and Gillespie, 1994). In July 1991 the faltering talks process initiated 19 months earlier by Peter Brooke, the Secretary of State for Northern Ireland, ground to a halt; by the end of the year there were 94 deaths arising from the conflict - the largest number since 1982; the Provisional IRA returned to a bombing campaign throughout the province and in Britain with renewed determination; and the number of British troops serving in Northern Ireland was increased to over 11,000. During the first six months of 1992 when the second, qualitative phase of the survey was conducted, the first glimmering of any political progress appeared with the recommencement of all-party talks in the wake of the General Election of 9th April. However, the first quarter of that year had been punctuated by a series of devastating sectarian murders, notably at

Teebane in Co. Tyrone on 17th January, where seven Protestant workmen were killed outright by a massive PIRA bomb and an eighth died from his injuries four days later. Less than three weeks later, five Catholics were killed and a further seven injured following a retaliatory attack by loyalist gunmen on a bookmaker's shop in Belfast. By the 1st March, 33 people had been killed and against this deteriorating background the number of British servicemen in the province was massively increased to over 18,000.

In this gloomy and polarised context, the preoccupation of the respondents who were re-interviewed was clearly with the seeming endlessness of 'the troubles' and the inability or unwillingness of the region's political leaders to overcome the impasse. Notwithstanding the incidence of cross-community activities that was especially apparent among the female respondents, activists of both sexes tended to see the future through a glass darkly. However, consistent with the attitudes both of women in the general population and voters, the female activists did tend towards the view that an increase of women in public office could improve the situation in Northern Ireland - and in two ways.

First, and irrespective of their political alignment, they commonly expressed the view that women in general are more tolerant of the opinions of others, that they are better listeners, less motivated by the pursuit of power and more inclined towards a conciliatory posture than are men. This was not an unreflective belief but rather was based upon their actual experiences as political activists. For instance, a number of the female respondents commented upon men's proclivity to become engaged in 'power games', to be more concerned with self-esteem and generally to try and exert dominance within the groups and organisations to which they belonged. Equally, the female activists who were wives and mothers not infrequently referred to their role as 'peacekeeper' within the domestic realm and their felt responsibility to steer their children away from involvement at either extreme of the political spectrum. In this respect, women commonly portrayed themselves in the guise of mediators, finding practical ways of solving problems no matter how seemingly inconsequential they may be. In effect, women activists drew a behavioural or stylistic distinction between themselves and men in both the public and private realms.

Secondly, while there was a broad, but not an unqualified, fit between women aligned with one or other of the parties and the latter's approach to gender policy issues, there was a frequently expressed belief that the failure to achieve a political settlement marginalises a raft of issues of particular interest to women. Irrespective of their party preferences, women activists believed that issues like health, education and welfare would be accorded a much higher priority if there were more female representatives in public office. Thus, there is evidence from among the activist women of a belief in interest representation; that female representatives can, in sufficient numbers, make a substantive change to the policy agenda in Northern Ireland as well as a stylistic or behavioural change to the political process. Neither was an untrammelled belief, however, and there were those who considered that the situation in the province was 'too far gone' for women to make any real change.

On balance, though, the weight of opinion was in the other direction. In an altered political context and with the prospect of an established peace on the horizon, the implications of these views are of real significance. This leads us to the discussion of the stereotypes of politicians, both female and male, identified by the respondents and which themselves bear on the wider debate concerning 'sameness' and 'difference' between women and men.

Notes

1. Given the focus of the chapter on the region's political parties, together with the mutual exclusivity of its voting blocs, this chapter concentrates on the views of voters. Among other things this enables the exploration of the extent to which there is either convergence or divergence among the electorates in Northern Ireland concerning the reasons for the underrepresentation by women. A more detailed analysis of the wider sample's attitudes towards the parties is included in Chapter 7.

2. 'EMILY's List' - 'Early money is like yeast' - is a Democratic Political Action Committee in the USA dedicated to raising finance for, and funding the campaigns of women running for political office. Its tactics have recently been emulated by the Labour Party in Britain. See Carney, 1994.

3. This is a rather remarkable result. The Worker's Party is, *via* the Republican Clubs, the descendant of the Official IRA. It was the latter's decision in January 1970 to recognise future Parliaments in Belfast, London and Dublin that formalised the split in the republican movement leading to the emergence of the PIRA. In February 1992, the Party split: a breakaway group, headed by its leader, Proinsias de Rossa, announced the formation of a new party, initally called 'New Agenda' and subsequently 'Democratic Left'. The rupture was caused by de Rossa's failure to persuade the Workers' Party to repudiate its links with the Official IRA (Bew and Gillespie, 1993).

4. The six departments with female heads are: Education; Foreign Affairs; Publicity; Trade Unions; Women; and Youth.

5. Letter from the Director of Sinn Fein's Women's Department, Joan O'Connor, to the author, February 1995.

6. For the current session of the European Parliament elected in 1994 the PES has set itself the task of achieving 'women's right to work' and their 'access to decision-taking and to positions of responsibility in all aspects of society'. In its manifesto, the SDLP aligns itself with the group's commitments to: 'the strict application of the principle of equal pay for equal work'; 'identical treatment within the social security system'; 'equality of opportunity in education, training and work'; 'equal opportunities for men and women to combine a career with family life, with special emphasis on the availability of high quality childcare to all parents who need it'; and 'fighting poverty which particularly affects single mothers' (SDLP, 1994).

7. Brook clinics offer a non-directive counselling service, especially to young people, on sex and pregnancy related matters.

7 Stereotyping politicians

Introduction

In the preceding chapter it was noted that a plurality of female respondents (45 per cent) agreed that women can make a difference to the public sphere, a view shared by one-in-three of male respondents (32 per cent). Though these proportions are not commanding they are, nevertheless, impressive votes of confidence in the ability of women to improve the character of politics in Northern Ireland. Against that background, this chapter reports the popular images of politicians that were identified by the sample population.

Respondents were furnished with a list of (pre-tested and piloted) traits and invited to select those they believed to characterise different types of politician: *viz* female and male politicians; successful politicians; and those that defined desirable and undesirable politicians. By exploring the interactions of these characteristics the opportunity is created to identify in more detail the nature of any differences ascribed to women and to discuss their implications for both the substance and style of politics.

Such images, while stereotypical, in effect bear on the issue of interest representation and as such assist in fleshing out the explanations for the widespread belief that Northern Ireland's political parties have failed women. It is also apparent that the general population are in favour of increasing the numerical representation of women. Before turning to the stereotypes, therefore, a more detailed analysis of the support for enhanced representation by women is presented.

The latter findings, besides establishing the nature and extent of support for more women in elected office leads, *via* the stereotypes, to explanations for the absence of women from elected office. Are women themselves blamed for their underrepresentation, or are respondents more inclined to attach responsibility to wider situational and structural practices and attitudes? Thus, there are three related issues explored below. The extent to which there is support within the sample population for increased representation by women; the reasons endorsed for such an increase; and the preferred explanations for the absence of women from the public realm. Underpinning these issues is the extent to which support for an increase rests on a belief in numeral and/or interest representation.

More women in politics?

The opinions of the respondents concerning the numerical representation of women were tested in relation to three tiers of public office: cabinet; parliament; and local government.

Table 7.1
Attitudes concerning women's representation (%)

	Female	Male	All
Majority of women in cabinet	2.9	2.4	2.8
Half of cabinet posts held by women	35.4	18.3	27.5
Some women in cabinet	38.3	18.3	42.3
No definite proportion of women in cabinet	21.4	30.6	23.5
No women in cabinet	2.0	2.1	2.1
Total	100.0	100.0	100.0
More women in parliament	61.5	49.6	55.8
Fewer women in parliament	3.6	4.2	3.7
Same number of women in parliament	34.9	46.2	40.3
Total	100.0	100.0	100.0
More women in local government	64.4	51.4	58.5
Fewer women in local government	3.0	4.4	3.3
Same number of women in local government	32.6	44.1	37.8
Total	100.0	100.0	100.0

As can be seen in Table 7.1, respondents were generally more reluctant to endorse an increase of women in cabinet than in other tiers of representation. Moreover, there is a gender gap in the levels of support. Male respondents are generally less supportive than female respondents in relation to each tier, especially cabinet: women are twice as likely to adopt an equality perspective towards the top political table. Local government, the least powerful tier of representation - and the only one in Northern Ireland in which women have achieved an increasing presence - is only marginally preferred by both women and men to the parliamentary sphere. On that basis, and especially among female respondents, there is no apparent belief that women should be shunted into the impoverished realm of the province's local council chambers.

While there is a palpable gender gap in support of women's increased representation, its extent is though structured by other variables.

Table 7.2
Support for women's representation: by age
(all respondents) (%)

	Aged < 30	Aged 30-44	Aged 45-59	Aged 60 >
Majority of women in cabinet	2.5	2.9	3.9	1.3
Half of cabinet posts held by women	29.8	28.9	21.9	27.0
Some women in cabinet	39.4	37.3	49.7	44.6
No definite proportion of women in cabinet	27.8	28.9	22.4	23.1
No women in cabinet	0.5	1.9	2.0	4.0
Total	100.0	100.0	100.0	100.0
More women in parliament	60.7	57.9	51.5	51.9
Fewer women in parliament	1.6	4.7	3.5	5.8
Same number of women in parliament	37.7	37.4	45.0	42.3
Total	100.0	100.0	100.0	100.0

Overall, younger respondents were more supportive of increased female representation in both cabinet and parliament, while older respondents were more likely to opt for 'some' or 'no definite proportion'. The lowest level of support for women in Cabinet came from those aged between 45 and 59. Indeed, this group was also the most likely to opt for maintaining the present number of women in Parliament. Men aged between 45 and 59 also adopted this position, with over half opting for the *status quo*, in comparison with just over one third of women. Indeed, while support for increasing the number of women in parliament declined steadily with age among women (from 68 per cent among women under to 40 to 52 per cent among women over 60), men were, on the whole, far less supportive, with support hovering at or around the 50 per cent mark.

Table 7.3
Support for increasing women's representation: by educational attainment (all respondents) (%)

	No formal quals	'O' Levels	'A' Levels	Degree
Majority of women in cabinet	3.2	4.1	0.5	1.1
Half of cabinet posts held by women	28.5	28.7	24.2	34.8
Some women in cabinet	47.6	38.9	27.7	33.1
No definite proportion of women in cabinet	18.1	26.1	44.3	31.0
No women in cabinet	2.7	2.2	3.3	0.0
Total	100.0	100.0	100.0	100.0
More women in parliament	48.8	55.6	66.2	70.0
Fewer women in parliament	5.5	4.9	0.0	2.1
Same number of women in parliament	45.8	39.5	33.8	27.8
Total	100.0	100.0	100.0	100.0
More women in local government	52.9	58.1	63.6	76.4
Fewer women in local government	4.8	3.8	0.5	2.1
Same number of women in local government	42.3	41.9	35.9	21.5
Total	100.0	100.0	100.0	100.0

Support for women holding half or more of Cabinet posts does not rise uniformly with educational attainment. Whilst respondents with degrees lend greatest support, those with no formal qualifications and 'O' levels are more supportive than respondents with 'A' levels. By contrast, support for increased female representation at both national and local levels does increase steadily with educational attainment. While a large majority of degree holders endorse an increase in the number of women in parliament, those with no educational qualifications are almost equally divided between supporting an increase and maintaining the current level of representation. Similarly, three-quarters of degree holders favour increasing the number of women councillors, compared with just over half of respondents with no formal educational qualifications. In effect, younger, better educated respondents favour increased female representation, particularly in parliament and in local government. Those with no formal educational qualifications, who comprised more than half of the sample, were also more likely to be older and were almost evenly divided between increasing the number of female public representatives or maintaining the *status quo*.

Table 7.4
Support for women's representation: by
socio-economic status (all respondents) (%)

	1	2	3	4	5	6
Majority of women in cabinet	0.0	2.5	0.8	2.7	4.8	2.3
Half of cabinet posts held by women	12.2	18.3	25.4	27.9	31.6	24.7
Some women in cabinet	37.6	35.4	44.3	44.3	40.4	50.5
No definite proportion of women in cabinet	46.1	39.2	29.5	23.5	21.7	20.8
No women in cabinet	4.1	4.5	0.0	1.7	1.5	1.7
Total	100.0	100.0	100.0	100.0	100.0	100.0
More women in parliament	55.3	42.8	67.5	59.1	52.3	42.5
Fewer women in parliament	3.5	0.6	2.0	3.3	5.1	9.2
Same number of women in parliament	41.2	56.6	30.4	37.5	42.5	48.2
Total	100.0	100.0	100.0	100.0	100.0	100.0
More women in local government	65.0	46.5	70.9	60.4	55.5	46.1
Fewer women in local government	2.7	0.6	2.6	4.4	3.7	4.8
Same number of women in local government	32.3	52.9	26.5	35.2	40.8	49.1
Total	100.0	100.0	100.0	100.0	100.0	100.0

Key: 1 = Professionals, Managers and Large Employers
      2 = Small Employers and Managers
      3 = Intermediate non-manual employees
      4 = Skilled manual and Junior non-manual employees
      5 = Semi-skilled manual employees
      6 = Unskilled manual employees and agricultural workers

Turning to socio-economic status (Table 7.4), the greater proportion of men in higher socio-economic positions lends some bias to the data, so that the categories which are the most supportive of increased representation by women tend to be those in which women predominate. Conversely, where there is a smaller proportion of women, the levels of support are lower. This is most pronounced in socio-economic categories 1 and 2 in which only eight per cent of the female sample are employed, compared to 18 per cent of the male sample. The higher proportions of women in categories 4 and 5 helps to explain their greater support for increased female representation. Thus, we find that intermediate non-manual categories are the most supportive of an increase at national and local level, while the greatest support in relation to cabinet posts comes from those who are in semi-skilled occupations.

Among the different religious groupings (see Table 7.5), Methodists and Catholics, together with those of no stated religious affiliation, emerge as clear advocates for more female politicians. One-third of Methodists and Catholics stated they wished to see half or a majority of cabinet posts held by women, while two-thirds of Methodists endorsed more female representatives at national and local level. A smaller proportion of Catholics wished to increase the number of women at both national and local levels, while those with no stated religious affiliation gave greatest support of all: at least 70 per cent stated they wished to see more women in both parliament and local government. The religious differences are perhaps explicable, given the history of Catholic participation in the civil rights movement and the struggle for equality. However, the position of Methodists and those with no stated religious affiliation provide evidence of a more complex picture.

Table 7.5
Support for women's representation: by
religious affiliation (all respondents)

	CI	Pres	RC	M	OP	None
Majority of women in cabinet	2.5	2.3	3.3	2.3	0.0	3.5
Half of cabinet posts held by women	24.9	20.8	34.2	35.3	16.1	27.9
Some women in cabinet	49.1	45.7	38.5	30.6	55.3	30.5
No definite proportion of women in cabinet	20.8	28.6	21.9	31.8	28.5	38.1
No women in cabinet	2.8	2.5	2.2	0.0	0.0	0.0
Total	100.0	100.0	100.0	100.0	100.0	100.0
More women in parliament	54.4	51.8	57.3	66.5	46.6	69.9
Fewer women in parliament	2.5	4.5	5.0	3.3	2.8	1.0
Same number of women in parliament	43.1	43.7	37.7	30.1	50.5	29.1
Total	100.0	100.0	100.0	100.0	100.0	100.0
More women in local government	53.3	51.6	63.1	70.3	52.8	73.0
Fewer women in local government	3.5	4.2	3.2	5.9	1.4	0.0
Same number of women in local government	43.2	44.2	33.7	23.8	45.8	27.0
Total	100.0	100.0	100.0	100.0	100.0	100.0

Key: CI   = Church of Ireland
Pres = Presbyterian
RC   = Roman Catholic
M   = Methodist
OP   = Other Protestant
None = No Stated Religious Affiliation

Overall, what emerges from the data is that while respondents were reluctant to support an increase in the representation of women at cabinet level, majorities wished to see more women in office, especially those who are younger and more highly educated. Despite the existence of generalised support for a numerical increase by women, there is, however, evidence of a preference for male politicians to represent the interests of respondents (Table 7.6).

Respondents were asked whether they had more confidence in a male or female politician to represent their interests, or whether the sex of a representative was irrelevant to the level of confidence she/he enjoyed.

Table 7.6
Confidence in female and male politicians to represent interests:
by sex and age (%)

	All	F	M	Aged < 30	Aged 30-44	Aged 45-59	Aged 60 >
More confidence in female MP	11.8	15.7	7.6	12.6	12.2	8.4	13.6
More confidence in male MP	21.4	21.3	21.7	16.7	15.5	23.3	32.3
No difference	66.8	63.0	70.8	70.7	72.3	68.3	54.2
Total	100.0	100.0	100.0	100.0	100.0	100.0	100.0

While similar proportions of women and men expressed confidence in a male politician, support for a female representative was greater among female than male respondents by a ratio of two to one. Younger respondents were more likely to adopt a 'gender neutral' position than older respondents, especially those aged over 60. Indeed, this last group is the most supportive of a male politician, but the converse is not the case: the group least in favour of women politicians are those aged between 45 and 59. Among female respondents, those older than 45 are far more likely to express confidence in a male representative than are younger women. Furthermore, slightly greater proportions of younger women expressed preference for a female, rather than a male, politician. For example, in comparison with the 21 per cent of all women who preferred a man, only 14 per cent of women aged under 30 and 15 per cent of those aged between 30 and 44 shared that preference. It should be noted, too, that younger women were also most likely to adopt a gender neutral stance, while women aged at least 60 were the least likely to take this position. Older women were more like male respondents in preferring a male rather than a female representative. What is compelling about these findings, though, is that a majority of all respondents adopt a gender-neutral stance on this question.

The adoption of a gender neutral position also tends to increase with educational attainment, such that 'A' Level and degree holders are most likely to state that they have no preference for either female or male politicians. The educational category most likely to express confidence in women are those with no formal qualifications, who are also those expressing the highest level of confidence in a male representative.

195

Table 7.7
Confidence in politicians: by educational qualifications
(all respondents) (%)

	No ed quals	'O' Level	'A' Level	Degree
More confidence in female rep.	13.3	11.0	10.6	9.5
More confidence in male rep.	27.3	17.6	11.8	14.1
No difference	59.4	71.4	77.6	76.4
Total	100.0	100.0	100.0	100.0

In relation to socio-economic status, the occupational category who are the most likely to have confidence in female politicians are unskilled manual workers.

Table 7.8
Confidence in politicians: by socio-economic status
(all respondents) (%)

	1	2	3	4	5	6
More confidence in female rep.	12.4	5.2	9.0	11.8	12.7	18.3
More confidence in male rep.	16.2	19.6	12.7	17.7	26.1	36.7
No difference	71.4	75.2	78.3	70.5	61.2	45.0
Total	100.0	100.0	100.0	100.0	100.0	100.0

Key: 1 = Professionals, Managers and Large Employers
     2 = Small Employers and Managers
     3 = Intermediate non-manual employees
     4 = Skilled and Junior non-manual employees
     5 = Semi-skilled manual employees
     6 = Unskilled manual employees and agricultural workers

Like those with no formal educational qualifications, unskilled manual workers are also most likely to support male representatives. The tendency to adopt a gender neutral position does increase with higher socio-economic status; the categories most likely to adopt this perspective are those in intermediate and small managerial occupations. These are also the occupational categories *least* likely to support female MPs.

A number of questions arise from the tendency towards gender neutrality evident among respondents. First, do respondents consider that women would *not* make a difference, although they would like to see more women as public representatives? Secondly, what are these interests which politicians are meant to represent? Thirdly, are the interests of women and men the same, and does it make no difference, therefore, who represents them?

Perceptions of difference

As can be seen from Table 7.9, while a plurality of respondents agreed that women will make a difference to the public realm, women were more likely to support this proposition than men.

Table 7.9
Do women make a difference to politics: by sex and age (%)

	All	F	M	Aged < 30	Aged 30-44	Aged 45-59	Aged 60 >
Strongly agree/agree	41.6	48.1	34.6	40.5	46.6	43.6	49.6
Neither	34.5	31.4	38.0	40.4	34.5	30.8	24.4
Strongly disagree/disagree	23.9	20.5	27.5	19.1	19.0	25.6	26.0

The age groups most likely to agree were those aged between 30 and 44 and those aged over 60, while almost a plurality of younger respondents adopted a neutral position. In some ways this could be seen to mirror the stance of these respondents in favouring neither a female nor male politician, and certainly the greater tendency of those aged under 30 to neither agree nor disagree would appear to indicate their propensity to adopt a gender neutral position. While older respondents were the most likely to disagree that women made a difference to the political realm the differences between the age groups were not great.

Turning now to an analysis of this question by educational attainment (Table 7.10), a majority of degree holders agreed that women would make a difference to the political realm, and were also the least likely to disagree. 'A' level holders were more likely to adopt a neutral position, while for the other educational categories there were majorities in support of the proposition that women make a difference to politics.

Table 7.10
Do women make a difference to politics: by educational qualifications (all respondents) (%)

	No ed. quals	'O' levels	'A' levels	Degree
Strongly agree/agree	46.5	42.4	38.9	55.8
Neither	28.8	36.3	40.5	30.3
Strongly disagree/disagree	24.6	21.3	20.6	13.9

In terms of religious affiliation (Table 7.11), Methodists again were most likely to agree that women make a difference, whereas Presbyterians and Other Protestants were the most likely to disagree. Secularists, that is those with no religious affiliation, are those most likely to embrace a gender-neutral view.

Table 7.11
Do women make a difference to politics: by religious affiliation (all respondents) (%)

	CI	Pres	M	RC	OP	None
Strongly agree/agree	49.2	40.2	54.9	46.5	37.5	40.3
Neither	31.7	32.6	29.6	31.5	37.0	39.4
Strongly disagree/disagree	19.1	27.2	15.5	22.0	25.5	20.4

While majorities of respondents are in favour of increasing women's representation at both local and national level, they do not state an overwhelming preference for either a male or a female politician to represent their interests in the public realm. Female respondents, however, were more likely both to support an increase in the number of female representatives and to agree that women made a difference to politics, as were Methodists and Catholics. Men and younger respondents were more likely to adopt a gender neutral position, whether in terms of the proposition that women can make a difference to politics or in favouring either female or male politicians. Respondents with degrees were most likely to agree that women made a difference to the public realm, but were among those least likely to favour one sex over the other as public representatives. The relative unimportance of a politician's sex creates a certain ambiguity for selectorates, however. On the one hand, it suggests that there is no marked aversion within the electorate towards female candidates and thus little reason for them to prefer a man on the ground of assumed voter hostility to women. On the other hand, the greater level of confidence expressed in a male candidate, especially by men, coupled with the high proportions stating that the sex of a candidate is largely irrelevant, hardly amounts to a resounding clamour for selectorates to break the mould of male-dominated candidacy.

Of what, then, does this perceived difference consist, and are female politicians *really* perceived to be different from male politicians? Moreover, are female MPs perceived to represent better the interests of women (Daly, 1978, Ruddick, 1980, Sapiro, 1981), and therefore to make a difference to the substance and 'style' of politics (Norderval, 1985, Hedlund, 1988, Skjeie, 1993)? What characteristics, therefore, do respondents associate with female and male politicians? Are women more or less likely to be perceived as desirable or successful political animals?

Stereotypes of politicians

In order to explore the images of politicians in some detail, respondents were asked to choose from five separate lists those characteristics they considered appropriate to each type of representative. The lists, or sets, of characteristics, which were placed at intervals in the survey instrument were:

- those which they find *desirable* in politicians;
- those which they find *undesirable* in politicians;
- those which they believe are possessed by *successful* politicians;
- those which they believe are possessed by *male politicians*;
- those which they believe are possessed by *female politicians*[2]

Respondents were asked to nominate all of those characteristics that they believed to apply in each case. They could name all or none, and were not asked to rank the characteristics. Women, in fact, tended to name more characteristics than men,[3] but for each of the five lists, the correlations of the relative rank orderings of the characteristics named by women and men is very high.[4]

Perhaps symptomatic of the turbulence and instability of Northern Ireland, strong leadership emerges as the most desirable trait of a politician among both female and male respondents (Table 7.12). However, this characteristic does not necessarily imply dogmatism, as is reflected in the placing of the ability to compromise. Taken together, each suggests a desire among women and men for a style of leadership that is both assured and flexible. The one major gender difference that emerges from the results is in relation to a belief in sexual equality: women were much more desirous of this trait in a politician than are men. It is worth noting, too, the low ranking of religiosity, suggesting a shared distaste for zealotry between both sexes.

Table 7.12
Ratings of desirable and undesirable characteristics of politicians: by sex (%)

Desirable traits	F	M
A strong leader	74.1	76.0
The ability to compromise	58.5	54.7
Belief in sexual equality	55.8	36.2
Respect for the environment	50.8	46.9
Ambition	26.8	27.9
A strong religious faith	15.2	14.1
Ruthless	2.8	4.7
Named no characteristics	1.5	1.8
Undesirable traits		
Ruthless	80.7	77.1
A strong religious faith	25.7	25.5
Ambition	15.1	15.1
The ability to compromise	2.5	4.2
Belief in sexual equality	1.4	2.3
A strong leader	0.7	1.0
Respect for the environment	0.5	0.3
Named no characteristics	7.8	9.9
(N)	(1301)	(384)

Respondents found it difficult to identify the undesirable[5] traits of a politician. For the most part, such characteristics were a negative image of those they deemed desirable. Yet, the combination of ruthlessness and a strong religious faith at the top of the list confirm a rejection of bigotry.

The broad pattern of agreement between the sexes also extends to the ratings of the characteristics believed to epitomise 'successful' politicians. Women and men stipulate the same five leading characteristics of 'winning' politicians: honesty, capacity for hard work, the ability to lead, the ability to compromise and approachability. Thereafter women are more likely to apply what might be conceptualised as a more 'feminised' set of traits including the capacity to care; respect for the environment; valuing the family; and a belief in sexual equality. Men, by comparison, tend to elevate confidence as a defining attribute of a successful politician.

Table 7.13
Ratings of 'typical' characteristics of male politicians: by sex (%)

	F	M
Ambitious	51.0	43.0
Ability to lead	48.7	44.8
Ruthless	42.6	30.7
Confidence	41.3	44.3
Hardworking	31.3	31.0
Corrupt	20.5	24.2
Approachable	14.2	16.7
Honest	13.4	13.5
Self-disciplined	12.8	12.0
Ability to compromise	11.5	13.8
Principled	11.1	12.0
Respect for the environment	10.1	10.2
Practical	9.9	13.8
Values the family	6.1	4.4
Caring	5.6	3.9
Strong religious faith	4.2	3.4
No answer	3.4	6.5
(N)	(1301)	(384)

There is also substantial agreement between the sexes in their configuration of male politicians (Table 7.13). 'Power' characteristics - ambition, the ability to lead, ruthlessness, confidence and the capacity for hard work - constitute the dominant syndrome of men in politics among both female and male respondents, although women are much more likely to ascribe a ruthless streak to them.

While the pattern of agreement persists between the sexes in rating the characteristics of female politicians, the dominant traits are strikingly different from those applied to male politicians.

Table 7.14
Ratings of 'typical' characteristics of female politicians: by sex (%)

	F	M
Values the family	54.6	50.3
Caring	53.5	39.8
Approachable	38.8	29.7
Hardworking	31.9	28.9
Honest	30.3	26.0
Practical	25.9	18.5
Respect for the environment	24.3	20.6
Ability to compromise	23.6	17.2
Ambitious	18.1	19.5
Confidence	17.0	16.9
Self-disciplined	16.7	11.7
Principled	15.4	15.4
Ability to lead	13.7	13.3
Strong religious faith	5.7	5.2
Ruthless	3.5	5.7
Corrupt	1.5	3.6
No answer	4.5	7.8
(N)	(1301)	(384)

In contrast to the 'power' characteristics perceived to typify male politicians, their female counterparts are imbued with rather "softer" qualities. The typical female politician is believed primarily to value the family, to be caring, approachable, hardworking and honest.

If we compare the different sets of ratings, there is a negative correlation between those characteristics considered desirable and undesirable in politicians. An encouraging lack of cynicism in Northern Ireland's electorate is apparent when noting, on the one hand, the high positive correlation between those qualities believed to epitomise successful politicians and desirable characteristics and, on the other, the high negative correlation between successful and undesirable traits.

Perhaps the most thought-provoking findings reside in the different ratings accorded to 'typically' male and female politicians (Table 7.15). Neither female nor male politicians are perceived to monopolise either desirable traits or those considered to delineate a successful politician. The stereotype of the male politician does though fit more closely with the extreme ends of the ratings of desirability and success. While the most desirable characteristic is a 'strong leader', and the 'ability to lead' is the second most popular trait ascribed to male politicians, 'ruthlessness' - the third-highest of the typically male characteristics - is nominated as the most undesirable of "qualities". Moreover, 'ambition', the leading characteristic ascribed to male politicians, occupies a rather ambiguous position in the scale of desirability: though a quarter of all respondents name it as a desirable quality, 15 per cent deem it undesirable.

Table 7.15

Correlations[a] of politicians' characteristics

	Desirable	Undesirable	Successful	Typical of male	Typical of female
Desirable	-	-0.640[d]	0.963[b]	0.283	0.703[d]
Undesirable	-0.738[d]	-	-0.582	0.230	-0.629
Successful	1.000[b]	-0.738[d]	-	0.136	0.474[d]
Typical of male pol.	0.429	-0.036	0.341	-	-0.282
Typical of female pol.	0.643	-0.821[c]	0.547[c]	-0.183	-

[a] Pearson's r above diagonal, Spearman's *Rho* below diagonal.
[b] Significant at $p < 0.001$.
[c] Significant at $p < 0.01$.
[d] Significant at $p < 0.05$.

Closer inspection of the correlations between ratings, however, provides an antidote to the tendency to focus upon extremes. As might be anticipated, while the characteristics considered typical of male and female politicians are negatively correlated, they are not statistically significant. This is *not* the case when one examines the correlations between the ratings of male and female politicians and success and desirability. In general, the sample holds a much more positive view of *female* politicians. Their characteristics correlate positively, and significantly, with both those considered desirable in politicians ($r = .703$) *and* those considered typical of successful politicians ($r = .963$). Concomitantly, there is a negative correlation between undesirable characteristics and those traits attributed to female politicians. This is not the case for the stereotype held for male politicians. The correlation between desirability and success is weaker and tends to be less statistically significant. Notably, there is *no* evidence of a negative association between undesirable characteristics and those believed to be typical of male politicians. In general, however, the characteristics that the electorate value as desirable, and those which they associate with successful politicians, fit *better* with the characteristics ascribed to female politicians.

Factor analysis

Table 7.16
Factor analysis* of desirable and undesirable characteristics in politicians

Desirable traits	Ruthless	"PC"	Religious	Ambition	Leader
Ambitious	0.082	0.162	0.045	**0.812**	0.034
Ability to compromise	-0.209	**0.531**	-0.130	-0.019	0.063
Strong religious faith	0.112	0.127	**0.715**	0.041	-0.107
Ruthless	**0.759**	0.132	0.012	-0.036	0.086
Belief in sex equality	-0.036	**0.702**	-0.018	-0.003	-0.127
Respect for the environment	0.122	**0.738**	0.071	-0.046	0.042
Strong leader	0.117	-0.003	-0.037	0.068	**0.709**
Undesirable traits					
Ambitious	0.160	0.273	0.087	**-0.738**	-0.001
Ability to compromise	**0.437**	0.012	0.313	0.135	0.058
Strong religious faith	0.161	0.260	**-0.741**	0.131	0.061
Ruthless	**-0.683**	0.216	0.326	0.148	0.173
Belief in sex equality	**0.456**	-0.099	0.114	0.003	0.140
Respect for the environment	**0.295**	-0.007	-0.106	0.123	-0.193
Strong leader	0.027	0.028	0.120	0.024	**-0.734**

* Oblique rotation. Varimax rotation yields the same substantive results. Analysis based upon male and female samples weighted to give equal Ns. Kaiser-Meyer-Measure of sampling adequacy = 0.54793.

The analysis of the above data provides only indirect information about the composite images held by respondents. Some combinations of traits are unlikely or even mutually contradictory.[6] Factor analysis, designed to identify statistical congruences or patterns in the responses to questions, provides a means of identifying groups of characteristics that are likely to be named by the same respondents. Firstly, combined factor analyses were conducted on the desirable and undesirable characteristics, followed by separate analyses of the characteristics of successful politicians, male politicians, and female politicians.[7]

The combined analysis of desirable and undesirable characteristics of politicians produced five factors. The first of these, labelled *Ruthless*, attracts a high loading from those who gave ruthlessness as a desirable characteristic of a politician and who also nominated the ability to compromise and a belief in sexual equality as undesirable characteristics.[8] The second factor, labelled *PC* (i.e., politically correct), consists of agreement that 'respect for the environment', a 'belief in sex equality' and an 'ability to compromise' are desirable traits in a politician. The remaining three factors are essentially unidimensional: *Religious*, where a 'strong religious faith' is considered desirable; *Ambition*, where 'ambitious' is regarded as a desirable characteristic; and *Leader*, where an ability to be 'a strong leader' is deemed desirable.

Table 7.17
Factor analysis* of characteristics of successful politicians

	PC	Zealot	Upright
Honest	0.018	-0.346	**0.619**
Principled	**0.404**	0.220	0.172
Ambitious	-0.035	**0.540**	0.264
Ability to compromise	**0.821**	-0.144	-0.330
Approachable	0.286	-0.084	**0.448**
Practical	0.353	0.065	**0.403**
Caring	0.325	-0.083	**0.511**
Ability to lead	0.053	0.100	**0.464**
Strong religious faith	-0.077	**0.630**	0.005
Ruthless	0.082	**0.654**	-0.189
Hardworking	-.111	0.070	**0.649**
Values the family	**0.476**	0.038	0.276
Belief in sex equality	**0.615**	0.024	0.057
Self-discipline	**0.472**	0.334	0.165
Respect for the environment	**0.546**	-0.037	0.259
Confidence	0.075	0.248	**0.521**

* Oblique rotation. Varimax rotation yields the same substantive results.
   Analysis based upon male and female samples weighted to give equal Ns.
   Kaiser-Meyer-Measure of sampling adequacy = 0.88782.

Turning to the analysis of 'successful' politicians, three factors emerged. The first of these, *PC*, consists of six leading characteristics: the ability to compromise; a belief in sexual equality; respect for the environment; valuing the family; self-discipline; and being principled. The second, *Zealot*, exhibits three main components and tends to exude a rather regional flavour: ruthlessness; a strong religious faith; and ambition. The final factor, *Upright*, contains seven components: hardworking; honesty; confidence; caring; ability to lead; approachability; and practicality. Respondents seem, in effect, to acknowledge three contrasting routes to political success: a 'soft', caring approach; ruthless fundamentalism; and hard, honest graft.

Table 7.18

Factor analysis* of typical characteristics of male politicians

	New man	Leader	Villain	Saintly
Honest	**0.369**	-0.038	-0.321	0.323
Principled	**0.497**	0.180	0.055	-0.086
Ambitious	-0.192	**0.671**	0.209	0.007
Ability to compromise	**0.602**	-0.131	-0.032	-0.104
Corrupt	0.137	-0.078	**0.767**	0.033
Approachable	**0.597**	0.027	-0.145	-0.021
Practical	**0.322**	0.253	-0.035	0.063
Caring	0.275	-0.062	-0.051	**0.539**
Ability to lead	0.108	**0.582**	-0.224	-0.179
Strong religious faith	-0.239	0.047	-0.003	**0.848**
Ruthless	0.027	0.095	**0.765**	-0.072
Hardworking	0.268	**0.471**	-0.234	0.069
Values the family	**0.660**	-0.049	0.149	0.165
Respect for the environment	**0.649**	-0.021	0.063	0.015
Self-discipline	**0.337**	0.201	0.139	0.171
Confidence	-0.011	**0.646**	0.056	0.082

* Oblique rotation. Varimax rotation yields the same substantive results. Analysis based upon male and female samples weighted to give equal Ns. Kaiser-Meyer-Measure of sampling adequacy = 0.79313.

Four factors emerged in relation to stereotypes of male politicians. The first of these can be labelled the *New Man*: typically, he values the family, respects the environment, is able to compromise and is perceived to be both approachable and principled. The second is the *Leader*, who is characterised as ambitious, confident, able to lead and hardworking. The third, the *Villain*, is a negative stereotype, perceived to be both ruthless and corrupt, while the fourth may be styled as *Saintly* and is portrayed as having a strong religious faith and also to be caring.

Table 7.19
Factor analysis* of typical characteristics of female politicians

	Queen Bee	Conventional	Villainess
Honest	0.226	**0.419**	-0.101
Principled	**0.377**	0.283	0.085
Ambitious	**0.643**	-0.297	0.030
Ability to compromise	0.276	**0.319**	0.123
Corrupt	-0.051	0.021	**0.817**
Approachable	**0.345**	0.316	-0.167
Practical	0.269	**0.353**	-0.071
Caring	-0.152	**0.599**	-0.094
Ability to lead	**0.643**	-0.036	0.117
Strong religious faith	-0.070	**0.443**	0.304
Ruthless	0.170	-0.153	**0.738**
Hardworking	**0.583**	0.034	-0.127
Values the family	-0.198	**0.660**	-0.034
Respect for the environment	0.232	**0.487**	-0.028
Self-discipline	**0.445**	0.261	0.185
Confidence	**0.662**	-0.050	0.045

* Oblique rotation. Varimax rotation yields the same substantive results. Analysis based upon male and female samples weighted to give equal Ns. Kaiser-Meyer-Measure of sampling adequacy = 0.80079.

The analysis of characteristics perceived by the sample to be typical of female politicians generates three stereotypes that correspond to the three leading images of male politicians. The first of these, mirroring the *New Man*, may be labelled *Conventional* or, perhaps, *Essential*. She values the family, respects the environment, has a strong religious faith, is caring and honest. The *Queen Bee* stereotype is confident, ambitious, able to lead, hardworking and self-disciplined. Finally, the *Villainess* is, like her male counterpart, understood to be corrupt and ruthless.

The analyses of the stereotypes suggests that any imputed differences women may make to the public realm would be both substantive and stylistic. A positive correlation emerged for characteristics associated with female politicians and respondents held a more positive overall view of them. Though there is a negative female stereotype (the 'Villainess'), support for it is extremely low, and certainly lower than that ascribed to the male equivalent. Male politicians are more likely to be perceived as corrupt and ruthless. Thus, not only is there a perception that women would make a difference, but that it would be a positive one: the images of female politicians are more positively correlated with the characteristics deemed desirable in a public representative.

At the same time, however, similar stereotypes for both female and male politicians are evident, suggesting that respondents are not entirely unambiguous about any perceived differences women might make to the public realm. This seems consistent with the majority view of both female and male respondents that the confidence they have in a representative to serve their interests is largely unrelated to her/his sex. This suggests that support for more women in office rests upon a combined belief in both numerical and interest representation, although greater weight appears to be attached to the former. But if there is widespread support for an increase in their presence, allied with a buoyant belief in difference, how does the sample population explain the absence of women from public office?

Explaining underrepresentation

To ascertain the reasons for women's underrepresentation respondents were provided with nine plausible explanations which, for the purpose of analysis, are grouped into three categories: individuated; situational; and structural (see Table 7.20). The respondents were invited to reply to each of the possible explanations, rather than to state a preference for any one or combination of them.

The results demonstrate that, in general, respondents were more likely to agree with structural and situational explanations than with individuated explanations. For example, over two thirds of female respondents and over half of all male respondents agreed that women encountered generalised discrimination in public life, although one-third of men compared to one-in-five women disagreed with this explanation. Slightly lower proportions of respondents also agreed that the failure of political parties to provide women with the opportunity to enter politics was a major cause of underrepresentation.

Table 7.20
Explanations for women's underrepresentation (%)

	Agree/strongly agree		Neither		Disagree/strongly disagree	
	F	M	F	M	F	M
Structural explanations						
Discrimination against women	68.7	54.0	10.1	12.1	21.1	33.9
Political parties don't give women the opportunity	62.8	51.8	13.2	13.1	24.1	35.1
Women lose votes	36.6	32.9	13.0	17.7	50.4	49.5
Situational explanations						
Women put families first	65.5	69.4	12.6	10.3	21.8	20.3
Hours and working conditions suit men and not women	64.9	62.1	10.4	8.2	24.7	29.8
Individuated explanations						
Women lack experience	25.6	25.0	11.7	10.7	62.6	64.3
Women lack interest	24.8	26.6	13.3	13.8	61.9	59.7
Women lack confidence	32.9	26.1	13.0	9.1	54.1	64.7
Women don't come forward	80.3	78.4`	6.3	6.1	13.4	15.6

The structural explanation which elicited the highest level of disagreement among respondents was the proposition that women candidates lose votes. Yet, approximately one-third of both the female and male respondents agreed that women candidates are, in effect, an electoral liability. From among the structural explanations, however, respondents are more likely to 'blame' both the political parties and wider social practices than their sister or fellow voters for the underrepresentation of women. Such reluctance to endorse voter hostility is consistent with the findings concerning stereotypes of politicians. 'Typical' female politicians were generally viewed in a positive light, while the confidence invested in a politician to represent one's perceived interests was generally regarded to be independent of sex.

Turning to situational explanations, while male respondents were rather more inclined to agree that women prioritised the needs of their families before a career in politics, a majority of female respondents also endorsed this possible explanation, a finding corroborated by the views of women councillors in Northern Ireland (Wilford et al, 1993). The latter not only agreed that women put their families first, but that they *should* do so. Similarly, the respondents who were re-interviewed during the second phase of the study also tended to agree that the needs of the family, especially the needs of young children, should come before the entry of women into the public sphere, whether as workers or politicians.

A majority of respondents, both female and male, also agreed that the hours and working conditions of political institutions were biased in favour of men. During the re-interviews, it was apparent that women not only find it more difficult, though not impossible, to reconcile the needs of their families with the demands of a 'public life' but also that in relation to Parliament the peripherality of Northern Ireland was seen to impose an additional and differential burden on women, especially those with children.

The most heavily supported of the individuated explanations was the proposition that 'women do not come forward to be considered as candidates'. The weight of agreement with this option among both female and male respondents suggests that the 'blame' for the absence of women from the public realm is laid squarely at their own door. Such an interpretation is, though, somewhat misleading. The apparent blameworthiness of women needs to be set in the context of the other reasons favoured by the respondents, not least the remaining individuated explanations.

The latter in fact tended to provoke disagreement rather than agreement. For instance, approximately two-thirds of both female and male respondents disagreed that women lack either the interest or the experience appropriate to a career in politics. However, the female respondents were less likely to disagree that women suffered from a shortage of confidence: indeed, almost one-third agree that a lack of self-esteem is a factor explaining their absence from elected office. This perceived lack of confidence is though explicable in both historic and cultural terms rather than in terms of any innate disposition among women to shrink from the public realm.

The traditional pattern of female underrepresentation in its public, male-dominated spaces, coupled with the martial character of politics in Northern Ireland, have served to exclude women from tiers of representation. They have, in short, been denied the opportunities to gain the confidence bestowed by serving in public office: not least by the less than woman-friendly selection procedures adopted by the province's parties in the past. Evidence from the study of Northern Ireland's female councillors (Wilford et al, 1993) also tends to confirm the effect of candidacy upon self-esteem. While few actively sought public office, having agreed to stand for election the public realm became a less forbidding prospect for them. The sheer experience of running for office inspired a felt growth in confidence among the councillors and led to the abdication of the view that politics properly belonged to men.

Overall, women and men converge in favouring a combination of structural and situational causes rather than individuated ones to explain the underrepresentation of women. There is, though, an exception to the relative unimportance of the individuated explanations *viz* the apparent belief that women have only themselves to blame by refusing to make themselves available as candidates. This, however, has less to do with deference than deterrence. While it may plausibly be supposed that the most potent deterrent is the appreciation of the risks, either to themselves or their families, of entering Northern Ireland's public realm, there is little evidence from the findings to suggest that this is the case. Rather, women are deterred by the interaction of the structural and situational factors already noted. The belief that they are generally discriminated against in public life; that the political parties deny them the opportunities to seek election; that they shoulder an inequitable share of domestic labour; that the routines of political institutions exert a disparate impact upon them; all are seen to combine in erecting a formidable set of obstacles in their paths.

Moreover, the widespread belief that women possess the relevant experience, the interest and, to a lesser extent, the confidence to enter politics indicates that they do not lamely adopt the guise of shrinking violets, meekly accepting that politics is men's work. Women 'don't come forward' largely because they face a series of practical hurdles that deter them from doing so. But because they are practical obstacles they are, of course, remediable. The widespread provision of affordable child-care facilities, reforms to the operating conditions of political institutions, the reform of candidate selection procedures and the more equitable division of domestic labour, would each contribute to enhanced representation by women. Their absence from the public realm is not then understood as the product of collective self-abnegation, but rather because respondents are sensitive to the interaction of structural and situational constraints upon women.

The political parties in Northern Ireland, which are widely perceived to have failed women (see Chapter 6), bear a particular responsibility for promoting increased female representation. The results from the survey suggest a number of reasons why the parties should actively recruit women. The finding that female politicians are viewed in a positive vein, that they are more closely associated with the traits deemed to be desirable in a public representative, plus the fact that they are not regarded as certain vote losers, provide several inducements for the parties to field greater numbers of women as candidates at national as well as local level. Equally, the view adopted by a plurality of respondents that women can improve politics in the province consolidates the arguments in favour of their increased presence in the public realm.

Sameness and difference: what respondents say about women in politics

The belief that female politicians are somehow different found corroboration during the re-interviews with sub-sets of respondents. This implied belief in some sort of 'sisterhood', which is explored in more detail in the following chapter, is illustrated by the following brief extracts from two of those in-depth interviews.

One respondent, a part-time teacher who conforms to the image of a 'family feminist' (see Chapter 8) and who subscribed to the 'conventional' stereotype of female politicians, understood the potential contribution of women to be a substantive one, based largely upon their maternal role: 'I think women probably have a greater insight into the needs of families and just the way we live...that's going to affect education and crèche facilities and those sort of things'. She understood there to be a common bond uniting women revolving around the experience of motherhood which, among other things, made them 'more peaceful' than men. There is more than a thread of female essentialism running through her views. It appears, for instance, in the belief that mothers should postpone a career in politics until their children reach at least secondary school age, a sentiment that is also shared by many of the region's female councillors (Wilford et al, 1993). However, this does not mean that women should vacate the public arena and leave men in sole control: not least because she is unpersuaded that men recognise the constraints that confront women:

> I think that at the end of the day in every family, even the so-called liberated men, at the end of the day it's the mother who works out who's going to babysit, who's going to collect the children from school and who's going to be there when they're sick. I think if there are *some* women politicians, all of that is going to be taken into consideration.

A maternalist basis of unity among women is also recognised by the second respondent, also a self-regarding feminist and a proponent of the 'conventional' stereotype. The bond which she believes to exist among women springs from their child-rearing responsibilities: 'I think there is a solidarity there among women, that they can get together and bemoan their mutual sort of shortcomings...they help each other out. I see a very big friendship there because they look after one another's children'. Like the previous respondent she also believes women to be naturally 'peace-loving', a characteristic that in her view clearly distinguishes them from men and which springs from their other-directedness:

> I would see it [their peace-loving nature] to be natural, and I think it's almost biological. I think the leading motivation in women's lives is people. Women are people-orientated where men are more ideas orientated. But that doesn't put one above the other. I think that as in every other aspect of male and female, it's complementary.

Her belief in both female and male essentialism encourages her to adopt an 'equal but different' approach to the matter of women's representation. Reminiscent of an earlier generation of welfare or evangelical feminists (Banks, 1981), her confidence that women would improve the tenor of politics is inspired by the belief that they would supply a corrective to the excesses of men:

> Women in general have a less aggressive attitude and I also think they are basically less aware of themselves as being a power person…I think there's an awful thing between men about succeeding one over the other and I think this happens not just in politics [but] that it's very important for men to be seen to be powerful by other men. It's part of their nature, it's important for them and it's where their self esteem comes from. And that very attitude may encourage them to think more of that than the actual issue at hand. I think the motives of women in politics would be to actually handle issues that they feel are important and would be less aware of themselves in doing so.

The practical, problem-solving nature of women together with their freedom from self-possession and the preoccupation with 'power games' which she ascribes to men would, in her view, enable the 'gentler values' to be expressed in the public world of politics. Such beliefs may seem unduly simplistic, even old-fashioned. Yet it was noted (Chapter 4) that among the female activists a sense of other-directedness, fuelled by an essentialist notion of sisterhood, was commonplace. Women who are involved in a range of organisations related to health, welfare and educational matters, do understand their activities to be an expression of some underlying and distinctly womanly set of values. Such values, whether they relate to substantive policy issues or the differences of style which they believe distinguish women from men, underpin the conviction that women carry the potential to fashion changes in the public realm.

This surfaces in the frequently expressed view among women that they are better listeners than men, a belief that is understood by some to have clear policy implications: women's voices would, they insist, be heard by other women rather than falling on the ears of men who remain largely deaf to their needs. Such uncluttered views are consistent with the stereotype of the 'typical' female politician: someone who is approachable, caring and who has a particular concern with family needs. Equally, the perception that female politicians are better able to compromise carries clear implications for the resolution of high policy matters.

However, respondents are not entirely starry-eyed about women's potential. While there is a widespread recognition of a shared agenda of needs among them, the implication that there is a submerged 'sisterhood' in the province is not entirely unqualified. There is an appreciation that unity among women is tempered by the cleavages of national and religious identity which have structured, and frustrated, efforts to forge a non-sectarian women's movement. Given the widespread support for increased representation by women and the generally favourable images of female politicians that are held by respondents, how do they perceive the women's movement, feminists and feminism? Are women in Northern Ireland 'women-identified' in such a way as to enable sisterhood to surface and flourish? By exploring these issues in the following chapter the discussion of the kinds of differences women could make to the public realm is developed further.

Notes

1. At the time of the survey there were 43 women in the UK parliament while the Cabinet, John Major's first, was a male monopoly. In comparison, there were 60 women local councillors in Northern Ireland out of a total of 566 local representatives.
2. The lists of characteristics were developed during the pretesting and piloting phases of the interview schedule. Initial lists of characteristics were produced through culling the literature and discussion amongst the researchers and with respondents during the pretesting phases. These lists of characteristics were refined during analysis of pilot results by removing overlaps between characteristics found to elicit similar responses from the majority of respondents.

The exact questions were:
1) **Which of the following, in general, would you consider to be desirable characteristics of a politician? Any others?;**
2) **And which of these would you consider to be undesirable? Any others?;**

3) **Now, please look at this list and tell me what you think are the characteristics necessary for a successful politician in Northern Ireland? Any others?;**

4) **Of the characteristics on this list that a politician might possess, which ones would you consider to be characteristic of a male politician rather than a female politician? Any others?;**

5) **And which ones would you consider to be characteristic of a female politician, rather than a male politician? Any others?**

In the interview schedule, the ratings of desirable and undesirable characteristics came together and were followed immediately by those for the successful politician. Those for male and female politicians were in a different location in the schedule. The traits of politicians appeared after the characteristics deemed to be *typical* and *untypical* of feminists (see Chapter 8).

3. For desirable characteristics, men named on average 2.6 characteristics, women, 2.8 (difference statistically significant, $p < 0.001$); for undesirable, men and women both named 1.3 characteristics, for successful politicians, men nominated 5.4 characteristics and, women 6.0 ($p < 0.01$); for those considered characteristics typical of a male politician, men identified 3.2, and women, 3.3; for a female politician, men named 3.2, and women 3.7 characteristics ($p < 0.001$).

4. For desirable characteristics in a politician, Pearson's $r = 0.996$; for undesirable characteristics, $r = 0.999$; for the characteristics of a successful politician, $r = 0.973$; for characteristics typical of a male politician, $r = 0.971$; for a female politician, $r = 0.976$. All of these correlations were highly significant ($p < 0.001$). Spearman's *Rho* rank-order correlations yield very similar results.

5. Almost ten per cent selected no characteristics.

6. This is most obvious for the characteristics that can be considered desirable and undesirable. The same characteristic (e.g., ambition) should not be named as both desirable and undesirable by the same respondent.

7. Factor analyses carried out separately on the female and male samples produced results resembling those for the combined sample; particularly if the substantive patternings of results, rather than the exact factor weightings, are compared. Because of the high level of agreement between the relative weightings of the characteristics mentioned by female and male respondents, all of the factor analyses have been carried out on combined samples of female and male

respondents. Weights have been applied to this combined sample so that the numbers of women and men approach parity.

8. An individual scoring highly on this factor presumably feels that it is desirable that politicians be ruthless. Note that it is also implicit that some people score low on each factor. So, there should be individuals in the sample who believe the contrary, i.e. that it is not desirable that politicians are ruthless. In presenting the factor results in this section, the risks of using confusing double negative phraseology needed to be avoided. In these cases the signs of factor components (though not absolute values) have been reversed to make discussion less convoluted.

8 Feminism and woman-centredness

Introduction

The background to the historically unhappy marriages that shaped the relationships between feminism and both nationalism and unionism in Northern Ireland was noted earlier (Chapter 1). More recently, these miserable liaisons were epitomised by events in the later 1960s. While second-wave feminism was burgeoning in the United States and latterly in western Europe, in Northern Ireland the issue of the moment was civil rights: its predominance effectively swamped the question of women's rights.

In some respects this experience was not unlike that in the United States where the campaign for black civil rights had diverted women's needs into the margins of struggle. In America, however, marginalisation had fostered a new radical feminism notably among women who found that their 'place', whether within the civil rights or the anti-Vietnam war movement, was a subordinate one. Yet, while inspired by the American model of the struggle for civil rights, the activists in Northern Ireland's Civil Rights Association (NICRA) were seemingly oblivious to the external influence of a rekindled feminist movement. In a society where conservative attitudes towards women were integral to both religious and secular institutions, and where 'armed patriarchy' (McWilliams, 1995) was the norm, the prospects for a nascent women's movement were distinctly unpromising.

With the benefit of hindsight, always a cheap commodity, it is tempting to blame the NICRA activists for their neglect of the gendered dimensions of citizenship. This, however, would be to dismiss the energy, fervour and commitment to the struggle for what were perceived to be basic group rights effected through opposition to anti-Catholic discrimination. Yet the priority attached to civil rights did arrest the possibilities for a more women-focused activism. Moreover, the increasingly nationalist character of NICRA also sharpened divisions among women. Those associated with the civil rights movement were branded as nationalists, generating a perception - not least among women drawn from the majority, Protestant, community - that republicanism and feminism were two sides of the same coin. (Ward and McGivern, 1980, Ward, 1986, McWilliams, 1991)

One event from the early phase of 'the troubles' exemplifies that association. In 1971 the British government abolished free school milk for children, a decision swiftly emulated by the government in Northern Ireland. This led to the emergence of a group of women, the 'Mothers of Belfast', who campaigned actively and vociferously against the decision. Originally a cross-community campaign, against the background of increasing sectarian tension it was soon abandoned by Protestant women who perceived the protests to be an expression of anti-state and, thus, disloyal sentiment by Catholics.

The linkage, whether actual or perceived, between an evolving feminist discourse and republicanism has had a divisive effect upon the women's movement in the province. The lack of unity has not, however, meant that women have been inert. As Evason (1991) and McWilliams (1995) demonstrate, campaigns on behalf of community welfare, housing issues, prisoner's rights, women's rights and in the interests of peace have been a feature of women's activism throughout 'the troubles', even if it has not always been expressly feminist in its inspiration. (Rooney and Woods, 1992)

Whether accidental or deliberate, the activism of women has, though, been structured by the wider political conflict. (Ridd and Calloway, 1986) The history of the umbrella 'Northern Ireland Women's Rights Movement' (NIWRM) is testimony to its effects. During the height of its activities, between the mid 1970s and the early 1980s, it adopted a variety of stances reflecting its vulnerability to the broader political context. In its early days it veered towards a welfare perspective, later displaced by a more radical agenda espoused by, for instance, 'Belfast Women's Aid' and the 'Socialist Women's Group' (SWG) during the mid 1970s. However, by 1977 both organisations left the NIWRM on the grounds that it lacked a clear focus on pertinent issues: Women's Aid arguing that it should focus on women's liberation rather than equality; while the SWG maintained the necessity of achieving socialism as a precondition of women's liberation. Moreover, the SWG became disaffected with the NIWRM's support for the 'Peace People' (see Chapter 1) as well as its refusal to endorse the 'Troops Out Movement'. The issue of the rights of women prisoners in Armagh jail also proved divisive. While the NIWRM chose not to regard these rights as a feminist issue, other organisations, including 'Women Against Imperialism', took a completely contradictory view (Loughran, 1990).

Besides the immanent ideological diversity of the wider feminist movement - the coexistence of, for example, liberal, socialist, Marxist and radical feminism - the context of Northern Ireland has compounded the divisions among women. Among other things, as McWilliams (1995, p. 27) so acutely observes, the priority lent to nationalism by the 'dominant voices' within its women's movement 'has served to silence the voices of Protestant women'. Against this turbulent and fractious backdrop, how are feminism and feminists perceived by the sample population? What, if any, are the appeals of feminism(s) in Northern Ireland? This chapter explores these questions by identifying the different faces of feminism (Banks, 1981) found among the respondents; assesses the impact of the wider political context on feminist politics; and seeks to develop the understanding of 'sisterhood' articulated by the more active women in the sample population.

'Are you now....?'

As an initial measure of the views of the respondents towards feminism, they were asked an explicit question: i.e., whether or not they would describe themselves as a feminist. (Table 8.1) In addition, and to probe whether there was any felt difference between the adoption of this 'label' and support for the aims of the women's movement, they were also asked to locate themselves on a ten-point scale: a score of one indicating no support and a score of ten complete endorsement for the perceived 'aims of the women's movement'.[1]

Table 8.1
Support for feminism and women's movement

	Identification with feminist label	Mean rating on women's movement scale (1-10)
Female	23.9%	6.2
Male	13.5%	5.8

Among all female respondents, virtually one-in-four embraced the feminist label, compared to 14 per cent of the male respondents. While this is undoubtedly a crude measure - as we shall see below, feminist identity is a multi-faceted phenomenon - the proportion of women who are self-identified feminists is not unimpressive. In terms of the mean support for the women's movement, the gender difference was narrower and somewhat marginal, suggesting the widespread diffusion of moderate support for its perceived aims.

Among women, who are the focus of this chapter[2], only a few background variables were found to be significant in terms of both the adoption of a broad feminist identity and self-placement on the women's movement scale.

Table 8.2
Support for women's movement and feminist label
among women by age

	Identification with feminist label	Rating on women's movement scale (1-10)
Aged less than 30	17.0%	6.4
Aged 30-44	19.6%	6.2
Aged 45-59	31.1%	6.3
Aged 60+	30.0%	6.0
All Women	23.9%	6.2

Firstly, among the female respondents age (Table 8.2) is significant both for self-identification as a feminist and support for the women's movement, although in rather contradictory directions. The propensity to claim a feminist identity, for instance, increases with age: those over the age of 45 are far more likely to call themselves 'feminist' than younger women. Indeed, a significant cleavage is apparent at middle-age with younger women underrepresented and older women overrepresented as self-identified feminists. In relation to support for the women's movement, however, a rather different picture emerges. While the differences across the cohorts are not large, women under the age of 30 are the most supportive of its aims, whereas those aged 60 or more are the least supportive. These age differentials merit comment, in particular the yawning gap that exists between younger and older women in terms of their readiness to adopt the feminist label.

It may be conjectured that younger women were exposed to two sets of disincentives that made them reluctant to embrace a feminist persona.

Coming of age in Northern Ireland at a time when 'the troubles' were unfolding and subject during the 1980s to a wider backlash (Faludi, 1991) against feminist values, it is not implausible to propose that they succumbed to both a perceived association between feminism and Irish republicanism and the cultural effects of the backlash. Yet, during the re-interviews with both active and inactive women, whether younger or older, there was no evidence to suggest that feminists in Northern Ireland were routinely associated with republicanism. What did emerge, however, was the tenacity of media-inspired images of feminists as bra-burning man-hating sirens, clad in dungarees and sporting cropped hair. A 19 year old 'isolate' (Chapter 2) who leant above average support to the women's movement, while also rejecting the feminist label, epitomised this view:

> No, I'm not a feminist. I don't like the association it has with being active, marching for women's rights or being public about feminism. I wouldn't burn my bra and all that. That's what I associate with it. You know: 'Burn your bra! Be a feminist!' I don't see the sense of it, of being a feminist. I just agree with equal rights. A woman can do a man's job as well as a man, but I wouldn't go out of my way to protest about it.

Another respondent, a 'super activist' in her mid-thirties, leant another recurring dimension to the refusal to identify oneself as a feminist. A strong supporter of the women's movement, she had chosen to give up paid employment to look after her three young children which, she felt, attracted obloquy from feminists:

> I link feminism with 'women's libbers'. They put down women who stay at home to look after their children, but I feel I've done a lot that working mothers can't do. We women who choose to stay at home have a right to that choice and shouldn't be put down.

A second super activist, but in her mid-fifties, also saw no contradiction between motherhood and, in her case, virtually unqualified support for the aims of the women's movement:

> No, I'm not a feminist [but] on the other hand I do agree with them. My idea of a feminist is someone who's a wee bit radical, the ones who burn the bras...But at the same time, I'm delighted that women are being pilots, are in the judiciary and gradually moving into all areas of life, even MPs. So I do agree with the women's movement, even though I like to see women looking after their families.

The views of this last respondent are somewhat at odds with those of her cohort in the wider sample, both through her rejection of the feminist label and in terms of the strength of her support for the women's movement. It was noted in Chapter 4, however, that the activists who were re-interviewed were distinguished by above average support for the women's movement and also by their greater preparedness to lay claim to a feminist identity. While unrepresentative of her age-group, she does typify the attitudes of the activists in relation to both measures of gender consciousness. (Miller et al, 1988) But while activist women are more likely to identify themselves as feminists, this is still a minority phenomenon among them. Most are deterred by the populist connotations of feminism; however, whether young or old their adherence to an equal rights agenda is unmistakable. Yet, the greater tendency among older women to describe themselves as feminists is somewhat puzzling. This apparent conundrum is explored later where attitudes to a range of women-identified issues are discussed. But at this point it may be conjectured that older women are more inclined to conflate feminism and feminity and/or to subscribe to the welfare feminism that was more characteristic of the first wave of the movement, thereby lending their interpretation a more pro-family orientation.

Whilst there were age effects, neither educational attainment nor socio-economic status were statistically significant variables in explaining either the strength of support for the women's movement or the likelihood of defining oneself as a feminist. However, party affiliation, (Table 8.3) religious identity and geographical location did exert significant effects upon support for the women's movement, though not upon the likelihood of adopting a feminist identity.

Women who support the two major unionist parties emerge as below average supporters of the aims of the women's movement. Thus, while we noted in Chapter 6 that both the UUP and the DUP were regarded by their female party identifiers as having failed to represent women's interests, the intensity of support among them for a woman-identified agenda falls below the norm. This does tend to confirm the view that such perceived failure is related to issues other than those associated with a women's agenda; notably, the inability of their parties to effect a solution to the wider constitutional question. More surprising are the attitudes of Alliance supporters: though the party has made extensive efforts to promote gender equality issues, its female supporters also exhibit below average support for the women's movement.

222

Table 8.3
Support for women's movement among women by
political party affiliation

Political party	Level of support
Alliance Party	6.0
Democratic Unionist Party	5.8
Ulster Unionist Party	6.1
Other Unionists	5.1
SDLP	6.5
Sinn Féin	7.1
Workers' Party	6.5
Conservative Party	5.7
Green Party	7.1
Other	7.0
None	5.7
All women	6.2

The views of both SDLP and Sinn Fein supporters do, by comparison, help to explain their disaffection with their respective parties in more explicitly women-centred terms. Both female electorates demonstrate above average support for the women's movement, thereby contributing to the mutual antipathy they feel in relation to the representation of women's interests by their preferred parties.

Table 8.4
Support for women's movement among women by religion

Religious affiliation	Level of support
Baptist	5.4
Church of Ireland	6.2
Free Presbyterian	5.9
Methodist	6.1
Presbyterian	5.9
Other Protestant	5.8
Roman Catholic	6.5
Other	5.9
No religion	6.5
All women	6.2

The difference in the salience attached to the aims of the women's movement by unionists and nationalists also tends to be reinforced by the effects of religious affiliation. Along with secularists, Catholic women are the only ones to lend above average support to the women's movement. With the exception of those who belong to the Church of Ireland, women in each of the Protestant denominations fall below the average level of support. Interestingly, women who live in rural areas and in urban areas other than Belfast are more likely to endorse the aims of the women's movement than those resident in the Belfast area.

Table 8.5
Support for women's movement among women by
geographical location

Location	Level of support
Belfast	6.0
Other urban areas	6.3
Rural	6.4
All women	6.2

It may have been surmised that women resident in the province's capital, where there is a concentration of women's organisations and which has provided the context for innumerable women-led campaigns, would have exhibited above average support for the women's movement. In fact the opposite is the case.

What is beginning to emerge, at least tentatively is, as Hedlund (1988) observes, that a compound model which employs a range of variables is more reliable as a measure of orientations towards feminism than a simple, uni-dimensional question of the 'are you now, or have you ever been, a feminist?' variety. Among women in the general population it is evident that self-identification with the feminist label is an insufficient means of identifying the nature and extent of gender consciousness. The inclusion of a measure of support for the perceived aims of the women's movement generates a richer and more complex picture and also reveals that despite populist images, attachment to those aims is widely diffused throughout the female population, especially among Catholic nationalists. If a wider measure of 'politicisation' includes gender consciousness or identity, then unlike the findings of Inglehart (1981, See Chapter 1), Catholic women in Northern Ireland appear to be more politically interested and politicised than non-Catholics. However, this judgement needs to be treated with caution. The complexities involved in examining gender identity are manifold and require further exploration. In order to advance the analysis, the extent of adherence among female respondents to a women's agenda is now investigated.

A women's agenda

To explore the differential levels of support for the women's movement, a factor analysis was conducted in relation to the respondents' attitudes towards a range of woman-related questions.

The questions employed in the factor analysis were wide-ranging and included attitudes towards preferential treatment for women; the provision of child-care facilities; increased representation by women in public office as well as the preferred explanations for their absence from the public realm. (See Table 8.6 for the full list of items included in the factor analysis.)

As can be seen, nine factors were extracted in total, five of which (2, 3, 4, 6 and 7) were woman-identified while the remainder (1, 5, 8 and 9) were not. While there are variations among the combinations of attitudes comprising them[3], female respondents scoring highly on the woman-identified factors endorse the pursuit of careers by women, both within and beyond the political arena, agree that the government should adopt special measures to improve the social and economic position of women and perceive sex discrimination to be a major problem in Northern Ireland. In addition, they do not believe that equal opportunities strategies have gone far enough and are sensitive to the failure of political parties to recruit women as electoral candidates. Respondents adhering to the non woman-identified factors are broadly opposed to an increase in the representation of women, whether at cabinet, parliamentary or local government level and do not endorse the introduction of special measures by government to address the inequalities confronting women. These respondents also included those who do not belong to a women's group.

Table 8.6
Woman-identified and non woman-identified factors

	Woman-identified factors					Non woman-identified factors			
	Two	Three	Four	Six	Seven	One	Five	Eight	Nine
Q1A	.128	.368	.134	**.397**	.267	-.079	-.165	-.343	-.124
Q1B	-.038	.011	-.097	-.058	.002	.098	.097	**.759**	.039
Q2A	.143	.059	.223	**.504**	.185	-.078	-.375	-.389	-.098
Q2B	-.008	.103	-.086	**-.635**	-.139	.032	-.017	.070	.041
Q3A	-.134	-.051	**-.702**	-.101	-.110	.205	.226	.064	.123
Q3B	.204	**.675**	.126	-.090	.142	-.241	-.180	-.028	-.144
Q3C	.003	.371	-.234	-.121	.139	.014	**.393**	.246	.293
Q3D	.201	**.752**	.136	.029	-.140	-.197	-.144	-.056	.023
Q3E	.329	**.634**	.087	.044	-.125	-.213	-.178	-.104	-.067
Q3F	-.174	-.122	-.285	-.104	**-.473**	.217	.370	.207	.105
Q3G	.211	**.603**	.033	.124	-.160	-.196	-.228	.045	-.159
Q4	.210	.046	.212	**.397**	.377	-.082	**-.440**	**-.418**	-.057
Q12B	-.026	-.235	**-.611**	-.173	-.124	.066	.095	.058	-.079
Q13	-.157	.010	-.237	-.143	.051	**.470**	.246	.230	.282
Q14	-.160	-.266	-.129	-.106	-.074	**.796**	.168	.122	-.046
Q15	-.155	-.239	-.136	-.138	-.007	**.813**	.220	.116	-.065
Q16	.249	.174	.170	.046	.040	**-.589**	-.209	.002	-.154
Q17	-.175	-.031	-.346	-.189	-.107	**.694**	.206	.104	.109
Q18A	-.041	-.040	**-.676**	-.142	.031	.325	.176	.148	.072
Q18B	**.416**	-.082	-.156	.030	-.110	.153	-.102	**.486**	-.071
Q18C	**.468**	.232	-.298	-.023	.077	-.201	-.108	.204	-.008
Q18D	.126	.121	**-.559**	-.139	-.079	.209	-.008	.397	.147
Q18E	.353	.210	-.066	.003	**-.596**	.029	-.165	-.021	.018
Q18F	**.764**	.162	-.042	-.064	-.076	-.172	.005	.037	-.041
Q18G	**.717**	.277	.130	.049	-.049	-.271	-.133	-.039	-.059
Q18H	**.646**	.247	.106	.115	-.199	-.231	-.047	-.044	.052
Q18I	**.473**	.251	-.027	-.034	**-.496**	-.027	-.229	-.080	-.221
Q49	.031	-.099	-.165	-.015	-.035	.219	**.728**	.087	.019
Q50	-.128	-.284	-.118	-.086	.008	.304	**.697**	.026	.115
Q66	-.026	.145	-.291	**-.407**	-.029	.231	.277	.019	-.040
Q76A	.039	-.104	.010	-.003	-.021	.003	-.024	-.040	**.861**
Q102B	.064	-.161	-.121	**-.651**	.254	.195	-.021	-.057	-.008

Kaiser-Meyer-Olkin Measure of Sampling Adequacy = 0.83997

Key:
Q1A	Attempts to give equal opportunities to women have gone too far
Q1B	Women themselves should make a special effort to overcome sex discrimination
Q2A	Agreement with opinions and demands of the women's movement
Q2B	Self-identification with feminist label
Q3A	In general, women suffer from discrimination against them at work
Q3B	If there are lay-offs at work, women should go before the married men

Q3C	If women are under-represented at a place of work they should be appointed or promoted in preference to men
Q3D	Women are *by nature* happiest when making a home and caring for children
Q3E	Men are more suited *by upbringing* for jobs that have a great deal of responsibility
Q3F	Employers of women with children should provide day care facilities
Q3G	It is ridiculous for a woman to do a 'man's work'
Q4	Government should do everything possible to improve the social and economic position of women
Q12B	Sex discrimination is a problem in Northern Ireland
Q13	At least half of cabinet posts should be held by women
Q14	More women should be elected to parliament
Q15	More women should be elected to local government
Q16	More confidence in a female politician to represent interests
Q17	In general things would improve if there were more women in politics
Q18A	In general, there is discrimination against women in public life
Q18B	Women do not come forward to be considered as candidates in elections
Q18C	A woman candidate will lose votes
Q18D	Political parties do not give women the opportunity to enter politics
Q18E	Women put their families above a career in politics
Q18F	Women do not have the confidence for politics
Q18G	Women do not have the right experience for politics
Q18H	Women are not interested in politics
Q18I	Hours and working conditions of political institutions suit men and not women
Q49	More female workers should join trade unions
Q50	Women are suited to lead trade unions
Q66	Churches should do more to further the interests of women
Q76A	Member of a women's group
Q102B	Try to get own children to share own views about sexual equality

What is noticeable is that no relationship was found among the female respondents concerning self-identification as a feminist, supporting the aims of the women's movement and being a member of a women's group. (Here it is worth recalling the observation made in Chapter 3 that there is an association between belonging to such a group and activism on behalf of a church.) Moreover, there is no significant association between the adoption of an overtly pro-woman position and membership of a women's group. Church groups in general emerge as being rather inclement contexts for the espousal of pro-womanist attitudes, at least those tested here.

The question now arises: what sorts of women subscribe to either the woman-identified or the non woman-identified factors? To answer this question, a regression analysis was carried out on each of the factors (Table 8.7).

The characteristics of respondents who scored highly on each of the sets of factors can be briefly summarised. The more strongly woman-identified respondents tended to be young, and were certainly aged below 45. They enjoyed both high educational and high occupational status and were not housewives. They were more likely to live in Belfast and were also more likely to support the women's movement than to identify themselves as feminists. The younger respondents were also the most receptive to positive action measures and, in general, exhibited a greater level of gender consciousness.

Table 8.7

Regression analysis - showing significant variables for 'women-support' factors

	Woman-identified					Non woman-identified			
	Two	Three	Four	Six	Seven	One	Five†	Eight	Nine
WM support		.088^c		.566^a	.113^b	-.205^c		-.230^a	
Feminist				.498^a					
Age	-.157^a	-.487^a	-.108^c			.159^a			
Middle aged					-.144^b				
Ed & Occ		.225^a							
Return to ed				.075^c					
Working in home			-.081^c						
Living in Belfast		.103^a							
SDLP								-.101^c	
UUP									.117^b
r^2	.022	.358	.011	.663	.035	.078		.056	.012

^{a} = ≤.001
^{b} = ≤.01
^{c} = ≤.05

Key: WM Support = Supporter of women's movement
Ed & Occ = variable combining the effects of education and occupation
† = No variables were significant for this factor

Those scoring highly on the non woman-identified factors tended to be older and leant low support to the aims of the women's movement, which is consistent with the picture mapped out earlier. Among these factors, party affiliation emerged in two ways. First, not being an SDLP supporter was significant for those women who adopted a 'traditional' view (Factor 8); i.e., who are opposed to the adoption of special measures by government, who do not believe women should themselves make an effort to overcome discrimination and who agree that women do not make themselves available as candidates. Secondly, for those women who did not belong to a women's group (Factor 9), support for the UUP was significant. Both these findings are consistent with those reported in Chapters 3 and 6. To reiterate the relevant points: membership in a women's group (closely associated with church-based organisations) is not conducive to either support for the women's movement or self-identification as a feminist; while the UUP's female supporters are, to say the least, less than radical in their orientations towards women's issues.

The use of multivariate analysis clearly demonstrates the complexities that emerge in seeking to make sense of both a feminist and a woman-centred orientation. It also prompts the issue of the nature of feminisms that appear to coexist in Northern Ireland. It to this matter that the next section is addressed.

Images of feminism

In order to obtain a clearer picture of attitudes towards feminism, respondents were invited to inspect a number of listed attributes and identify those they considered to be both 'typical' and 'untypical' of feminists. The attributes were compiled from a variety of sources, including earlier studies of feminist profiles (McClain, 1987) and works that discuss popular perceptions of feminists (including Brownmiller, 1984, Phillips, 1987 and Wolf, 1990), which were pretested during the design of the interview schedule. This resulted in a final list of 17 traits, which were selected on the basis that they were the most frequently cited by respondents during the pilot survey, or which were composites of similar-meaning attributes.[4] A factor analysis was carried out on the characteristics in order to identify correlations among them and this yielded a number of prevailing stereotypes (Table 8.8).

In all, nine factors emerged corresponding to nine feminist images. Three of these - the Conventional (Factor 1), the Super (Factor 5) and the Upright (Factor 8) Feminist - were highly positive stereotypes. Three others were negative images: the Cold, Anti-Family and Amoral Feminist (respectively, Factors 2, 4 and 9). The remaining three enjoy a somewhat intermediate status that verges towards negativism: *viz* the Limp (Factor 3), Shy (Factor 7) and the Political (Factor 6) Feminist.

Table 8.8
Factors for stereotypes of feminists

	Positive			Intermediate			Negative		
	Conventional	Super	Upright	Limp	Political	Shy	Cold	Antifamily	Amoral
Honest	**.667**	.153	.041	.052	-.191	-.146	-.066	-.144	-.060
Principled	.296	**.551**	.048	-.025	.206	-.098	.246	-.133	.015
Manhating	-.173	-.213	-.194	.004	.032	.112	**.442**	**.523**	.174
Ambitious	.048	**.463**	-.149	-.009	-.292	-.314	.175	.081	.174
Able to compromise	**.561**	.249	.043	-.153	.043	-.001	-.289	.060	.012
Approachable	**.688**	.252	.040	-.088	-.029	.007	-.020	-.067	.105
Practical	**.484**	.365	.153	-.133	-.102	.052	.038	-.001	.221
Caring	**.695**	.083	.054	.076	-.141	.136	-.038	-.247	-.004
Political	.025	.314	-.070	.053	.332	-.104	**.534**	.173	.139
Able to lead	.135	**.620**	-.101	.001	.092	-.044	-.067	.129	.157
Strong religious faith	**.427**	.001	.009	.066	-.229	-.134	.033	.063	**-.449**
Ruthless	-.087	.033	-.147	.014	-.004	.020	**.461**	.519	.183
Hardworking	**.395**	**.413**	.026	-.019	-.352	-.067	.094	-.146	-.067
Sexist	-.127	-.031	-.137	.108	.153	.014	.590	.339	.223
Values the family	**.640**	.091	.008	.008	-.127	.109	-.059	-.275	-.038
Self disciplined	.352	**.545**	.032	-.176	-.102	.231	.008	.095	-.141
Confident	.189	**.599**	-.074	-.003	-.209	-.121	.215	-.067	.047
Not honest	-.064	.067	**-.642**	.094	.009	.137	.089	.139	.023
Not principled	.085	-.111	**-.632**	-.107	-.160	.031	.052	.175	.255
Not manhating	**.505**	.283	.072	-.039	.068	-.189	-.300	-.312	.069
Not ambitious	.065	-.003	-.104	.023	.077	**.740**	.022	-.110	-.108
Uncompromisg	-.133	.078	-.137	-.030	-.078	-.012	**.703**	.112	.039
Unapproachable	-.139	.125	**-.407**	.091	-.021	.030	**.461**	.252	-.189
Not practical	-.087	.133	**-.604**	.312	.153	-.018	.147	.064	-.091
Not caring	-.185	.023	-.280	.110	.097	-.036	.183	.671	-.133
Not political	.154	.099	.024	.062	**-.707**	.031	-.082	-.093	-.026
Unable to lead	.111	-.076	-.161	**.658**	-.270	.012	.119	-.055	.059
Not strongly religious	.082	.343	.005	-.016	.027	-.037	.120	-.037	**.600**
Not ruthless	**.491**	.145	.080	.044	-.163	-.063	-.206	-.344	-.109
Not hardwork'g	-.045	.034	-.051	**.740**	.127	.142	-.092	.233	.009
Not sexist	**.375**	.263	-.008	-.092	-.044	-.101	-.220	-.196	-.184
Does not value the family	-.199	.048	-.134	.144	.052	.011	.124	**.726**	-.005
Not self disciplined	.097	-.178	-.332	.230	-.145	.008	.215	.111	**.527**
Not confident	-.042	-.078	-.082	.157	-.181	**.554**	-.010	.140	.185

Kaiser-Meyer-Olkin measure of sampling adequacy = .84414

If we unpack these images, the Conventional feminist appears in an estimable light, akin to an idealised maternal figure. She is honest, able to compromise, approachable, practical and strongly religious. Neither man-hating nor ruthless, she is portrayed as both caring and as someone who values the family. The Super version emerges in rather different terms. She is principled, ambitious, a leader, hard-working, self-disciplined and confident. This image seems consistent with a power-dressing, executive stereotype. The final, 'positive' image, the Upright feminist, is perceived to embody the virtues of honesty and practicality and also to be both principled and approachable: a somewhat matronly figure, perhaps.

Cast against these images is the Cold feminist who epitomises the stereotype manufactured by the media during the early stages of the second wave of feminism, the bra-burner referred to earlier. She is typified as a man-hater and a sexist, and to be political, ruthless, uncompromising and wholly unapproachable. The Anti-Family feminist is somewhat similar: she too is a ruthless man-hater and unlike the Conventional feminist is uncaring and does not value the family. The remaining negative stereotype, the Amoral feminist, is characterised by just two traits: she is neither principled nor religious.

Poised somewhere between these two sets of images are the Limp, Shy and Political feminists. The first is neither able to lead, nor is she hard-working, while the Shy version is unconfident and lacks ambition. The final stereotype, the Political feminist, is defined simply as 'political': a somewhat elusive and allusive characteristic.

Before exploring these stereotypes in more detail, by means of a regression analysis it is possible identify the types of women who endorsed them (Table 8.9).

What the regression analysis reveals is that age, educational attainment and self-identification with the feminist label emerge as the most significant variables for the feminist stereotypes. Not surprisingly, the self-identified feminists were more likely to score highly on the images of the Conventional and the Super feminist, while those who disdained the feminist label were, equally unsurprisingly, more likely to support the Cold, Anti-Family and Political stereotypes.

However, a simple division between self-identified feminists and non self-identified feminists is too crude a device to distinguish between these respondents since they were themselves divided by other background variables. Supporters of the Conventional image, for example, were also the older self-identified feminists, while those endorsing the Super feminist stereotype were feminist identifiers with both a high educational and occupational status. Those identifying the Cold image, while possessing a high educational status, not only rejected the feminist label but also did not support the aims of the women's movement. The Anti-Family feminist identifiers also enjoyed high educational status and portrayed themselves as non-feminists. High educational status was also significant for those who identified the Amoral stereotype, while low educational attainment was characteristic of those subscribing to the Upright feminist image. Finally, the Shy feminist identifiers were typically middle-aged.

Table 8.9
Regression analysis showing significant variables
for feminist stereotypes

	Positive			Intermediate			Negative		
	Conven-tional	Super	Up-right	Limp†	Poli-tical	Shy	Cold	Anti-family	Amoral
WM							-.105^c		
Feminist	.276^a	.141^b			-.143^b		-.212^a	-.230^a	
Age	.129^b								
Middle age						.102^c	-.098^c		
Education			-.099^c				.176^a	.114^b	.115^c
Ed & occ		.116^c							
r^2	.099	.033	.009		.020	.010	.117	.066	.013

^{a} $\leq$ .001
^{b} $\leq$ .01
^{c} $\leq$ .05

Key: WM = Supporter of women's movement
     Ed & Occ = Variable combining effects of both education and occupation
     † = No variables were significant for this factor

Support, or lack of support, for the feminist label is not therefore a simple assignment according to age, educational and occupational status. Multivariate analysis demonstrates that identity with the label is higher among older respondents who are also those adhering to the Conventional stereotype. Both higher educational attainment and not being middle-aged are also significant for support of negative stereotypes. However, as was noted earlier, high educational attainment was also significant for the adoption of a woman-identified perspective. In other words, older women are more likely to harbour a Conventional feminist image and to themselves profess a feminist identity, while younger women are more likely to disown the feminist label but also lend higher than average support for a woman-identified perspective. Similarly, educated women, though more likely to support negative feminist stereotypes, are more supportive of a woman-identified agenda.

The coexistence of these images is consistent with the appearance of different kinds of women's activism in Northern Ireland (McWilliams, 1995). The nine faces of feminism that appear prevalent in the province, while reflecting the diversity of perceptions of the movement elsewhere, may also be more locally grounded. The Conventional form, for instance, while resonant with the image of the welfare or evangelical feminist of the first wave of feminism, is also consistent with Mitchison's (1988) portrayal of the province's ubiquitous family feminist, who is focused more upon family and community concerns than her own needs. The salience of communitarian activities among the more highly participative women also tends to confirm the popularity of this stereotype.

Unlike the Conventional image, the Super feminist is understood not to value religiosity and to that extent can be said to be a less traditional image (Cairns, 1991, Clark and Clark, 1986). She in fact resembles the Queen Bee stereotype of the female politician, whereas the Conventional feminist betrays an affinity with the Essentialist female politician. Supporters of the Super feminist stereotype are also akin to many of the female activists: each, for instance, exhibit high educational and high occupational status.

The anti-feminist stereotypes were also endorsed by those with high educational attainment and, in the case of the Cold feminist, with not being middle-aged. This latter finding seems surprising, given the documented tendency (Montgomery and Davies, 1991, Kremer and Montgomery, 1993) among younger women to both adopt more liberal views and to demonstrate a more pro-womanist perspective as noted earlier. This perhaps reflects the durability of media-inspired caricatures of feminists that were prominent in the early phases of second wave feminism. (Bouchier, 1979, Phillips, 1987, Griffin, 1989) Also, as McWilliams (1995) observes, the feminist label was generally an unacceptable one in Northern Ireland prior to the late 1980s, perhaps because of its implied association with Irish nationalism. But, when included as a variable this did not appear significant in the regression analysis. It may, however, be hinted at in the sense that among activists the term 'political' was associated with sectarianism in general, while in relation to perceptions of feminists within the sample population it was correlated with attributes such as misanthropy, ruthlessness and an inability to compromise. Being 'political' in Northern Ireland may not, in that respect, be seen as a womanly characteristic.

Perhaps the most salient point is that self-identification with the feminist label is more significant for the feminist stereotypes, whereas strong support for the women's movement is more significant for the women's agenda. The clear association between, on the one hand, younger women and support for the latter and, on the other, between older women and support for the former, suggests that younger women harbour greater expectations about their life chances. Thus, while they embrace negative stereotypes of feminists, this does not deter them from endorsing a pro-womanist agenda. In a sense, among the younger cohorts feminism appears to have become something of a victim of its own success. While more recently subject to a backlash, the aspirations it has engendered have survived unscathed: disdaining the label because of its negative connotations has not meant relinquishing the goals of equality and justice inspired by the wider women's movement. In that sense, feminism has virtually become mainstream, especially among young women.

Feminists, feminism and sisterhood

In addition to the age differentials concerning a woman-identified agenda, there was also greater support for woman-centred policies among Catholic women who support either the SDLP or Sinn Féin. One possible implication of this finding is that 'sisterhood' may be exclusive to some, rather than inclusive of all, women. Before turning to that issue, however, the views of the female activists towards feminists and feminism are explored. While unrepresentative of the sample at large, both in terms of the incidence of a feminist identity (31 per cent are self-identified feminists compared to 24 per cent of women in the general population) and a higher than average level of support for the women's movement, their perceptions help to set the context for a discussion of the nature and extent of sisterly unity in Northern Ireland.

While they were more likely to describe themselves as feminists than women in the sample population, the activists also tended to distance themselves from what was commonly voiced as the 'extremism' associated with feminists. One forty year old, intensively involved in a single issue campaign, explained her rejection of the feminist label in precisely those terms: 'No, I'm not a feminist. They are too extreme, so I wouldn't get involved with them. But', she added, 'I do support equal rights for women'. Another respondent, a Sinn Féin supporter in her early thirties, while lending complete support to the aims of the women's movement also refused to describe herself as a feminist and in similar terms to those of the previous respondent (a DUP member): 'A lot of them around here are extremist, terribly extremist and very forceful...Even slight [favourable] comments I've made about my husband, they try to make me feel as if I was a doormat'. A 35 year old SDLP supporter, who gave above average support to the women's movement, is equally forthright about her rejection of the feminist tag:

> To be a feminist you have to feel very strongly about all the issues pertaining to women's role and demand independence and autonomy. It's too strident, too dictatorial. I see women in terms of equality rather than feminism, so I do support women's rights and opportunities: but I'm not a feminist.

An Alliance supporter in her early forties perhaps encapsulates the views of those activists who, while identifying strongly with the aims of the women's movement, shrugged off a feminist identity:

> It's counter-productive to call yourself a feminist. To actively describe yourself as a feminist creates almost a barrier, it puts you into a negative relationship with other people. The aggressive nature of some of the women who are involved, I can't agree with them...It's sad that they become so assertive, so aggressive. They frighten people out of their skins: that doesn't achieve anything.

The ascription of epithets such as 'extremist', 'aggressive' or 'fanatical' were commonplace among the activists. Another Alliance supporter, in her mid-forties and, on our measures, a hyperactivist, captured the distinction between a feminist and support for the aims of the women's movement (which she endorsed fully) in representative terms:

> I would say that women should be taking a bigger role in business, in running the country both locally and nationally and there has to be some sort of organisation to foster that aim...[M]ovements like the women's movement who put women's issues to the fore have to be commended. But I don't agree with a lot of the issues that the feminists put forward. I mean, I believe we are all equal but...I'm not one of those people, 'we are the superior race', you know. I think we [women] are much better than we are given credit for, but both genders have their strengths and weaknesses and we have to recognise that. So I wouldn't like to be called a feminist because they're too extreme. If you're middle of the road you're not a feminist.

Others, about one-third of the activists, did embrace the label and some relished the association of women's strength with feminism. One young woman in her early thirties, a 'hyperactivist' involved in the UUP, the Orange Order and a wide range of local organisations, aligned herself with the Super feminist stereotype and was a strong supporter of the women's movement. Indeed, her identification with women in general was clear:

> Women are underdone by, they are the lower class. Even in the high class bracket women are treated as a maid, as a servant...There are a lot of very intelligent women and there are a lot of women that can be intelligent if they're given the chance but they never get it. That's just totally unfair that way. I like to push women's ideas. You know, if I see a girl sitting in a house all day with kids, not even wanting to go to a mothers and toddlers group, I'd go around to her door saying 'Why don't you come along', you know... I have to tell anybody that felt as if they were chained to something like that there's life after being married. A man, even if he's domineering, is not pressing the thumb that hard that you can't go out the door.

A 43 year-old Catholic woman, active in church and school-related organisations who endorsed the Conventional feminist image, drew a distinction between her own self-identity as a feminist and the populist stereotype:

> Yes, I am a feminist because women have been taken for granted for far too long. They haven't been able to realise their full potential. Now, I'm not the type to put all the men against the wall and shoot them: I wouldn't go that far, definitely not! But women should be given the opportunity, they shouldn't be discriminated against.

Even those who were self-identified feminists did tend towards ambivalence in representing themselves as such. In effect they recognised the diversity of feminist beliefs, but not in ways that reflected an association between the doctrine and the wider political conflict in Northern Ireland. Rather, the differences that they drew among feminists revolved around the preferred strategies for confronting patriarchy and for tackling the disadvantages and inequalities that afflict women. This also incorporated the so-called 'man-problem' in feminist discourse; i.e., whether men are perceived to be either allies or enemies in the pursuit of women's rights. Radical gynocentrism, however, was not extolled by the feminists among the respondents. Instead, a more conservative pro-family feminism was evident, laced by a strong belief in an equal rights strategy, which is consistent with the preference among women voters for gender recognition policies noted in Chapter 6.

That broad preference, together with an awareness of diversity within feminism and of the debate concerning the place of men within the struggle for women's equality, surfaced in the views of a 46 year-old respondent. A supporter of the UUP, intensely active in educational matters and an adherent of the Conventional feminist stereotype, she acknowledged her own difficulties in choosing to describe herself as a feminist:

> At one time I would have denied being a feminist, but my understanding of it now is different. Anyone who is pro-women, pro-equal opportunities, I would describe as a feminist. The problem is that some people's understanding of feminism is different from others. My own definition is pro the equality of women in society and women being able to take their rightful place alongside men...I went to a community development review organised by my employers where the position of women in Northern Ireland was being discussed. I took my earrings off before going in because all the women there were very strong feminists...True feminists would say that it is not possible for a man to be a feminist and some of the women at the review asked the men to leave. I thought that was horrifying because the two men concerned were really quite liberal in their views.

While there is, even among those who adopt it, an acute awareness of the negative connotations implied by a 'feminist' identity, in policy terms there is much that unites the activists. As remarked above, the mixture of welfarist and equal rights perspectives was commonplace. The achievement of equal rights and equal opportunities by women would, in the eyes of most, enable them to bring a more welfarist perspective to the public arena of politics.

The previous respondent, for example, who adhered to the Conventional feminist stereotype also endorsed the Conventional or Essentialist stereotype of the 'typical' female politician. For her, women's 'caring' nature would make a substantive difference to politics because they would propel family-centred issues up the agenda: 'Women are more caring; they would favour more help for families. There would be more stress on education, on health and less on defence and security'. Within the context of Northern Ireland, she also believed that in sufficient numbers women would, because of their moral superiority, apply a corrective to the excesses of men. She understood this superiority to be rooted in 'maternalism' which, besides spurring her own activities was, she believed, a common motivation among women and formed the basis for an all-encompassing sisterhood:

> I think that women quite often get involved in things simply because the mothering instinct is so strong. Anything that I have got involved in actually started with the protective instinct to make sure that nobody harmed my youngsters. Very frequently that is the way women become involved and find their feet and then step off from that. It is a trigger.

But while apparently subscribing to a maternal 'instinct', she did not believe that men were incapable of learning how to care: 'Men could be more caring. There is no reason why they can't take on some of the female attributes but at present they're brought up to be aggressive'. Such attributes would in her view not only influence the policy agenda, but also change the ways in which men act:

> Men are much more interested in power than women. In my opinion women's groups are more effective because men tend to build power structures very quickly, but women have no difficulty in working together, they have a good way of working that men should take on board. Two women's groups that I helped to set up worked quite happily without any hierarchical structures.

The stylistic differences she believes women can bring to the public realm are echoed by an SDLP supporter who also aligns herself with the Conventional feminist stereotype. Active on a wide range of committees concerning health and educational issues, she too ascribes to men a need to be seen 'to be dominant, in control, to be assertive', whereas women are more cooperative. But not all women: 'In positions of authority, women who do not have children are much less good at compromising and at working with people. Having a family enables you to see other people's points of view and to allow for differences'. An Ulster Unionist supporter echoes these sentiments. In her opinion, parenthood encourages women to be better listeners:

> [M]ore women can look at either side of what's going on, whereas the man, if he gets his teeth into something, that's it: he'll not listen to anybody else's point of view. A woman politician would sit and listen to both sides.

This view of motherhood - that it equips women with particular kinds of skills, supplies the motive for their participation and encourages them to identify sets of interests that men tend to ignore - presents the role as a resource rather than a constraint. A non-feminist, lending below average support to the women's movement, conveys such a perspective in the following terms:

> If there were more women in politics we'd have a more level-headed approach. Women are much better organisers than men. Let's be realistic, very few men have the ability to teach a child the multiplication tables, do the ironing and make the dinner all at once! It takes real organisational ability to do that.

While many of the respondents, whether or not they were self-identified feminists, referred to their domestic roles as making them more versatile, adaptable and practical, they were also acutely sensitive to the fact that women in general are effectively prevented from gaining entry into the public realm by the inequitable division of domestic labour. Such inequality explains the premium that most women place, whether unionist or nationalist, on the importance of child-care provision. (See Chapter 6)

There are, though, exceptions even among members of the same party family. One active member of the UUP, for instance, was highly critical of the party for its neglect of child-care: 'they just don't do enough. If you bring an idea to them on child-care, they wouldn't push it. They are not as forceful as I would like them to be. I'd set up a creche for anybody if I thought that women were getting a better deal out of it'. Another UUP supporter took a contrary view. An anti-feminist opposed to the women's movement, she had decided views about motherhood:

> I don't like women working outside the home. I mean, if you're going to have children, surely you should be in the home. When I came out of hospital with my daughter, they had the cheek to hand me a child-minding leaflet...A woman's place should be in the home. It's a woman's natural instinct to be at home. You're only making a 'ginny' out of a man if he stays at home, something he's not meant to be. Making a woman out of him, somebody who comes in and fusses about.

Such a prescriptive approach was extremely rare among the respondents. Moreover she, unlike most of the women who were re-interviewed, did not subscribe to any transcendent sisterhood among women. Her traditional views of gender roles were allied to an exclusive sense of community identity. Ensuring that her daughter remained within the unionist and Protestant fold was paramount. For that reason she was, for instance, opposed to religiously integrated education: 'She' (her daughter), 'could have a Roman Catholic sitting beside her and that wouldn't be right'. The respondent was also somewhat unusual in believing that women 'couldn't cope with politics'. This she ascribed to their asserted lability: 'If somebody said something to them, they could be very emotionally upset by it...where a man can be very determined and stick to his point far better than a woman could under pressure'.

Such views, whether among feminist or non-feminist identifiers, were though the exception. More commonplace were references to women's tenacity. A 43 year-old Catholic respondent (a self-identified feminist), in referring to the differences she believed women could make to politics, captured this ascription in graphic terms:

> I think they would just keep on and on and on - what a man would call nagging - until they've got some sort of discussion going or got something out of it. I think that's what they would do, just fall back on what every woman does, keep on and on at something until they've got their point across, you know; they wouldn't give up. If they were in politics...they've got the mandate to keep on and on, hammering on at a certain point until it's accepted and they've got it across.

Dogged persistence, whether or not it was expressed in such unflattering language, was often associated with women's decisiveness. One 40 year old non-feminist - 'I don't like women who don't like people to open doors for them or get up and give them a seat: that's wrong. It's nice to be feminine' - a Presbyterian supporter of the UUP, who leant below average support to the women's movement, had clear views on this matter. Not only did she perceive behavioural differences between the sexes but she also subscribed to the notion of mutuality among women:

> Generally speaking, women are prepared to talk and listen: they can listen to another point of view without coming to blows. I know that there are women on either side who are very staunch and strong but they do listen...And when they've made a decision they tend to act on it. Men, though, they tend to make a decision and sit for a while and change it around. But women, if they make a decision it would be acted upon...And women socialise easier with each other than men can, they understand one another better.

Commonality among women was a recurring motif among the respondents who were re-interviewed. Whether feminist or non-feminist; ardent or weak supporter of the women's movement; Catholic or non-Catholic; unionist, nationalist, other or non-aligned; the perception of an underlying unity was, as the following extracts suggest, a familiar theme:

> There is more that unites women than divides them. The groups I'm involved in, it's a need that unites us. Men aren't as united because women are more open with one another. I would certainly sit down and discuss things with a woman, but men, they don't want to know really. (65 year-old non-feminist, unequivocal supporter of the women's movement, Catholic, SDLP voter):

> There is a sisterhood of women...You can sit down with a group of women, it doesn't matter where they're from, there's always a common bond running between you, a common experience - and a lot of humour

as well. I mean, you have to laugh otherwise you wouldn't get through it.
(35 year-old Green Party supporter, no religious affiliation, a feminist lending below average support to the women's movement):

I think there is more that unites women, yes a sisterhood. Women make closer friends among their own sex than men do. And women find it easier to cross barriers, to form relationships with people who have different ideas than they have.
(49 year-old feminist, above average supporter of the women's movement, Church of Ireland, Ulster Unionist voter):

It's been my experience that women speak much more freely to each other, within the families, within the communities, within the schools. I see that as a feminine trait. Women unload to each other much easier and share much more than men. I think that's universal.
(38 year-old non-feminist, above average supporter of the women's movement, Catholic, SDLP voter.)

There were exceptions to these views. A strong supporter of the women's movement, but reluctant feminist, summed up the views of a small minority: 'I think that men sometimes cross the divide easier than women because women don't go out to work so much. If they do work most of their life is still centred around their families so they don't get the opportunity to mix'. Where they are locked into a family-centred lifestyle the respondent understood women to be equally, if not more strongly, attached to their own exclusive communities:

I think women can be very traditional. Very often it's the women that feel very strongly about their nationalist heritage or their unionist heritage: it's the women that are very strong. They take their children to the band practice or the Irish dancing, so they can be very polarised as well.

The latter respondent, while stating that there are 'women's issues', did not endorse the concept of interest representation; i.e., that only women can represent women, instead adopting a rather pragmatic approach: 'I think men are the best people to represent women's issues because there are more of them around to do so'. This, though, was not a widely shared view among the activists. Feminist or non-feminist, enthusiast or critic of the women's movement, most volunteered a set of interests that they believed women were better placed to articulate.

As mentioned above, they tended to reflect a welfarist perspective mixed with a commitment to the enjoyment of equal rights and opportunities. It is a familiar list: health, education, child-care and equal pay being particularly prominent. Many women talked in terms of 'social issues' which included a more personalised or intimate understanding of politics. The views of the following respondents reflect something of the span of agreement on a common agenda. The first, a Baptist and UUP voter who rejects a feminist label and is a below average supporter of the women's movement articulated the following range of issues that she felt women were better placed to articulate:

> Politics would improve if there were more women, particularly in the area of social issues - the likes of child abuse, rape, the vulnerability of women in marital break-ups and in issues like housing and unemployment. They have a lot more to give there. They'd be a lot more forceful in trying to push women's view which would ameliorate the situation, particularly in housing, child welfare and education of course. Women realise the necessity for more nursery provision because it is something that has been severely neglected.

Juxtaposed with these views are those of two Catholic, SDLP voters, each a self-identified feminist according above average support to the women's movement:

> Women would get down to the "nitty-gritty" of day to day issues and not be distracted into what men see as the big issues. They wouldn't lose sight of those but on the other hand women wouldn't lose sight of very important ongoing life issues: housing; welfare benefits; the elderly; child-care; all those sorts of things. We're a lot more practical about those things

> Women would listen to other women [they] can be more sympathetic of women's issues. Just take as an example the abortion rules. Why not give women the right to choose? Everybody should have that right. Women are more aware of that and more sympathetic of other women.

A Church of Ireland member and a Conservative voter who was an enthusiast of the women's movement but unequivocally rejected a feminist identity - 'Nobody would ever call me a feminist!' - argued:

> If there were more women in politics things would improve because they'd have much more awareness of a woman's side of things, a woman's view and how women think...They would make things easier for women to be able to work, better child-care facilities and give women more opportunities.

242

Summary

Among activists the articulation of a shared agenda does supersede self-ascription with a feminist label and also extends across a range of support for the women's movement. A 'womanist' rather than a feminist persona seems to be the fulcrum on which their identity is balanced. Within the wider sample population womanism also seems to be the essential pivot, especially among younger women. While women who are Catholic and vote either for the SDLP or Sinn Fein are more likely to lend higher levels of support to the aims of the women's movement, there is among such activists nothing to suggest that their sense of sisterhood is an exclusive one. Their greater level of support is perhaps explicable in terms of the associated and wider struggle for civil rights; the ideological space for equality issues provided by the socialist principles that inform both parties; the historic experience of women's marginalisation within the wider nationalist movement; and the patriarchy of the Church. Indeed, it was not unusual for Catholic women to criticise the Church for its failure to address women's needs. One respondent expressed her antipathy thus:

> I think that the sermons around Easter and Christmas which focus on men and drinking take the wrong approach. Priests don't ever stand up and say 'It's right for a woman to take her children away from a violent, drunken husband' - but they should be saying it. They should come down off the fence.

Another vented a broader range of criticism:

> I think the Church is the real traditionalist in the sense that it believes the woman's place is in the home and she should be bringing up her children. That she should be there to see them through to granny stage and even then to be there to support them...there's no place for women in the Church. Nuns aren't even treated with any respect. I don't think it does anything for women's rights.

Similar views were echoed by another Catholic who differed from the two previous respondents in being neither a self-defined feminist nor a supporter of the women's movement:

> The Church is biased against women. The tradition is that the woman's place is in the home and it doesn't take women seriously. The Church considers the woman's role to be a sort of super-being, taking everything on her shoulders, it doesn't matter what it is. You know, because you're a woman you're built to take everything, just grin and

bear it and carry on. The priests need to be more tolerant and understanding.

A fourth Catholic, a strong supporter of the women's movement but not a feminist identifier, drew a direct parallel between the treatment of women by political parties and the Church: 'Like them [the parties] the Church makes decisions relating to women and it's totally made up of men: that's wrong. You need both men and women'. This sense of being enveloped in a patriarchal web was not uncharacteristic of Catholic respondents. But far from being abashed or quelled by the weight of both tradition and contemporary practice, they aspired to a shared sense of sisterhood. Nor did they monopolise such an aspiration.

Women-centredness was apparent throughout the wider sample, whether or not respondents were self-regarding feminists. While the history of feminism has been structured by 'the troubles' - which some respondents believe have brought women together while driving men apart - women are effectively refusing to be defined solely in terms of being members of one or the other dominant tradition or 'community'. That activists, in particular, are characterised by a disposition to communitarianism itself represents a form of cultural resistance among women to the dominant public discourse in the province. This is not to imply that Northern Ireland has a gender cleavage, but rather that women of different religious and national backgrounds share a common understanding of the inequalities that confront them and the needs they require. While they are no more likely to agree about the future constitutional status of the province than are men, on other issues there is the potential for strategic coalitions to emerge and develop if the peace becomes established: and therein lies the problem.

The prospect for women-identified issues to become increasingly salient on the policy agenda is in large measure contingent upon the outcomes of the peace process. Such contingency is a stark reminder of the dependency of women upon men and as such represents the negative dimension of women's culture. The consociational formula (Lijphart, 1968, O'Leary, 1989) consistently adopted by successive British, and latterly Irish governments, only reinforces this dependency. While it has been tempered more recently by the proposal to create cross-border institutions, consociationalism limits thinking in both London and Dublin towards securing top-down or elite agreement among (male) political leaders representing what are perceived to be two, and only two, communities. While both governments underwrite and promote mutual tolerance, respect and understanding at the grass-roots level within the province, this goal is framed in terms of relationships between these two apparently monolithic blocs. Such a perspective glosses over diversities that exist among people of the same assumed tradition or 'community' within Northern Ireland, while at the same time obscuring the commonalities that unite them: in effect, people are constrained to think and calculate in 'them and us' terms.

To base high policy upon 'parity of esteem' between just two traditions effectively marginalises a whole raft of people (and issues) who share many aspirations in common: not least women, whose historic place at the periphery of debate throughout Ireland is a familiar one. That women, young or old, feminist or non-feminist, Catholic or non-Catholic, share certain aspirations, engage in similar communitarian activities and exhibit common interests tends, in official circles, to pass largely unremarked and go mostly unrewarded. While women have been active in the folds of 'the troubles', the opportunities created by the peace process have created other spaces in which women can articulate their needs and become fully-fledged participants in what may prove to be a period of transition in Northern Ireland. This is not to imply that women, unlike men, have the future in their bones nor that they are more likely to regard the past as a foreign country: the weight of history still bears heavily on both women and men. However, there is a submerged woman-identified agenda which, on the basis of the record of the parties, women themselves will have to advance, whether by achieving entry into the parties in greater numbers and/or by forging new campaigns and alliances in enlarged civic spaces they have already made largely their own.

Notes

1. The two questions were worded as follows: **Would you describe yourself as a feminist?;** and **In general, the women's movement seeks to raise women's status in various ways. People, men as well as women, may agree with some of its opinions or demands while disagreeing with others. On a scale of 1 to 10, where 1 means 'not at all' and 10 means 'completely', how much do you agree or disagree with the opinions and demands of the women's movement?**

2. The male sample was much smaller than the female sample and a factor analysis of 'woman-related' questions as well as of the stereotypes of feminists did not yield conclusive results.

3. The five **woman-identified factors** were as follows:
   Factor 2 These respondents **disagree**: that women do not make themselves available for a career in politics; that women candidates lose votes; that the hours and working conditions of political

institutions suit men and not women. They also **agree** that women have the interest, experience and confidence for a political career.

Factor 3 These respondents **disagree**: that women in employment should be made redundant before married men where there are redundancies at the workplace; that women are suited by nature to child-rearing; that men are suited by upbringing to occupations carrying high levels of responsibility; and that women are unsuited to undertake jobs traditionally regarded as 'men's work'.

Factor 4 These respondents **agree** that women suffer from sex discrimination at work; that sex discrimination is a major problem in Northern Ireland; that there is generalised discrimination against women in public life; and that political parties do not provide women with the opportunities to pursue a career in politics.

Factor 6 These respondents **disagree** that equal opportunities for women have gone too far. In addition they **agree** that the government should adopt special measures to advance the social and economic position of women; they are self-identified feminists; are supportive of the women's movement; and seek to transmit their views on sexual equality to their children.

Factor 7 These respondents while **agreeing** that women place the interests of their families before a desire to enter politics as a career also **agree** that the hours and working conditions of political institutions suit men and not women. They also **agree** that employers should provide day-care facilities for women with children.

The four **non woman-identified factors** were:

Factor 1 These respondents **do not support** parity of representation (or greater) by women at Cabinet level; they also **support** reduced representation by women in both parliament and local government; and express **more** confidence in a male rather than a female representative. They also **disagree** that an increase in female representation would lead to a general improvement in political life.

Factor 5 These respondents **do not support** either the adoption of positive discrimination measures on behalf of women or the promotion of special measures by government on women's behalf. They **do not believe** that women should join trade unions, nor that women are suited to lead trade unions.

Factor 8 These respondents **do not believe** either that women should themselves make a special effort to overcome sex discrimination or that the government should adopt measures designed to improve the social and economic status of women. They also **agree** that women do not make themselves available for a political career.

246

Factor 9 These respondents do not belong to a women's group.

4. The full list of characteristics in the order they appeared on the survey instrument were as follows: Honesty; Principled; Man-hating; Ambitious; Able to Compromise; Approachable; Practical; Caring; Political; Able to Lead; Strong Religious Faith (included because of the relevance of religion in Northern Ireland); Ruthless; Hard-working; Sexist; Values the Family; Self-discipline; Confidence. Respondents were also invited to nominate any other characteristics they considered either typical or untypical of a feminist.

9 Summary and conclusion

The origins of the study lay in the conviction that the then current state of work on the subject of gender and political activity was inadequate. While 'malestream' theorisation of the 'political' had been shown convincingly by feminist social theorists to be lacking - both in terms of its conceptual scope and the depth of its substantive grounding in empirical findings (Lovenduski, 1981; Bourque and Grossholtz, 1984; Goot and Reid, 1984; Siltanen and Stansworth, 1984; Jones, 1988) - these critiques had not, in our view, been applied in a practical and systematic way. The absence of a comprehensive investigation of a hypothesized terrain of participation that lay beyond more orthodox modes of activity was apparent, as was the attempt to map both its variety and its boundaries.

This study was a deliberate attempt to chart this *terra incognita* of participation. The methods chosen and their application were deliberate. The quantitative interview schedule was ambitious in the breadth of its combination of measures of activity derived from a variety of other studies. Furthermore, the interview schedule also included many novel measures of participation whose careful operationalisation comprised much of the background testing and piloting that preceded the main quantitative fieldwork. This gave the study a depth at its quantitative level that has not been equalled by other studies of gender and political activity. This expansive coverage, both in terms of the number and variety of quantitative measures of activities individuals actually engage in and in their application to representative samples of the general population was innovative.

The focus of the study upon the general population was not an unreflexive application of quantitative survey methods, but a deliberate strategy to avoid biasing our findings at the point of collection. While studies of political participation that focus upon activists can provide rich material on behaviour *as realised by these activists*, studies of activists

248

alone cannot provide insight into the actual parameters of the forms and extent of activism as they exist in the general population. Furthermore, studies of activists alone must be tautological: any findings about the nature of political activism will be influenced by the criteria employed to select the target group(s). In an activist-centred study, one must either approach existing organisations or groups and seek access to those in the hierarchies of these groups; or one must approach individuals already known to be 'active' by some *ad hoc* criteria. Individuals who may be active with other groups, or active in ways not anticipated at the start of the investigation, or not known prior to the study to be active, will be omitted altogether. In other words, significant types of political activism may be neglected by the bias caused at the point of selection of those deemed to be 'really' active. The only cast-iron solution to this difficulty is the use of large representative samples of the general population such as those employed by this study.

The activists

In this context it is significant that the active individuals unearthed by the study - the 'hyperactives', 'superactives' and 'intensives' who were subjected to in-depth interview at the second stage - do *not* match the stereotypical patterns of women (and men) who are normally deemed to be 'the active'. While most of the active women support the tenets and goals of the women's movement, those we term 'womanists', fewer label themselves as feminists. Rather than the young, the middle-aged predominate amongst the active. In fact, the study results imply that while the goals of a broadly-defined women's movement have been internalised by the general population of women of all ages and by men (particularly by younger men) a backlash, at least against activist pro-woman politics that can be termed feminism, may be extending itself to younger *women*.

In other ways, the women identified by the study as active do match general expectations. The active women were more likely than women generally to be in employment, particularly in the 'helping', 'caring' and 'educating' professions. They possessed educational qualifications and were of a higher socio-economic status than the population at large. In general, the possession of these resources of both a high level of educational attainment and a high occupational status provided the wherewithal for activity.

249

Situational explanations for activity

The study also threw light upon the nature of the obstacles to activity that are faced by women. Strikingly, situational explanations rooted in the differential responsibilities of women for child-rearing and domestic duties did not find support (at least when considered in the crude terms in which they are often advanced). (Note that in the regression models in Chapter 3 the category of "situational explanations" often does not even appear.) Marriage was associated with more, not less, activity. Moreover, parenthood, even of children of pre-school age, was not found to be a significant barrier to the active and in an impressive number of cases, actually was a spur to participation. A not insignificant proportion of the woman activists mentioned their children or a duty to future generations as important motives underlying their participation. Active individuals also tended to be active in multiple spheres and, just as a comparatively small proportion of people seem to shoulder the burdens of activity on behalf of an inactive majority, these same actives cope with the burdens of domestic responsibilities. At most, children cause for their mothers a temporary deferral of activity up to the time the children attain school age. Once the youngest child has entered school, women have more scope for juggling conflicting demands upon their time.

Interactional explanations for activity

Considering the factors that promote activity, the most interesting results arose from the more innovative measures employed. As can be seen in Figures 9.3, *interactional* or *personal dynamics* explanations were highly significant for explaining activity, particularly for the indicators of especially intensive activity or involvement. The most important of these interactional factors was the presence for men, *and for women,* of a supportive partner. This key resource of spousal support was neither unilateral nor unequivocal, but it was a key enabling factor for participation. When female activist respondents spoke about balancing public activities with domestic demands, the themes that emerged were not those of a 'zero-sum' game, but rather ones of negotiation, reciprocity and balance. Spouses were often active themselves and often had played an important role in encouraging their partners to assume or resume activities, particularly after the birth of children. Despite acknowledging the importance of the support of their partners, however, few if any of the female activists considered the 'balance' to completely equal or in their favour. The double burden of public and domestic responsibilities still falls more upon active women than active men. In this context, it is noteworthy that while activist men acknowledged the support of their spouses, the support they enjoyed did seem to be more unilateral. While there were exceptions, in general, the partners of activist men were themselves not active but limited to a supportive role. Furthermore, activist men neither mentioned reciprocity as a theme in their interviews nor expressed an obligation to return the support they received from their partners.

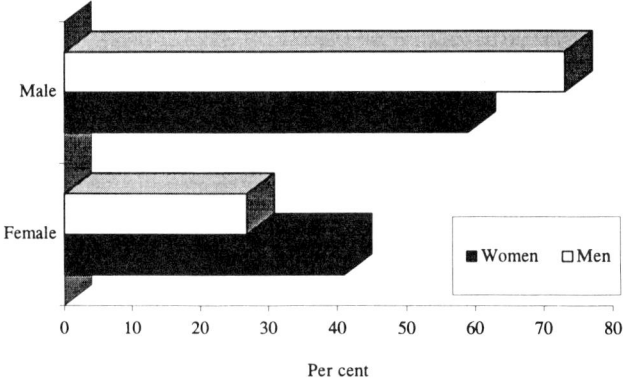

Figure 9.1a   Sex of 'significant other' by sex of respondent

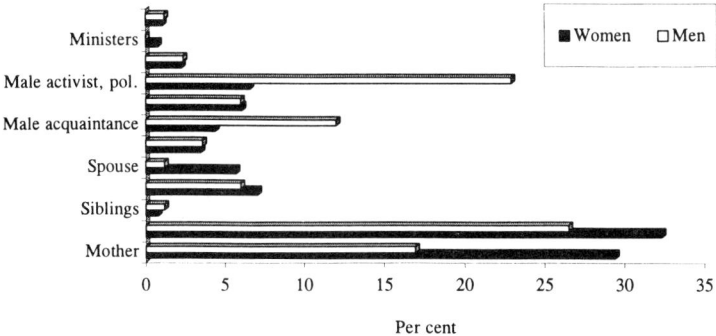

Figure 9.1b   Relationship of 'significant other' to female and male respondents

Other 'interactional' factors, in particular the presence of 'significant others' in the respondent's past or the lasting influence of prior significant events, also emerged as important for triggering activity. Those identified as 'high actives' were much more likely than the general population to

251

mention the influence of a 'significant other'. As with discussants, the 'significant others' were usually male if the respondent was a man and were equally likely to be female if the respondent was a woman.

In either case, their effect was usually a 'positive' one of having provided an example of public activity to be emulated and/or having had a seminal effect upon an individual's values that then has worked itself through the individual's own life. 'Significant events', which almost always stemmed from 'the troubles', tended to have acted as an incentive rather than a deterrent for subsequent, and increasing, public involvement over time.

The emergence of these significant interactional factors - the support of the partner, the significance of individuals and important events in the lives of the activists - leads to a different consideration of the generation of participation. Rather than a mechanical 'political arithmetic' of high socio-economic status and the like being squeezed in at one end of a black box and participation popping out of the other, a perspective of activity being created and recreated in an interplay of social structure and interaction emerges. Rather than the 'private' cramping activity in 'public' spheres in a unilateral and mechanical way, the two interact where 'private' support for public activity can be crucial for anything more than a superficial involvement. Other than dampening public involvement, the significance of the 'private' was the effects it had upon *promoting* involvement.

The significance of the inactives

As revealed in Chapter 2 and in Figures 9.2a and 9.2b below, while 'actives' appeared as exceptions to a general rule, the most inactive, the 'somnolent', can be seen as a modal type, almost as an expression of the most typical behaviour - apathy - rather than as the end of a continuum of activity/inactivity. Despite a carefully-designed quantitative instrument that probed for activity across a wide variety of potential spheres, lack of public involvement and a great reluctance to perceive one's activities as carrying political connotations were robust results of the study. In terms of characteristics, the inactives emerged as a 'negative image' of the actives. Where the actives tended to possess resources such as education and a high job status that made activity more feasible, the inactives tended not to possess such resources. Lack of resources mitigates against contact with others, so perhaps a better term for this category could be 'isolates'.

The reticence in Northern Ireland to define one's activities as being 'political' is rather problematic and can sometimes be taken as an indication of the penetration of sectarianism into life in the province. Nevertheless, for many this finding of reticence should be taken as being fundamentally a correct research finding.

The study discovered neither a reservoir of previously unremarked public activities with political meanings nor, without forcing square non-political self-definitions of activities into round holes of political participation, a hitherto unrecognised body of political involvement. These 'negative' results, however, should not necessarily be seen as disappointing. That there is (to exaggerate) a 'reservoir of apathy' rather than a reservoir of hidden and unremarked political activity is a fact worth knowing in itself. This is particularly the case because, as we discuss in Chapter 1, there has been much speculation about the true extent of behaviour with an unrecognised political meaning in the general population. Up to now, this speculation has been hampered by the lack of hard data about the level and distribution of public activity within the general population. Furthermore, the finding of a generally rather low level of activity highlights the extraordinary singularity of activists and provides a valuable corrective to the tendency to extrapolate from studies based only upon activists to an exaggeration of the true extent of participation within the population.

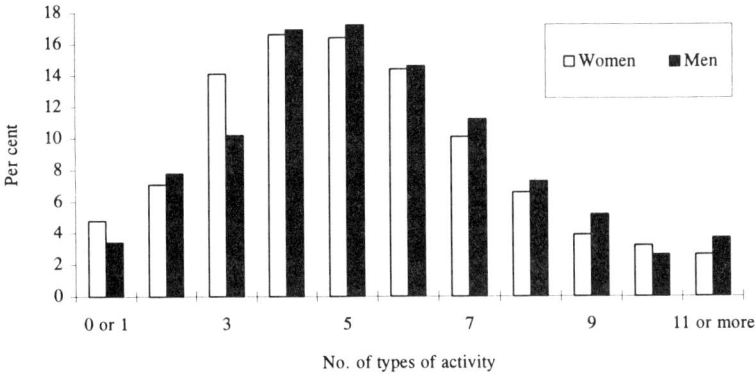

Figure 9.2a   Number of types of activity by sex of respondent

253

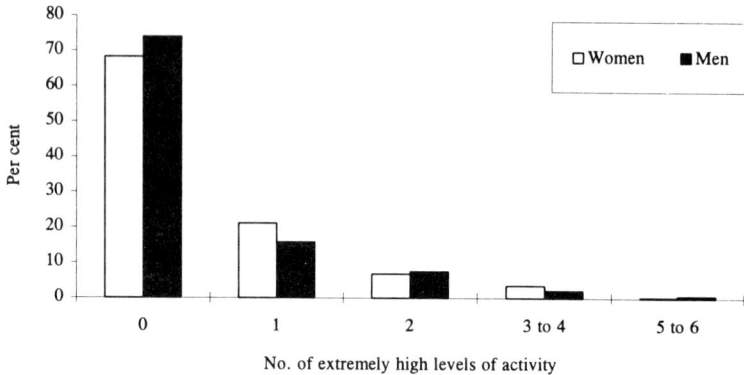

Figure 9.2b   Number of extremely high levels of activity by sex of respondent

How different are the two sexes?

One of the main sociological myths debunked by the findings is that of the nature of the differences between the two sexes; i.e., that women are inactive and men active. The great weight of the results is towards *similarity* rather than *difference*. As one can see from the results in Chapter 2, while there were some differences between the sexes in the average level of activity, the composition of the types of activity of the two sexes was strikingly similar - to the extent that for the purposes of the further causal analyses the varieties of activity can be treated as equivalent for both sexes.

Similarly, the results of these causal analyses in Chapter 3 demonstrate that the sex of an individual rarely emerges as a cause of increased or lowered activity. On the rare occasions when it did appear, its effects in comparison to other causes were weak and invariably in the direction of indicating *more*, not less, activity on the part of women. The differences between the sexes that do emerge must be seen in the light of their relatively small significance in comparison to other causal explanations; and the normally low levels of activity of both sexes within the population generally. Figures 9.3a to 9.3c provide a visual depiction of the relatively small effects of gender in comparison to the other varieties of explanation for the different levels of activity. Sex does not even appear as a significant effect in two of these charts.

254

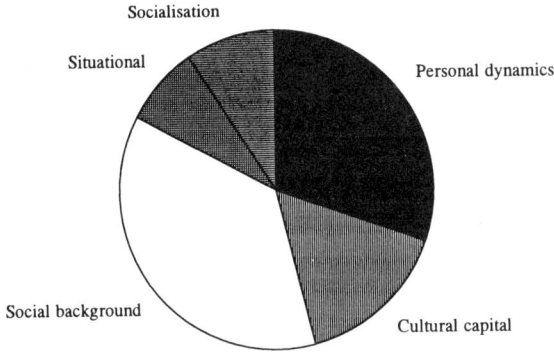

Figure 9.3a   Explanations for number of types of activity

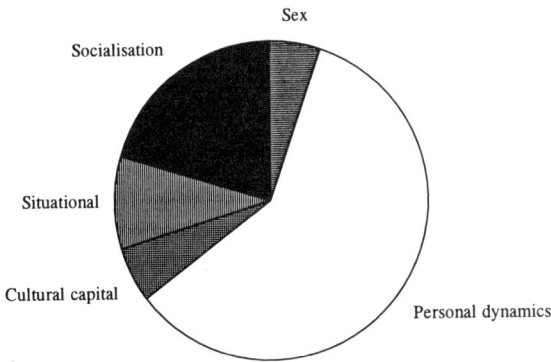

Figure 9.3b   Explanations for number of extremely high levels of activity

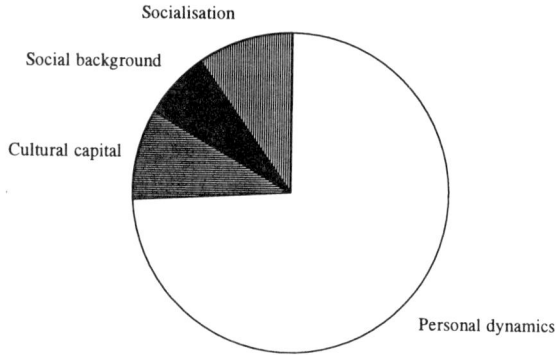

Socialisation

Social background

Cultural capital

Personal dynamics

Figure 9.3c **Explanations for maximum extent of organisational involvement**

The 'three perspectives'

These findings may be structured by recourse to the three perspectives of participation identified by Norris (1991) and others. In the interviews with the activists, particularly the older activists, we found evidence for sentiments in favour of 'family feminism' congruent with the traditional view of women's activity. The perspective most clearly supported, however, was that of the revisionist - women and men being more alike than different. As noted above, the norm for both sexes was a low level of political activity and a marked reluctance to consider any activities other than voting and (rare) political party activism to have a political content. The types of activities indulged in by both sexes were strikingly similar and in the multivariate models the variable of sex played only a very minor part in explaining variation in activity of any sort. The radical perspective was also confirmed in the multivariate models to the extent that women were found to participate *not less* than, but, arguably, *more* than men. The radical perspective also was supported by the finding that, while the types of participation were similar for both sexes, there were variations in the levels of participation within them: women were heavily involved in charitable activities, voting/socialisation and 'women's movement' activities; men were more heavily involved in direct and indirect political activism and were (or claimed to be) more assertive in personal relationships.

256

Communitarianism/women's culture

The radical perspective also found qualified support in the existence of evidence for a nascent 'sisterhood' and a common agenda that was shared by women from both sides of the communal divide. The position of feminism in Northern Ireland has always been weakened by the sectarian divide. As Chapter 8 discusses, when 'second-wave feminism' began to emerge, its reception in Northern Ireland was complicated by the conflation of feminist movements with the largely republican (female) relatives of prisoners support groups that sprang up at the same time. This legacy of Protestant suspicion of the true agenda of activist women's groups persisted at least until the 1980s. Many women, even those in the ranks of what we term the 'womanists' (the majority of women who identify substantially with the goals of a woman's movement) refuse to consider themselves as feminist. Today, the rejection of the label by many women in Northern Ireland is better attributed to the general legacy of a thirty years' campaign in the popular media throughout western society to portray all feminists as extremist man-haters than to the particular history of feminism in the province. The study did not find significant differences between Protestant and Catholic women in their rejection (or acceptance) of the feminist label, in their propensity to agree with a broadly-defined 'women's movement', in their responses to the battery of attitude questions on issues relating to equity for women, or in their stereotypical perceptions of the characteristics 'typical' and 'untypical' of feminists. The important result is not the acceptance or rejection of the feminist *label* but rather the broad acceptance by women of all persuasions of a pro-'womanist' perspective.

Women, religion and participation

An early, and significant, influence upon the study at its inception was the work of Inglehart (1981) on the differing levels of politicisation of Protestant and Catholic women in Germany and elsewhere in Europe. The possibility of testing in a different society her hypotheses concerning the translation of the different world views of women into differences in political interest and activity was intriguing. As Table 9.1 demonstrates, at a gross level the results do not confirm the work of Inglehart. In general, Protestant women do not demonstrate significantly higher levels of activity than Catholic women. This result was not altered when multivariate modelling of levels of activity was applied. The differences that remain in the activity levels of women that can be ascribed to the effects of religion are few and of minor significance.

Table 9.1
Mean activity by religion, women only

	Protestant	Catholic	Others
Political activism[d]	0.07	-0.12	0.07
Charitable activity[d]	0.03	0.03	-0.19
Voting/socialisation[c]	0.08	0.00	-0.25
Assertiveness[d]	0.28	1.34	-4.47
Environmentalist[d]	0.02	-0.05	0.05
Woman's movement[c]	0.13	-0.14	-0.16
Religious activist[a]	0.13	-0.18	-0.05
Number of types of activity[b]	5.32	5.14	4.63
Number of high levels of activity[d]	0.34	0.32	0.34
Number of low levels of activity[b]	1.74	1.87	2.07
Maximum extent of organisational involvement[c]	1.37	1.12	1.09

[a] $p < 0.001$
[b] $p < 0.01$
[c] $p < 0.05$
[d] Means not significantly different

Rather than showing Protestant women with a higher level of activity than Catholics, the main differences that remain are between higher levels of activity for *both* Protestant *and* Catholic women in contrast to the "Others", those who did not ascribe themselves to either broad Christian grouping. Furthermore, when one considers the *explanations* underlying the varying levels of activity, the validity of Inglehart's arguments, at least for Northern Ireland, must be questioned. The core of Inglehart's thesis is that being from a Protestant or Catholic culture will predispose women for or against interest in politics. While the study found some differences by religion, we found no evidence confirming that women participated more or differently due to variation in their personal outlooks that originated in the different world views that might be ascribed to being brought up in a Protestant or Catholic culture, or ethnic group, or to religious teachings themselves. For instance, the direct explanations for a higher level of church-related activity among Protestant women centres upon rather mundane causes, such as Protestant ministers in contrast to Catholic priests having wives who carry out much of the organisation of women's activities; or that there are no women-only lay groups in the Roman Catholic Church. To see the higher level of women's church groups in the Protestant faith as a confirmation of Inglehart, one would have to argue that, rather than from differential opportunity, the higher level stems from the more individualistic tenets of Protestantism translating into Protestant women being predisposed to form themselves into activist groups within their churches.

The Northern Ireland perspective - the peace context and the future

A study such as this has both an outer and an inner perspective. Looking outwards, the study had its origins in a debate over the extent and nature of women's political participation prompted by the general feminist critique of traditional assumptions in a variety of disciplines that had neglected to consider women: a pattern that is now (finally) recognised as having been to the detriment of the social sciences. Our findings will, we hope, feed back into the ongoing debate, providing as they do important and unique information about gender differences in the levels and types of political participation in a general population.

At the same time, the study has the potential to influence the local context of women's political participation in Northern Ireland. As such it arrives at a timely moment. The province has had to endure decades of political stagnation that, with the coming of the cease-fires, may be over. During this period, the opportunities for women's participation has been constrained, as have men's, by the imposition of direct rule. The greatest extent of women's (limited) electoral participation has been at the level of local government, precisely where the least power has resided over the last decades. Of more significance, however, has been the eclipse of any women's agenda in politics by the overriding significance attached to sectarian issues by all political players - be they parties, governments, commentators or paramilitaries. With the coming of the cease-fires, however, a window of opportunity is opening. The question for women's participation, however, is how far this window will open.

There can be no doubt that the overarching cleavages of nationality and religion have dwarfed the consideration of 'women's issues'. As discussed in Chapter 8 and elsewhere (Wilford et al, 1993), female politicians often felt that they shared both a common ground and approach with their counterparts from parties on 'the other side', but that constitutional issues marginalised any commonalities, which always had to take second priority to the 'more important' work of sectarian posturing. If the peace holds and a political settlement is reached, there is a real chance that women's issues may gain a higher profile in the province and that women who have been separated by the divide may find opportunities for working together. A major evaluation of the fair employment legislation[1] in Northern Ireland is underway and a result of this evaluation may be its extension to spheres of public participation. This extension could include women in its compass and could go so far as to impose mechanisms for guaranteeing women's participation in public life. Certainly the widely held dismay with the performance of the political parties, especially in relation to 'women's interests', together with buoyant support for gender-recognition policies, suggests scope for the emergence of strategic coalitions among women.

'Windows of opportunity', however, can also shut. The study found support for women playing an increased role in politics, but one should note that this support was based more upon the principle of numerical equity than upon interest representation. One of the reasons why women may have been comparatively successful at the local level in politics in Northern Ireland may be because the political power located at these levels has been so diluted. As noted in Chapter 6, many women entered local politics due to their parties seeking, and failing to find, male candidates. If power returns to local politics, it is likely that men will seek to do so as well. With peace, a relegation of women to the home and kitchen could occur in a manner analogous to that which happened at the end of the world wars. It is not enough for women in effect to wait on male politicians to reach a broad political consensus: women too must make the peace, else they risk marginalisation, an all too familiar experience throughout the island of Ireland.

Here, our findings have a particular relevance. The study found that attitudes towards women's increased participation in politics were favourable amongst both female and male electorates. Moreover, the stereotypes of politicians reported in Chapter 7 should demonstrate to the political parties that female candidates enjoy characteristics that *can* win elections, such as honesty and being perceived as hard working, caring and approachable This would be the case particularly if parties choose to centre their campaigns around issues that would advantage a female candidate. As reported in Chapter 7, one can hardly ignore the finding that stereotypical characteristics of female rather than male politicians match more closely with those considered both desirable in politicians *and* typical of successful politicians. If the cease-fires hold and the tenor of political debate in the province moves more towards normal political discourse, the most effective model for winning votes may not be that of the 'strong leader' but rather the 'caring friend'. While this may hold more so for the local level of politics where practical issues may come to dominate and where personal contact and knowledge are of more consequence, the clever and successful parties in Northern Ireland in the coming decade may be the ones that are most successful in developing and fielding female candidates. Moreover, the input that women could make to political activity in Northern Ireland could have a significance much more profound than petty political party advantage. The characteristics perceived as typical of women in politics can have a very special role to play in the future of the province - *humanising* politics and directing debate in a healing manner toward non-sectarian issues.

Notes

1. In Northern Ireland the phrase 'fair employment' refers to employment equity between the religions only. If the phrase 'equal opportunities' is used, what is generally meant is equity between the sexes. One may note that an effect of this phraseology is to direct the discussion of equity between religious groups towards employment issues.

Technical appendix

The research project was designed from the outset with a 'two-pronged', or 'triangulated' data collection strategy. This Appendix provides information on the conduct of both phases of the study. For the initial quantitative survey phase, details of the sample design, the background to the construction of the interview schedule, its content and the conduct of the fieldwork are given. For the qualitative phase, information on the selection of respondents for in-depth interview, the topic items covered during the interviews and the general perspectives adopted by the interviewers are given.

The survey samples and fieldwork

At the core of the first phase was a large probability sample of adult women in Northern Ireland who were interviewed about their 'political' activities and attitudes, employing a broad conception of 'the political'. During the writing of the research proposal, it became apparent that the types of information sought by the study had never been collected systematically for men either, so a smaller probability sample of male respondents was included in the research design.

The two samples, the main sample of 1,900 women and the supporting sample of 600 men, were multi-stage samples drawn from the electoral rolls. Polling districts were grouped into 53 areas which were stratified by geography (Belfast region and elsewhere). The selection of polling districts from within each area was taken with probability proportionate to population. Individuals were then selected by systematic random sampling. The same polling districts were used for both the 'female' and the smaller 'male' samples. Hence, the sample designs were the same, except that the selection interval for individuals in the 'male' sample was larger.

To facilitate an analysis of 'spouse effects' on activity and attitudes, interviewers were instructed to obtain an additional interview from the 'partners' of male respondents (if one was in the household) in order to obtain a subset of cases in which both spouses were interviewed. After weighting, these partners of male respondents have been included in the analyses presented here.[1]

Overall, the survey achieved 1,404 interviews with women and 386 interviews with men. Once those listed on the rolls who were not actually available for interview (moved from address, out of Northern Ireland for the duration of fieldwork, a small number of elderly not capable of answering an interview schedule etc) are taken account of, an overall response rate of 70% was achieved. Fieldwork on the survey took place over the summer and early autumn of 1991.

Development of the quantitative interview schedule

The interview schedule was developed through an extensive process of pretesting concluding with a pilot survey. The instrument went through seven drafts, three of them major redrafts, prior to fieldwork. The research team began by combing recent and current research reports for question items of relevance and by consulting with local networks of academics involved in gender and women's studies. The latter consultation led to extensive discussion about the items that should be included in a study of participation and the form that a quantitative instrument should take.

The final schedule collected standard background information such as educational attainment, economic activity/class position of the household and family structure. There was a broad range of attitude questions relating in the main to opinions of the 'women's movement' and issues surrounding women's participation in the political process, reasons both for women's lower participation in party political activity, their low incidence in public office, and the perceived characteristics of, respectively, male, female, 'ideal' and 'successful' politicians. Subjected to constraints on the average length of an interview and cognisant of other projects such as the Northern Ireland Social Attitudes Survey, the study elected, however, to adopt a strategy of concentrating on the area of its direct concern, *participation*, rather than attitudes. Hence, the core of the interview schedule was a series of items calculated to provide information on a wide range of activities that can be defined as 'political'. In each case, the 'activity type' concerned the actual behaviour of the respondents themselves, not aspirations or perceptions of what others might engage in.

The questions or scales designed to tap the areas of interest to the study often either did not exist or were deemed by the investigators to be wanting. In these instances, the study developed its own items from the 'ground up'. Items were tested through interaction with respondents selected for their activist backgrounds as well as women (and some men) drawn from the university sector. In certain areas of interest - particularly the socialisation of the young, tapping the ideas of 'sisterhood'/'brotherhood', an explicit feminist agenda and the political content or character of the domestic realm - many of the quantitative items that were pre-tested eventually had to be omitted from the quantitative instrument because of reliability problems. Draft versions of the interview schedule had asked about the division of household tasks; this area was not included in the final version of the quantitative instrument partly because of the constraints imposed by average interview time and the number of items necessary to investigate this issue reliably and partly due to the publication of a survey sponsored by the Equal Opportunities Commission for Northern Ireland, 'Women's Working Lives' (Kremer and Montgomery, eds., 1993) that, among other things, covered in detail the domestic division of labour. The main testing of these issues occurred during the qualitative interview phase carried out by the research team.[2] The less orthodox items that did remain on the interview schedule - the scale of informal activities, the listing of characteristics considered 'typical'/'untypical' of feminists and male and female politicians, the scale of items concerning political discussion and assertiveness in the domestic sphere, self-education and the ranking of factors when choosing a school for male and female children - survived this system of discussion, pre-testing, testing and re-testing.

Types of activities probed

1) Party political activity - Voting, party membership, nominated or holding public office, holding position within a political party;
2) 'Grassroots' party political activity - Contributing money, helping out in elections (canvassing, taking voters to polls, putting up posters);
3) 'Informal' political activities - Writing letters to Members of Parliament or other public officials, writing letters to newspapers about political issues, attending meetings of local councils or neighbourhood meetings about local issues, circulating petitions, attending political demonstrations or rallies, participation in some forms of political protest;

4) Organisational involvement - nature and type - both as a member of a stated organisation and as an official. Depending on the type of organisation (trade union, charity, church groups with 'welfare' roles, 'women's' groups, ecological groups, 'pressure' groups, etc), additional questions about levels of involvement were posed;

5) (If parent) Attempts to socialise children into a political or moral 'tradition' - Direct questioning, control of television viewing, monitoring church-going, reasons for choosing one secondary school over another;

6) Consumer activism - Buying 'green' or participation in consumer boycotts;

7) Expression of personal political opinions - Frequency of discussion of political topics with spouse, family and friends, willing to argue with same, efficacy or expectation of winning a discussion or argument;

8) (If 'with partner') Financial arrangements in household - Pooling all money, partially pooling money, spouses completely independent financially, giving or receiving an allowance.

The latter items of 'political activity' occasioned some of the most intensive pretesting, with a variety of strategies for collecting the desired information being tried out and discarded. Those active in at least one organisation were asked about ways that their involvement have affected them, about family constraints on involvement and whether their spouse supported their involvement. Respondents were also asked about whether there had been any significant others or events that had influenced their activity or political opinions.

Variables comprising indices of participation

- Discusses politics: Frequency of talking about media news story; political discussion in last two weeks; introduction of politics into a conversation;
- Persuades others: Ability to persuade others to adopt one's view; to disagree or argue about politics; ability to win an argument;
- Ecological consumer activism: Buying or preferring three 'ecology friendly' products; engaging in three 'environmentally friendly' activities;
- Non-institutional political activities: Writing letter to MP; writing letter to other public official; writing letter on political topic to newspaper; attending local council meeting; attending other meetings about public issues; other activities to solve community problems; circulating

petition; attending political rally/demo; withheld taxes as protest; other political protest activity - all 'once' or 'several times';

- Union activism: Strike activity; attendance on a picket line; frequency of union meeting attendance; voting in union elections; proposing motions at union meetings; holding union office;
- Charitable activities: Non-trivial donation; voluntary work; paid charitable work;
- 'Grassroots' activity on behalf of a political party: Contributed money; election work; fund-raising; clerical-type assistance;
- Socialisation of children: Encouraged child to join youth groups/societies; monitoring child's attendance at religious services; intensity of attempting to mould child to respondent's views on religion, political party preferences, sexual equality and sexual morality; importance for selection of school of: (i) moral education; mixing by (ii) class, (iii) sex and (iv) religion; (v) liberal or (vi) disciplined ethos;
- Voting: In last General, District Council and/or European Parliament elections

The qualitative phase

Sub-sets of respondents from the quantitative phase (59 women and 15 men) were re-interviewed in depth by the four members of the research team. These sub-sets were not chosen haphazardly. As the first priority when the quantitative data became available in a clean form, the responses to the batteries of participation questions were subjected to extensive analyses to establish the parameters of participation. Following this step, scales of intensity of involvement were developed so that both 'high actives' and different types of highly active individuals could be identified for in-depth re-interview. In addition, some individuals were chosen from the large numbers of 'low actives' on the expectation that the contrast between the extremes would be an effective strategy. There was a very marked and uniform correlation between the indices of participation arrived at from the quantitative data and the levels and types of activity found when individuals were re-interviewed in depth. We believe that this correlation is neither an artefact nor that we have missed genuinely active individuals in the survey samples.

Prior to the in-depth re-interviews, an informal interview schedule was developed as a guide to the research team. This schedule was designed to illuminate issues that could not be adequately covered by the quantitative instrument and was designed with reference to preliminary analyses of the quantitative data from the first phase. The informal interview schedule and interviewing procedure were pre-tested with activists not in the survey samples.

Prior to conducting a re-interview, the member of the research team charged with the interview drew up a profile of the relevant respondent that was derived from her/his responses to the survey interview schedule. This profile was sensitive not only to the actual activities each respondent engaged in but also to the various cues peppered throughout the initial survey instrument that concerned particular issues and the political situation in Northern Ireland.

Summary of topics covered during the qualitative interviews

The informal interview schedule was a lengthy document designed both to probe responses to the quantitative instrument and, *via* a series of signifiers that the quantitative instrument included, to open up other areas of enquiry. The interviews normally began by establishing the background and origins of the respondents: a discussion of significant others (especially parents) and the relative weights that could be accorded to home, school and peer group influences upon beliefs and activities. A second area concerned sources of identity - cultural, national, political and religious - and perceived linkages between them. Significant events - personal, local, national and international - and their effects upon respondents were explored. Respondents were asked to assess their relative importance: had they precipitated activities or deterred them from becoming involved? What effects had the nominated events had upon their beliefs and opinions?

Another area explored was a detailed consideration of the actual public activities that respondents were involved in. How had they become involved?; why?; whether there was a perceived sexual division of labour in the groups they were involved in; the effects on self of involvement; how activities fit in with other roles, notably within the context of the family; would the roles they occupy be different if the respondent was of the opposite sex?

In relation to both the partner and/or parents, respondents were asked to identify and discuss differences and similarities of opinion and belief about a range of issues - Northern Ireland's constitutional status, national issues, international issues, women's issues, civil rights, class, religion, environmental issues and security policy in Northern Ireland. Relatedly for some, the importance of political agreement between prospective partners was explored. In relation to their children, parents were invited to assess the extent to which they sought to transmit a sense of cultural identity. This included specific questions relating to events in the Northern Irish political calendar: whether, for instance, children were or were not expected to attend the Twelfth of July and other Orange Order marches; the anniversaries of Bloody Sunday and the introduction of internment; and the commemoration of the 1916 Easter uprising. Did they perceive such events as political? In relation to education, respondents were asked their opinions about the compulsory cross-cultural theme of 'education for mutual understanding' and state support for religiously integrated education. In a related vein, respondents were asked whether they thought that children of mixed marriages suffered or gained in terms of their cultural and political identity. Parents were asked about their attitudes to the Irish language, Irish dancing and music and whether they encouraged their children to involve themselves in such activities. Similarly, they were asked to explain the extent to which they sought to inculcate partisanship and attitudes about equality, including sexual equality, in their children, including the extent to which children of both sexes were expected to help around the house. Parents were also invited to explain the kinds of activities they would like their children to engage in. This led on to a discussion of their attitudes towards paramilitary organisations and whether they would countenance the involvement of their children in them. Did they make any distinction between the activities considered appropriate for sons and daughters?

Respondents were invited to amplify their responses to the questions concerning the women's movement and their attitudes to feminism. How did they understand feminism?; was there a women's agenda?; what did they understand as women's rights?; to what extent did their partner support women's rights?; how did this translate into the domestic division of labour? Relatedly, respondents were invited to discuss the existence of a 'sisterhood'/'brotherhood' in Northern Ireland: what did they consist of?; was the potential for a common identity among women/men structured by the cleavages of nationality and religion?

The respondents were asked whether and in what ways Northern Ireland would be affected if more women were involved in the public realm of politics; i.e., would more women make a difference?; and what kinds of differences, if any? Why did they think so few women occupied roles in the public realm? Did they associate women in Northern Ireland with peace-seeking movements?; what were their attitudes towards women who became involved in paramilitary activities? Were the latter somehow 'unnatural'?; did they consider it more 'natural' for men to be involved in political violence and women to be involved in peace movements?; and why?/why not?

Attitudes towards the churches in Northern Ireland and their influence on women were also explored. Should the churches do more to further the interests of women?; in what ways could/should they pursue these interests? How did the respondents perceive politics and political activity? Were their attitudes about political issues and institutions governed by others within the family? In what contexts did they discuss politics?; did their political views determine who they socialised with? Did the troubled nature of Northern Ireland supply constraints or opportunities for political activity?

The conduct of the interviews and the relationship between the qualitative and quantitative phases

The qualitative phase, indeed the whole project, was informed by the perception that politics is a seamless web rather than a limitless activity, and particularly was concerned to explore the interactions between 'private' and 'public' spheres of activity. Such interactions related not only to the current domestic/household situation of the respondents - whether in respect of partners, children or significant others (identified during the quantitative phase) - but also to their own family backgrounds. This involved not merely the perceived opportunities and/or constraints upon overt involvement in the public sphere created by the immediate domestic situations of respondents and the political situation in Northern Ireland, but also whether respondents held the same or different attitudes toward a range of issues - women's rights, 'women's interests', civil rights, the national question, international issues, class politics, political violence - from those held by their relevant 'significant others'. Thus, the range covered during the qualitative phase included questions relating not only to activities within both the public and private realms, but also to respondents' attitudes and opinions on a number of issues.

A key sub-text of the qualitative phase was whether respondents believed women could make a difference to both the style and agenda of politics in Northern Ireland. Thus, in addition to supplying a raft of information concerning, for instance, the pathways to participation - or indeed non-participation - of the re-interviewees, the study was also able to explore the extent of a 'women's culture' within Northern Ireland. The first phase provided part of the answer both by indicating that there are certain types of activities that women are more likely to engage in than men - that there are gender-differentiated arenas of participation - and by signalling perceived differences in the attributes of female and male politicians, perceptions of feminists, identification with the women's movement and whether respondents believed 'things would improve if there were more

269

women in politics'. The responses to the latter items did enable the study to explore at some length during the qualitative phase people's opinions on whether women tend to speak in a distinctive or different voice; i.e., whether women identify with 'women's interests' and/or emerge as more caring, egalitarian and 'connected' than men. The re-interviews ranged freely, with the question areas intended to act more as a guide or checklist than as a fixed itinerary. During the latter in-depth interview phase, we relied to a considerable extent upon respondent's self-definitions of politics and political activity, rather than leading them to consider whether certain issues are 'political'. This created the opportunity for respondents to speak for themselves, albeit sometimes nudged and prompted as each interview unfolded. This strategy, to create a context in which the political content of issues could emerge in the free-flow of conversation, was adopted deliberately on the grounds that their emergence could then be accorded greater authenticity and legitimacy. Depending upon the respondent, the re-interviews often tended to concentrate upon particular activities or issues, some of which had emerged from the first phase while others surfaced or appeared as especially salient during the re-interview itself. Thus, the two phases should be viewed as 'belt and braces': during its initial phase, the study concentrated upon participation and conceptualised politics as an expansive or seamless activity; then, during the qualitative phase which placed more emphasis upon attitudes, this conceptualisation was used to provide a variety of cues to elicit discussion. In this way, we hope that a balance has been maintained between the study of respondents' behaviours and their opinions.

Notes

1. An alternative strategy could have been to interview the male partners of female respondents, but the primary focus of the study was upon the activities of women with men being included mainly in order to provide a basis of comparison with the women.
2. One should note that the survey had very large samples and the fieldworkers employed on the survey, while experienced interviewers and thoroughly briefed by the research team, were not themselves trained social scientists.

Bibliography

Andersen, K. (1975), 'Working Women and Political Participation, 1952-1972', *American Journal of Political Science,* Vol. 19, pp. 448-52.

Ballhausen, A., Brandes, U., Karrer, M. and Schreiber, R. (1986), *Zwischen Traditionellem Engagement und Neuem Selbstverständnis - Weiblich Präsenz in der Offentlichkeit,* Kleine Verlag, Bielefeld.

Banks, O. (1981), *Faces of Feminism: A Study of Feminism as a Social Movement*, Martin Robertson, Oxford.

Barnes, S. and Kaase, M. et al (1979), *Political Action: Mass Participation in Five Western Democracies*, Sage, London.

Beale, J. (1986), *Women in Ireland: Voices of Change*, Gill and Macmillan, Dublin

Bean, C. (1991a), 'Gender and Political Participation in Australia', *Australian Journal of Social Issues*, Vol. 26, No. 4, pp. 276-93.

Bean, C. (1991b), 'Participation and Political Protest: A causal model with Australian evidence', *Political Behavior*, Vol. 13, No. 3, pp. 253-83.

Berry, M.F. (1988), *Why ERA Failed*, Indiana University Press, Bloomington.

Bew, P. and Gillespie, G. (1993*), Northern Ireland: A Chronology of the Troubles 1968-1993*, Gill & Macmillan, Dublin.

Bjornsdottir, I.D. and Kristmundsdottir, S. (1995), 'Purity and Defilement: Essentialism and Punishment in the Icelandic Women's Movement', *The European Journal of Women's Studies*, Vol. 2, No. 2, May, pp. 171-84.

Blondel, J. (1970), *Voters, Parties and Leaders*, Penguin, Harmondsworth.

Bouchier, D. (1979), 'The Deradicalisation of Feminism: Ideology and Utopia in Action', *Sociology*, Vol. 13, No. 3, pp. 387-402.

Bourque, S. and Grossholtz, J. (1984), 'Politics an unnatural practice: political science looks at female participation', in Siltanen, J. and Stanworth, M. (eds.), *Women and the Public Sphere*, Hutchinson, London, pp. 103-21.

Brownmiller, S. (1984), *Femininity*, Hamish Hamilton, London.

Bruce, S. (1986), *God Save Ulster! The Religion and Politics of Paisleyism*, Oxford.

Cairns, E. (1991), 'Is Northern Ireland a Conservative Society?', in Stringer, P. and Robinson, G. (eds*.), Social Attitudes in Northern Ireland*, The Blackstaff Press, Belfast.

Carney, E. Newlin (1994), 'Weighing In', in Githens, M., Norris, P. and Lovenduski, J. (eds.), *Different Roles, Different Voices: Women and Politics in the United States and Europe*, Harper Collins, New York, pp. 93-8.

Chamberlayne, P. (1993), 'Women and the state: Changes in roles and rights in France, West Germany, Italy and Britain, 1970-1990', in Lewis, J. (ed.), *Women and Social Policies in Europe*, Edward Elgar, Aldershot, pp. 170-93.

Chapman, J. (1993), *Politics, Feminism and the Reformation of Gender*, Routledge, London.

Christy, C. (1987), *Sex Differences in Political Participation: Processes of Change in Fourteen Nations,* Praeger, New York.

Clark, C. and Clark, J. (1986), 'Models of Gender and Political Participation in the United States', *Women and Politics*, Vol. 6, No. 1, pp. 5-25.

Clark, J. (1994), 'Getting There: Women in Political Office' in Githens, M., Norris, P. and Lovenduski, J. (eds.), *Different Roles, Different Voices: Women and Politics in the United States and Europe*, Harper Collins, New York, pp. 99-110.

Collins, P.H. (1990), *Black Feminist Thought*, Allen & Unwin, London.

Conge, P.J. (1988), 'The Concept of Political Participation: Toward a definition', *Comparative Politics*, Vol. 20, pp. 241-49.

Converse, P. (1969), 'Of Time and Partisan Stability', *Comparative Political Studies*, 2, July, pp. 139-71.

Coole, D. (1993), *Women in Political Theory: from Ancient Misogyny to Contemporary Feminism*, Harvester Wheatsheaf, Brighton.

Coote, A and Pattullo, P. (1990), *Power and Prejudice: Women and Politics*, Weidenfeld and Nicolson, London.

Corrigan, M. (1991), Interview on BBC Radio Ulster's Series, 'The History Makers', July.

Daly, M. (1978), *Gyn/Ecology: The Metaethics of Radical Feminism*, Beacon Press, Boston.

272

Darcy, R., Welch, S. and Clark, J. (1994), *Women, Elections and Representation*, 2nd edition, University of Nebraska Press, Lincoln.

Dawson, K. Smith (1980), 'Political Socialization and Behavior', in Smith, D. Horton, Macauley, J. et al (eds.), *Participation in Social and Political Activities*, Jossey Bass, San Francisco.

Donaghue, F., Miller, R.L. and Wilford, R.A. (1993), 'Careerist, Manhating or Family-oriented: Stereotyping the feminist in Northern Ireland', paper presented at Women and Politics in Ireland Inaugural Conference, Trinity College, Dublin, March.

Donaghue, F., Miller, R.L. and Wilford, R.A. (under review). 'The Orange and the Green: Feminism and women in Northern Ireland'.

Ellis, P.B. (1987), *A Dictionary of Irish Mythology*, Constable, London.

EOCNI (1986), *Response to the Consultative Document*, EOCNI, Belfast.

Equal Opportunities Commission Northern Ireland (1991), *Where Do Women Figure?*, EOCNI, Belfast.

Evason, E. (1985), *Right Brothers! A Study of Women and Trade Unions in Northern Ireland*, unpublished manuscript, University of Ulster, Coleraine.

Evason, E. (1991), *Against the Grain*, Attic Press, Dublin.

Fairweather, E., McDonough, R. and McFadyean, M. (1984), *Only the Rivers Run Free. Northern Ireland: the Women's War*, Pluto Press, London.

Faludi, S. (1991), *Backlash*, Crown Publishers, New York.

Freeman, B.C. (1976), 'Power, Patriarchy, and 'Political Primitives', in Roberts, J.I. (ed.), *Beyond Intellectual Sexism: A new woman, a new reality*, McKay, New York.

Galligan, Y. (1993), 'Party Politics and Gender in the Republic of Ireland' in Lovenduski, J. and Norris, P. (eds.), *Gender and Party Politics*, Sage, London, pp. 147-167.

Gillespie, U. (1994), 'Women in Struggle' in *Women in Struggle: 25 Years of Resistance*, Sinn Fein Women's Department, Sinn Fein, Dublin, pp. 17-9.

Gilligan, C. (1982), *In A Different Voice*, Harvard, London.

Githens, M., Norris, P. and Lovenduski, J. (eds.) (1994), *Different Roles, Different Voices*, HarperCollins, New York.

Glendinning, C. and Millar, J. (eds.) (1992), *Women and Poverty in Britain in the 1990s*, Harvester Wheatsheaf, London.

Goel, M. Lal and Smith, D. Horton (1980), 'Political Activities', in Smith, D. Horton and Macauley, J. et al (eds.), *Participation in Social and Political Activities*, Jossey Bass, San Francisco.

Goldthorpe, J.H. and Hope, K. (1974), *The Social Grading of Occupations*, Oxford, Clarendon Press.

Goot, M. and Reid, E. (1975), *Women and Voting Studies: Mindless Matrons or Sexist Scientism?*, Sage, London.

Goot, M. and Reid, E. (1984), 'Women: if not apolitical then conservative', in Siltanen and Stanworth, (eds.), op. cit., pp. 122-36.

Griffin, C. (1989), '"I'm not a Women's Libber, but...": Feminism, Consciousness and Identity', in Skevington, S. and Baker, D. (eds.), *The Social Identity of Women*, Sage, London.

Gustafsson, S. (1994), 'Childcare and Types of Welfare States', in Sainsbury, D. (ed.), *Gendering Welfare States*, Sage, London, pp. 45-61.

Hakim, C. (1979), 'Occupational Segregation', *Department of Employment Research Paper No. 9*, Department of Employment, London.

Hedlund, G. (1988), 'Women's Interests in Local Politics', in Jones, K. and Jonasdottir, A. (eds.), *The Political Interests of Gender: Developing Theory and Research with a Feminist Face*, Sage, London, pp. 79-105.

Hinds, B. (1995), 'Women in Politics', Submission to the Forum for Peace and Reconciliation, Northern Ireland Women's European Platform, Belfast.

HMSO (1986), *Equality of Opportunity in Employment in Northern Ireland: Future Strategy Options*, HMSO, Belfast

HMSO (1992), *The Northern Ireland Census 1991: Summary Report*, HMSO, Belfast.

Hooks, B. (1981), *Ain't I A Woman: black women and feminism*, South End Press, Boston.

Inglehart, M. (1981), 'Political Interest in West European Women', *Comparative Political Studies*, Vol. 14, No. 3, 299-326.

Jennings, M.K. (1983), 'Gender Roles and Inequalities in Political Participation: Results from an eight-nation study', *Western Political Quarterly*, Vol. 36, No. 3, pp. 364-85.

Jones, K.B. (1988), 'Towards the Revision of Politics', in Jones, K.B. and Jonasdottir, A.G. (eds.), *The Political Interests of Gender*, Sage, London, pp. 11-32.

Kavanagh, P. (1988), *Irish Mythology*, Goldsmith, Newbridge.

Kelly, R.M. (1991), 'Female Public Officials: A Different Voice?', *Annals of the American Academy of Political and Social Science*, 515, May, pp. 77-87.

Kinghan, N. (1975), *United We Stood: The Story of the Ulster Women's Unionist Council, 1911-1974*, Appletree Press, Belfast.

Kolinsky, E. (1993), 'Party Change and Women's Representation in Unified Germany' in Lovenduski, J. and Norris, P. (eds.), *Gender and Party Politics*, Sage, London, pp. 113-46.

Kremer, J. and Montgomery, P. (eds.) (1993), *Women's Working Lives*, HMSO, Belfast.

Land, H. (1980), 'The Family Wage', *Feminist Review* 6, pp. 55-7.

Lane, R. (1959), *Political Life*, Glencoe, Illinois.

Lee, M. (1976), 'Why Few Women Hold Public Office: Democracy and Sexual Roles', *Political Science Quarterly*, Vol. 91, pp. 297-314.

Lee, R.M. (1994), *Mixed and Matched Interreligious Courtship and Marriage in Northern Ireland*, Volume 2 of Series, *Class, Ethnicity, Gender and the Democratic Nation*, University Press of America, London.

Leijenaar, M. and Niemoller, K. (1991), 'Equality in Political Participation and Decision Making', in Tabak, F. (ed.), *The Implementation of Equal Rights for Men and Women*, Onati Institute, Onati, pp. 79-112.

Lijphart, A. (1968), *The Politics of Accomodation: Pluralism and Democracy in the Netherlands*, University of California Press, Berkely.

Lorde, A. (1984), *Sister Outsider*, Crossing Press, Trumansburg.

Lorde, A. (1994), 'The Master's Tools will Never Dismantle the Master's House', in Evans, M. (ed.), *The Woman Question*, 2nd edition, Sage, London, pp. 366-68.

Loughran, C. (1990), 'Armagh and Feminist Strategy', in Lovell, T. (ed.), *British Feminist Thought*, Blackwell, Oxford, pp. 170-83.

Lovenduski, J. (1981), 'Towards the Emasculation of Political Science: The Impact of Feminsm', in Spender, D. (ed.), *Men's Studies Modified*, Pergamon, London, pp. 83-97.

Lovenduski, J. (1986), *Women and European Politics: Contemporary feminism and public policy*, Wheatsheaf, Brighton.

Lovenduski, J. (1993), 'Introduction: The Dynamics of Gender and Party', in Lovenduski, J. and Norris, P. (eds.), *Gender and Party Politics*, Sage, London, pp. 1-15.

Lovenduski, J. (1994), 'Difference and Feminist Politics', in Githens, M., Norris, P. and Lovenduski, J. (eds.), *Different Roles, Different Voices: Women and Politics in the United States and Europe*, HarperCollins, New York.

Lovenduski, J. and Randall, V. (1993), *Contemporary Feminist Politics*, Oxford University Press, Oxford.

McClain, E. (1978), 'Feminists and Non-Feminists: Contrasting Profiles in Independence and Affiliation', *Psychological Reports*, Vol. 43, pp. 435-41.

McCrory, M. (1994), 'Women Took the Lead', in *Women in Struggle: 25 Years of Resistance*, Sinn Fein Women's Department, Sinn Fein, Dublin, pp. 15-16.

McDonagh, E.L. (1982), 'To Work or Not to Work: The differential impact of achieved and derived status upon the political participation of women, 1956-1976', *American Journal of Political Science*, Vol. 26, pp. 280-97.

McWilliams, M. (1991), 'Women in Northern Ireland: an overview', in Hughes, E. (ed.), *Culture and Politics in Northern Ireland: 1960-1990*, Open University Press, Milton Keynes, pp. 81-100.

McWilliams, M. (1995), 'Struggling for Peace and Justice: Reflections on Women's Activism in Northern Ireland', *Journal of Women's History*, Voi. 6, No. 4, Winter, pp. 13-39.

Milbrath, L. (1968), *Political Participation: How and Why Do People Get Involved in Politics?*, Rand McNally, Chicago.

Milbrath, L. and Goel, M. (1977), *Political Participation: How and Why Do People Get Involved in Politics?*, 2nd edition, Rand McNally, Chicago.

Miller, R. and McDade, D. (1993), 'Trade Union Involvement', in Kremer and Montgomery (eds.), *op. cit.*, pp. 113-30.

Miller, R.L., Wilford, R.A. and Donaghue, F. (1992), 'Gender and Estimates of Political Activity in Northern Ireland', paper presented at the First European Conference of Sociology, Vienna, August.

Miller, R.H., Hildreth, A. and Simmon, G.L. (1988), 'The Mobilization of Gender Group Consciousness', in Jones, K. and Jonasdottir, A. (eds.), *The Political Interests of Gender: Developing Theory and Research with a Feminist Face*, Sage, London.

Mitchison, A. (1988), 'Ulster's Family Feminists', *New Society*, 19 February, pp. 17-9.

Moloney, E. and Pollak, A. (1986), *Paisley*, Swords.

Montgomery, P. (1993), 'Paid and Unpaid Work', in Kremer and Montgomery (eds.), *op. cit.*, pp. 15-42.

Montgomery, P. and Davies, C. (1991), 'A woman's place in Northern Ireland', in Stringer, P. and Robinson, G. (eds), *Social Attitudes in Northern Ireland: 1990-1991*, Blackstaff Press, Belfast.

Morgan, V. and Fraser, G. (1994), *The Company We Keep: Women, Community and Organisations*, Centre for the Study of Conflict, University of Ulster.

Mueller, C. (1988), *The Politics of the Gender Gap: The Social Construction of Political Influence*, Sage, Newbury Park, California

Müller, W., Karle, W., König, W. and Luttinger, P. (1988), 'Education and Class Mobility', CASMIN Working Paper No. 14, Mannheim.

Norderval, I. (1985), 'Party and legislative participation among Scandinavian women', in Bashevkin, S. (ed.), *Women and Politics in Western Europe*, Frank Cass, London.

Norris, P. (1985), 'Women in Legislative Elites', *West European Politics*, Vol. 8, No. 4, October, pp. 90-101.

Norris, P. (1990), 'Gender Differences in Political Participation in Britain: Traditional, Radical and Revisionist Models', ECPR Conference Paper, Ruhr University, Bochum.

Norris, P. (1991), 'Gender Differences in Political Participation in Britain: Traditional, Radical and Revisionist Models', *Government and Opposition*, Vol. 26, No. 1, Winter, pp. 56-74.

Norris, P. (1993), 'Conclusions: Comparing Legislative Recruitment', in Lovenduski, J. and Norris, P. (eds.), *Gender and Party Politics*, Sage, London, pp. 309-30.

Norris, P. (1994), 'Political Participation', in Githens, M., Norris, P. and Lovenduski, J. (eds.), *Different Roles, Different Voices: Women and Politics in the United States and Europe*, Harper Collins, New York, pp. 25-6.

NIO (1995), Private Correspondence, Central Information Unit, Northern Ireland Office, Belfast.

Okin, S. M. (1991), 'Gender, the Public and the Private', in Held, D. (ed.), *Political Theory Today*, Polity Press, Cambridge.

O'Leary, B. (1989), 'The Limits of Coercive Consociationalism in Northern Ireland', *Political Studies*, Vol. 37, pp. 562-88.

O'Leary, C., Elliott, S. and Wilford, R.A. (1988), *The Northern Ireland Assembly 1982-1986: A Constitutional Experiment*, Hurst, London.

Oppenheim, C. (1993), *Poverty: The facts*, Child Poverty Action Group, London.

Pankhurst, S. (1977), *The Suffrage Movement*, Virago, London.

Parry, G., Moyser, G. and Day, N. (1992), *Political participation and democracy in Britain*, Cambridge University Press, Cambridge.

Pateman, C. (1983), 'Feminist Critiques of the Public/Private Dichotomy', in Benn, S.I. and Gaus, G.F. (eds.), *Public and Private in Social Life*, Croom Helm, London.

Pateman, C. (1992), 'Equality, difference, subordination: the politics of motherhood and women's citizenship', in Bock, G. and James, S. (eds.), *Beyond Equality and Difference*, Routledge, London, pp. 17-31.

Phillips, A. (1987), *Divided Loyalties: Dilemmas of Sex and Class*, Virago, London.

Phillips, A. (1991), *Engendering Democracy*, Polity Press, Cambridge.

Phillips, A. (1993), *Democracy and Difference*, Polity Press, Cambridge.

Pitkin, H. (1967), *The Concept of Representation*, University of California Press, Berkeley.

Pollock, A. (ed.) (1993), *A Citizen's Inquiry: The Opahl Report on Northern Ireland*, Lilliput Press, Dublin.

Randall, V. (1982), *Women and Politics*, St. Martin's, New York.

Randall, V. (1987), *Women and Politics*, Macmillan, London.

Randall, V. (1991), 'Feminism and Political Analysis', *Political Studies*, Vol. XXXIX, No. 3, September, pp. 513-32.

Randall, V. (1991), 'Feminism and Political Analysis', *Political Studies*, Vol. XXXIX, No. 3, pp. 513-32.

Rhode, D. (1992), 'The politics of paradigms: gender difference and gender disadvantage', in Bock, G. and James, S. (eds.), *Beyond Equality and Difference*, Routledge, London, pp. 149-63.

Ridd, R. and Callaway, H. (eds.) (1986), *Caught up in Conflict: Women's Responses to Political Strife*, Macmillan, London.

Rooney, E. and Woods, M. (1992), Women, Community and Politics in Northern Ireland: A Research Project with an Action Outcome, Centre for Research on Women, University of Ulster.

Ruddick, S. (1980), 'Maternal Thinking', *Feminist Studies*, Vol. 6, pp. 342-67.

Rule, W. (1981), 'Why Women Don't Run: The Critical Contextual Factors in Women's Legislative Recruitment', *Western Political Quarterly*, Vol. 34, March, pp. 60-77.

Rule, W. (1987), 'Electoral Systems, Contextual Factors and Women's Opportunity for Election in Twenty-Three Democracies', *Western Political Quarterly*, Vol. 40, September, pp. 477-98.

Rule, W. and Zimmerman, J.F. (eds.) (1992), *US Electoral Systems: Their Impact on Minorities and Women*, Greenwood Press, Westport.

Sapiro, V. (1981), 'Research Frontier Essay: When Are Interests Interesting? The Problem of Political Representation of Women', *American Political Science Review*, Vol. 75, September, pp. 701-16.

Sapiro, V. (1983), *The Political Integration of Women: Roles, socialization, and politics*, University of Illinois Press, Urbana.

SDLP (1994), *European Parliamentary Election Manifesto*, SDLP, Belfast.

Shannon, E. (1989), *I Am Of Ireland: Women of the North Speak Out*, Little Brown, Boston.

Siltanen, J. and Stanworth, M. (eds.) (1984), *Women and the Public Sphere: A critique of sociology and politics*, Hutchinson & Co., London.

Siltanen, J. and Stanworth, M. (1984), 'The politics of private woman and public man', in Siltanen and Stanworth (eds.), *Women and the Public Sphere, Hutchinson*, London, pp. 185-208.

Sinn Fein (1994), *Women in Struggle: 25 Years of Resistance*, Sinn Fein Women's Department, Dublin.

Skjeie, H. (1993), 'Ending the Male Political Hegemony: the Norwegian Experience', in Lovenduski, J. and Norris, P. (eds.), *Gender and Party Politics*, Sage, London, pp. 231-62.

Squires, M. (1993), 'Ulster Unionism and Women's Issues: A Political and Historical Overview', Conference Paper, Women and Politics in Ireland Conference, Trinity College Dublin.

Stacey, J. (1986), 'Are Feminists Afraid To Leave Home?: The Challenge of Conservative Pro-Family Feminism', in Mitchell, J. and Oakley, A. (eds.), *What is Feminism?*, Blackwell, Oxford, pp. 219-48.

Taillon, R. (1992a), *Directory of Women's Organisations in Northern Ireland*, Women's Support Network, Belfast.

Taillon, R. (1992b), *Grant-Aided or Taken for Granted?*, Women's Support Network, Belfast.

Thomas, S. and Welch, S. (1991), 'The Impact of Gender on Activities and Priorities of State Legislators', *Western Political Quarterly*, Vol. 44, June, pp. 445-56.

Thompson, W. (1983 [1825]), *Appeal of One-Half of the Human Race, Women*, Virago, London.

Titmuss, R.M. (1970), *The Gift Relationship*, Allen and Unwin, London.

Tong, R. (1989), *Feminist Thought: A Comprehensive Introduction*, Unwin Hyman, London.

Trewsdale, J, and Toman, A, (1993), 'Employment', in Kremer and Montgomery (eds.), *op. cit.*, pp. 85-112.

Turner, I. (1993), 'Childcare', in Kremer and Montgomery (eds.), *op. cit.*, pp. 151-74.

Vallance, E. (1982), 'Where Power Is, Women Are Not', *Parliamentary Affairs*, Vol. 35, Spring, pp. 218-219.

Verba, S. and Nie, N. (1972), *Participation in America: Political Democracy and Social Equality*, Harper and Row, New York.

Verba, S., Nie, N. and Kim, J. (1978), *Participation and Political Equality: A seven-nation comparison*, Cambridge University Press, Cambridge.

Verba, S., Nie, N. and Kim, J. (1980), *Participation and Political Equality*, Cambridge University Press, Cambridge.

Ward, M. (1983), *Unmanageable Revolutionaries: Women and Irish Nationalism*, Pluto Press, London.

Ward, M. (1987), *A Difficult, Dangerous Honesty*, Women's Book Collective, Belfast.

Ward, M. and McGivern, M.T. (1980), 'Images of Women in Northern Ireland', *The Crane Bag*, Vol. 4, No. 1, pp. 66-72.

Walby, S. (1988), 'Gender Politics and Social Theory', *Sociology*, Vol. 22, No. 2, pp. 215-32.

Walby, S. (1990), *Theorizing Patriarchy*, Blackwell, Oxford.

Welch, S. (1977), 'Women as Political Animals? A Test of Some Explanations for Male-Female Political Participation Differences', *American Journal of Political Science*, Vol. 21, No. 4, pp. 771-30.

Welch, S. (1980), 'Sex Differences in Political Activity in Britain', *Women and Politics*, Vol. 1, No. 2, pp. 29-46.

Welch, S. (1984), 'Are Women More Liberal than Men in the U.S. Congress?', *Legislative Studies Quarterly*, Vol. 10, February, pp. 125-34.

Welch, S. and Studlar, D.T. (1986), 'British Public Opinion Toward Women in Politics', *Western Political Quarterly*, Vol. 39, pp. 138-54.

Wilford, R. (1992), 'Inverting Consociationalism? Policy, pluralism and the post-modern', in Hadfield, B. (ed.), *Northern Ireland: Politics and the Constitution*, Open University Press, Buckingham, pp. 29-46.

Wilford, R. (1994), 'Feminism', in Eccleshall, R. et al, *Political Ideologies: an introduction*, Routledge, London, pp. 252-83.

Wilford, R., Miller, R., Bell, Y. and Donoghue, F. (1993), 'In their own voices: women councillors in Northern Ireland', *Public Administration*, Vol. 71, No. 3, Autumn, pp. 341-55.

Williams, F. (1993), 'Gender, "Race" and Class in British Welfare Policy', In Cochrane, A. and Clarke, J. (eds.), *Comparing Welfare States: Britain in international context*, Sage, London, pp. 74-104.

Wolf, N. (1990), *The Beauty Myth*, Vintage, London.